MRS. WITTY'S
HOME-STYLE
MENU
COOKBOOK

ALSO BY HELEN WITTY

Fancy Pantry

Mrs. Witty's Monster Cookies

Better Than Store-Bought
(with Elizabeth Schneider Colchie)

The Garden-to-Table Cookbook
(Compiler and Editor)

The Cooks' Catalogue
(Editor)

MRS. WITTY'S
HOME-STYLE
MENU
COOKBOOK

BY HELEN WITTY

WORKMAN PUBLISHING, NEW YORK

A few of the recipes in Mrs. Witty's Home-Style Menu Cookbook *have appeared, in different form, in periodicals that include* Cuisine, The International Review of Food & Wine, The Home Garden, *and* Bon Appetit.

Witty, Helen.
Mrs. Witty's home-style menu cookbook /: family dinners good enough for company / by Helen Witty.
p.   cm.
ISBN 0-89480-819-2   ISBN 0-89480-690-4 (pbk.)
1. Cookery, American.   2. Menus.   I. Title.
TX715.W8453   1990
641.5973—dc20   89-40729
                                          CIP

Book design by Lisa Hollander and Regina Dalton-Fischel
Cover design by Charles Kreloff
Cover illustration by Margaret Cusack

Workman Publishing
708 Broadway
New York, New York 10003
Manufactured in the United States of America

First printing May 1990
10 9 8 7 6 5 4 3 2 1

This book is for those who have shared, in every place that has been called home . . . My parents, and all their children; Richard, Anne, and George; and the good friends who have become family.

CONTENTS

MRS. WITTY'S HOME-STYLE MENU COOKBOOK

WHY HAS MRS. WITTY WRITTEN THIS BOOK, AND WHAT'S _IN_ IT?

---

*O*nly at the end of a long and varied life can one profess to know
much about food.

—P. MORTON SHAND, *A BOOK OF FOOD*

Of cookbooks: There are so many, and most of them so bad.

—E. S. DALLAS, *KETTNER'S BOOK OF THE TABLE*

Don't go into a restaurant for something you can do better at
home.

—NICOLAS FREELING, *THE KITCHEN*

o one has a better right to ask *why-what-who* than you,
dear and hungry reader, so Mrs. W will try to say who she
is, what's in this book, and why she hopes you'll invite it
into your kitchen.

First, though, you should know a little about the person who
comes with this food, because there's no such thing as a dish (or a
menu) without its author. (As John Thorne, the sage of simple
cuisine, has pointed out.)

The gastronomical Mrs. Witty—like all cooks who write things
down—is the product of family influences, long-evolving tastes, and
hands-on experience. She springs from "California Midwesterners":
her people became Americans on the eastern seaboard before the
Revolution and took their westward journey in slow stages, moving
past the dividing mountains to the midlands—Illinois, Michigan,
Missouri. Eventually her parents-to-be took the long jump to the
Pacific Northwest, Dad as the Illinois-born infant son of a Methodist
farmer-preacher, Mother much later as a young teacher making
what we'd now call a career move from Michigan. And there, on
Whidbey Island in Puget Sound, they met, married, and produced
the first three of seven children. From Seattle, where Dad worked for
Boeing Aircraft, the family moved to Southern California, where he

was joining the fledgling company in Santa Monica that became Douglas Aircraft.

Growing up, the children took as their due the clear sun of pre-smog California, the blue Pacific two or three miles away, the mountains in the other direction, and in between the enormous open spaces and orange groves and nut orchards that are now paved with houses and laced with freeways.

We lived in "California"-style houses on streets edged with palm trees, acacias, and jacarandas; there was a many-doored oak icebox in the kitchen (later, a clunky Frigidaire) and a vegetable garden in the backyard. There were pets—Paws the Airedale, a cat, a flock of droll bantams, a few mallard ducks, and even, for a while, two baby goats and a quarrelsome goose.

The grocery stores were stores, not supermarkets, and had clerks and counters. Mr. MacCampbell, the egg man, came around with eggs, chickens, and walnuts from his place in the San Fernando Valley; the Watkins man visited every few months to sell spices and flavorings; milk and cream came from the Adohr dairy in chilly bottles with little pleated caps that were delivered daily to the built-in box by the back door. Peddlers' trucks full of vegetables and fruits appeared all year, and in summer, entrancingly, our street was visited every other day by a tin-lizzy ice-cream wagon piloted by a woman with flaming-red hair....

CALIFORNIA FOOD, THEN

———

The gentle climate made available in abundance some good things that must have been rarities "back East" (which was anywhere beyond the blue mountains). We consumed such exotica as artichokes, persimmons, avocados, plain and fancy kinds of citrus, eggplant, loquats (the earliest of the spring fruits, which made delicious jelly if they weren't all eaten up raw), apricots melting-ripe from the tree, quinces, pomegranates, ground cherries, guavas, and even such exotica as cherimoyas and a fruit (properly the feijoa) we called "pineapple guava." There were such veggies (some from the backyard) as salsify, chayotes, "celery" (Chinese) cabbage, banana squash, fennel, perennial New Zealand spinach, and Swiss chard, as well as the usual garden stuff. From the ocean, we had halibut, fair-to-middling barracuda, sea bass, California mackerel (not much good unless brined and smoked), and a special delicacy, abalone.

KITCHEN PLAY, AND LEARNING

———

We young ones were allowed, even encouraged, in the kitchen; some of us were interested, some not (but nobody has starved since, for lack of kitchen skill). For food lore there were the women's magazines Mother subscribed to (Ann Batchelder was a shining light), and a budding cook could write away for excellent booklets and mini-cookbooks (the ring-bound one from Pet Milk is fondly remembered). Some were free, some cost ten cents or a quarter. *Sunset* magazine—a slim publication then—ran monthly pieces on food that included cartoonlike how-to's; I thought they were wonderful. Mother (her generation took kitchen competence for granted) had a one-volume culinary library, the *White House Cookbook*, and didn't seem to need it often (but surely she looked *some* things up?).

My father often spoke of and sometimes fixed the dishes he'd grown up on—Puget Sound clam chowder, salmon steaks, fried oysters, bean-hole beans, venison (we only heard about the last two), and a few other things, which you'll find in this book.

WHAT WE MISSED...

———

Not until later were we to meet up with garlic, olive oil, Parmesan, cilantro, fresh ginger, and other things now thought of as essential to cuisine, nor had kiwis yet come along. We didn't really know how to cook spaghetti, and Chinese food was still over the horizon.

But people still cooked (and knew how to cook) as a matter of course, although the can opener had made inroads. TV dinners were yet to come as the answer to "What's for dinner?" The future Mrs. Witty grew up with (and never grew out of) a liking for simple, flavorful, just-plain-good dishes; it has never been permanently derailed by the newest foods or latest culinary fashions, despite a lot of worktime spent in the New York "foodie" world. (Oh, yes, Mrs. Witty has tasted—and cooked—her share of the fine and the fashionable, and enjoyed much of it, being a curious soul; but she has sometimes been tempted to repeat the famous line, "I say it's spinach, and I say the hell with it.")

FOOD PAST, AND FOOD (PERHAPS) TO COME

Now that I've got myself started on the subject, what about that gastronomic "spinach"? In the last decade or so we've *had* nouvelle cuisine, whose sillier manifestations (not all of the food was silly) are receding fast. But since nouvelle began to wane we've been told regularly—by new superstar chefs, drop-dead caterers, and the "writers" of books consisting mostly of four-color food photos— that the only thing that should pass our lips at a given moment is twisted Cajun, or "new" Californian food or other dubious regionalia, or dishes from remote Thailand or other places farther east, or smoke-and-fire charrings (this perhaps to balance the only slightly seared raw fish being pushed in other quarters). And we're not even counting the health-related food fads, which are outside the scope of this collection— if eating oat bran does something for you, I'm not going to argue. (I'm also not going to refrain from writing recipes that call for beef, or eggs, or butter.)

Some restaurant menus—which quite accurately reflect the ebbings and flowings of "in" cuisine—have become fearful and wonderful reading. (And so has some of the fancier food writing.) Which brings to mind some dead-accurate words on the subject, from Jean-Francois Revel's *Culture and Cuisine:*

The function of this toplofty jargon [e.g., "Rillettes of Tuna," "Rumpsteak of Sole"] is to disconcert and thereby create the illusion of originality, a more facile solution than the honest execution of tried and tested recipes. But there is another function, which we might call (if we are being nasty) that of intimidating or (if we are being kind) that of spellbinding.

The chef's art is precisely the art of knowing what he can borrow from various traditions without betraying them.

That just about winds up the case for paying more attention to our own traditions—what we *like* to eat, no matter why we like it—and less to what trendmongers tell us we *should* like. Of course, as a nation we've been traveling and tasting, and our culinary horizons have expanded enormously since (for instance) I was first aware that not all families ate the same food my family did. So we've collectively gained a lot of good things, but at the same time there has been a tendency to shove into the chimney corner the Cinderella dishes of real merit that most of us grew up on.

It's time to get Cinderella off to the ball, or at least to the family table. With pleasure, it's noted that some enlightened restaurateurs are doing exactly that; and I suspect that many good home cooks never left home in the first place.

WHAT'S IN THIS BOOK, AND HOW TO USE IT

There are forty menus (plus variations) built around dishes that have been favorites of my own young (and now grown) family just because, I believe, they're *good*. They're things I still like, myself, not least because they're an antidote to over-trendiness at the table. It's time to get a grip again on such Americana as perfect mashed potatoes, lobster stew, peerless pot roast, upside-down cake, real lemonade, buttermilk biscuits, maple mousse, country sausage, summer fruit shortcake, baked beans, chicken and veal loaf, chili con carne, angel biscuits, corn oysters, Boston cream pie, turkey stuffed with such native foods as wild rice and black walnuts, cranberry and raisin pie, seafood chowder.

The menus and the roughly two hundred recipes that accompany them are grouped in five sections—breakfasts (family and/or company); luncheons/cookouts/picnics; dinners; suppers; and two or three festive gatherings, which include a full-scale Thanksgiving.

Some recipes are my own renderings of American classics, some are dishes of my own devising, and there are a few adaptations of admired recipes written by others—all, I hope, fully and gratefully acknowledged. Finally, there are some good things from other cuisines.

The menus are simply suggestions; drop any dish you wish, fatten up a menu with an added course, or restructure any menu by using the Index and the Seasonal Recipe Lists starting on page 289. You're the one who knows what you like best, and how copious (or how spare) a meal you want to serve.

HOW WE FEAST AT OUR HOUSE

If there's enough for company, company is welcome—you'll notice that the recipes are written for six people. (Some "keepable" dishes will serve more.) So we reckon that taking potluck will be no hardship, all other things being equal.

If it's a gathering (which is going to be informal, these days), there will be no platters of what James Beard dismissingly called "doots" to nibble with drinks, but there *will* be one or two good things to which people can help themselves. If we're having a buffet (highly likely, now that we live in a small house that used to be a weekend cottage), the watchword will be *plenty*, because built into our genes there's a strong repugnance toward running out of food when people are still hungry.

AND HOW DID THE KIDS TURN OUT?

Anne and George grew up as members of the Clean Plate Club—no problems are recalled in that department, probably because it was established quite amicably, just after the baby-jar stage, that what you see is what you eat.

Now that they're out in the world, both young people have signed up for the Dial-a-Cook Club, whose half-dozen members phone Mrs. Witty when they want guidance on a cooking project. Calls from offspring are infrequent, however; they seem to know how to feed themselves and their friends, and, so far, they have shown no symptoms of becoming culinary yuppies.

But be it noted that their tastes, like those of most children, have evolved. Anne, at age six, chose for her birthday party Dione Lucas's famous chocolate roll, which she had seen big-eyed and had a taste of. A year or so later she browsed in books and wrote down, for her mother's benefit, a recipe for fudge that looked good, hint, hint.... By the time she had finished college and was planning a joint bon voyage party for a friend heading for Oxford and for herself, off abroad on a traveling fellowship, she asked for—what? Chili con carne.

George was a seafood fellow, not a chocolatier, when young—at eight, he composed a fish cookbook, with illustrations, that began, "For many years I have been interested in fish." At eighteen, enrolled at Cornell, he found himself cooking frequently for housemates after he'd been sprung from the freshman dorm; he seems to have learned kitchen skills by osmosis. He was, and is, attached to family food traditions—turkey for Thanksgiving, roast beef for Christmas dinner, sugar-dusted loaves of stollen for Christmas breakfast.

HOW DO I COOK? THE PLEASURES OF INCONSISTENCY

———

When cooking for pleasure—which means most times, for I enjoy the process as well as the product—I make no special effort to cook a dish exactly the same way twice unless the recipe is intended for publication. In that case it's tested and retested by being made exactly according to directions, no matter how much I may yearn to improvise. At all other times, the motto of the kitchen is something Emerson is supposed to have said—"The truly consistent person changes his mind whenever occasion offers." That's the way recipes seem to evolve and/or improve, at least at our house, and if you'll try it, you'll discover a dandy way to keep out of a culinary rut.

When using any recipe in this book or from any other source: Touch, look, listen (yes, food makes noises when it cooks); sniff (the nose *does* know).

REGRETS...

———

Alas, there's no space for some dishes dearly (or sneakily) loved. Maybe next time.

ANYBODY ELSE FOR BREAKFAST THREE TIMES A DAY?

*"What is for breakfast?" asked Mr. Betts, coming in with boots
and gaiters—up, of course, since dawn. Mrs. Betts produced a
mighty steak of salmon.
"What's a pound of salmon to a man like me?—Bring me
six boiled eggs."*

—NICOLAS FREELING, *THE KITCHEN*

I'm just joking about multiple breakfasts, although, truth
be told, this is my favorite meal, especially when I'm
traveling. It's the most restorative meal of the day and, in
some countries, it can be the best, too. So I *like* breakfast and hope
you like it, too, at least when there's leisure to fix and enjoy something interesting as a change from everyday.

Perhaps because our American breakfasts are so hurried and perfunctory when we're too busy for our own good, this meal seems to improve even more than lunch or dinner when it's given a little loving care. According to me, a truly restorative breakfast, perhaps late on Sunday morning, cries out for "foods of the heart," dishes of a certain timelessness that haven't been chosen for their chic or their rating in this year's health-food competition. There's nothing chic for its own sake in this section (or any other part of this book), and there's even one breakfast (or supper), on page 241, that consists of a single dish—what could be more alluring on a June morning than a breakfast of strawberry shortcake or, in August, a shortcake of dripping-ripe peaches?

CHOOSING ALTERNATIVES, AND FINDING BREAKFAST IN OTHER CHAPTERS

Some of the menus offer alternative dishes to suit alternative moods or likings—Finnan Haddie in Cream, if you're not in a position to serve calves' brains; Corn Oysters in place of Scrapple; bacon instead of Updated Home-Style Sausage, and so on. In other chapters you'll find dishes that are delightful for breakfast as well as the meals they're placed in.

Among them are Amber Apples, which could top an extra-crisp waffle or a slice of buttered whole-wheat toast; Angel Rolls, a make-ahead hybrid between hot biscuits and yeast rolls; Cinnamon-Capped Apple Muffins; Bread & Butter Pudding with Berries; Fresh Corn Popovers; Blueberry Corn Bread (or muffins); Swiss-Style Skillet Potato Cake; Sautéed Red & Green Tomato Slices; Uncooked Lime or Lemon Curd, to go on toast in place of jam; Richard's Celtic Soda Bread with Raisins & Caraway; Ambrosia; and, for a cool but spicy fruit dish as a change of pace on a summer day, Gingery Melon Mold.

The Index and the Seasonal Recipe Lists will yield more ideas.

BREAKFAST (OR SUPPER) WITH A SASSY COOK

Chipped Beef in Cream Ann Batchelder's Way (below)

*with poached eggs (see the note after the recipe) and
slow-toasted multigrain bread (for breakfast), or spooned into
split baked potatoes (for supper)*

*Pickled peaches, pears, or crab apples, from the pantry or the
fancy-foods shop*

*Supper dessert, optional: Pineapple Cake (page 81) or the
Rhubarb Variation of Green Tomato Fool (page 108)*

To drink: Tea, coffee, or other breakfast beverage

A t about the time I did my first real cooking—making hot biscuits in honor of a grandmother who had just arrived for a visit—I discovered the sassy food writing of Ann Batchelder in *The Ladies' Home Journal*. "The cook in me," as the novelist Günter Grass would have described the inner being of that youngster, was about eight; the biscuits were meant to show Grandmother "what a big girl am I."

Ann Batchelder's food pieces appealed a lot to that budding cook. Ann was to be an editor of the *Journal* for many years and, as she later wrote, she adored food and "the ways to do something about it," and was in love with words. She was no bumpkin in her tastes—"Into each life some caviar comes, some lemons are bound to fall"—and she knew what to do with the caviar; but she never dismissed the merits of simple dishes just because they were simple.

It would have been enjoyable, I've often thought since acquiring some of her inimitable books, to have had a meal with Ann Batchelder—perhaps a Sunday breakfast starring her Chipped Beef in Cream, certainly a simple dish but one that's pleasing to any palate unprejudiced by the awful jokes about the versions perpetrated by Army cooks....

Also pleasing is an old-style and cockle-warming supper of baked potatoes topped with chipped beef in cream. Just squeeze each hot baked potato in a towel to mash its insides to fluffiness, slash an X in the top, spread it open, and fill it generously with the beef and sauce. Minced parsley (which tastes good) or paprika (which looks pretty) might go on top.

SHOPPING FOR DRIED BEEF: Dried or chipped beef, packed in jars, was once ubiquitous in grocery stores, but today it must be sought out. Supermarkets tend to put it, if it's stocked at all, somewhere near the bacon. Before buying, check the label and peer at what you can see of the slices—if the meat is the real thing, shaved from a chunk of solid meat and not from a block of pressed-together scraps, it will have visible grain. Most beef I've sampled is very salty; it's a good idea to rinse the slices quickly and drain and pat them dry before proceeding.

CHIPPED BEEF IN CREAM ANN BATCHELDER'S WAY

Ann Batchelder's recipe is adapted below with only one or two added touches— rinsing the beef to decrease saltiness, adding a touch of steak sauce or hot pepper sauce, and proposing the poached eggs as an option.

Her method is different from my family's; our beef was frizzled in butter, then stirred with flour before milk went in. Frizzling can toughen the beef if it's not done gently, but if you'd like to try you'll need 4 tablespoons each of butter and flour and 4 cups of half-and-half or milk. Back home, if my father was cooking, he'd put in a lot of parsley at the end, because he loved that gentle herb.

Serves 6

6 to 8 ounces high-quality dried (chipped) beef
All-purpose flour for coating the beef
1 quart half-and-half, or milk and cream in preferred proportions
Freshly ground pepper
Few drops of steak sauce or hot pepper sauce, optional
Optional accompaniment: *Eggs poached in the creamed beef, 1 per person (see right)*

Separate the slices of beef, stir them in warm water for a few seconds, drain, and pat dry with paper toweling; this gets rid of excess salt. Tear the beef into 1-inch scraps; blot them again if still damp.

Scatter flour over the pieces and toss them until well coated; shake off surplus flour in a sieve.

Put the beef into a cold, ungreased heavy skillet over medium heat and stir for a moment to warm and separate the pieces. Stir in the liquid gradually; cook about 3 minutes until the sauce has thickened smoothly, then boil for a minute or two more. If the sauce is too thick, add a little milk; if too thin, reduce it by simmering.

Season generously with pepper and, optionally, a few drops of steak sauce or hot pepper sauce.

Poached eggs: Poach eggs separately, or slip them on top of the creamed beef, cover the pan, and leave it over the lowest possible heat until the whites have set and the yolks have glazed, about 5 minutes.

NUTTY HOTCAKES & FRUITED SYRUP

Grapefruit, cranberry, or pineapple juice, either chilled or half frozen and "slushed" in a blender

Banana-Nut Pancakes (below) with Whipped Cottage Cheese (page 270) or whipped sweet butter and Chunky Orange Syrup or Sauce (below), warmed

Broiled bacon, either thick-cut or Canadian-style

To drink: *Tea, coffee, or other breakfast beverage*

A pancake feast isn't very festive for the cook if it involves shuttling between stove and table to keep the vittles coming, so for a breakfast of these nutty cakes we dig out an electric frying pan or electric griddle that can come to the table.

If the bacon is ready, the syrup is hot, and the plates warm before the batter ever hits the pan, the chief cook can sit down, pour a mug of coffee, and enjoy breakfast with the rest.

OUTWITTING THE AGGRAVATING BANANA: Like the jam in *Through the Looking-Glass*—jam yesterday, jam tomorrow, but never jam today—bananas are never ripe just when they're wanted.

The freezer is your best hope if you'd like to have ripe bananas when you need them.

Peel the bananas, wrap each in plastic, and freeze them in a sealed bag. They'll keep for months; thawed, they will be soft but still flavorful.

Makes 12 large pancakes or 2 dozen or more "silver-dollar" pancakes

2 large eggs
2 medium, fully ripe bananas, sliced
⅓ cup granulated sugar
3 tablespoons vegetable oil
1 cup milk
1 cup all-purpose flour
1½ teaspoons baking powder
½ teaspoon salt
¼ teaspoon baking soda
⅓ cup chopped pecans or walnuts

BANANA-NUT PANCAKES

wo small suggestions for these griddle cakes: Use bananas that have a good crop of freckles on their skin to indicate that they are lusciously ripe—it doesn't matter if the flesh is a bit soft so long as the flavor is okay (a taste will tell). Then, if you want extra-nutty nuts, toast them as described on page 275, if you have a few minutes to fiddle while the coffee drips. The toasting makes a difference.

Beat the eggs in a mixing bowl; mash the bananas and add them, with the sugar, oil, and milk; beat well.

Sift together the flour, baking powder, salt, and soda. Add the flour mixture and nuts to the liquid mixture and stir until the dry ingredients are just dampened; don't overmix.

Heat an electric griddle, or heat a stovetop griddle over medium-low heat, until drops of water sizzle slowly when flicked on. If the drops hop and skip, let the griddle cool a little before pouring the batter; the pancakes should bake slowly and brown only lightly.

For 4- to 5-inch pancakes: Ladle scant ⅓-cup measures of batter onto the griddle 2 inches apart; bake until half the bubbles on top are "set" and stay open. Turn the cakes and bake until they feel firm and springy to a fingertip.

For silver-dollar-size cakes: Measure the batter with a spoon holding 2 to 3 tablespoons.

Serve the pancakes on warmed plates and, if sheer perfection is your goal, with syrup that has also been warmed.

YES, WE HAVE NO BANANAS: As an alternative to the tropical fruit, try the temperate apple. One large, tart apple, pared and grated, will be enough; add a pinch of cinnamon to the batter and bake the cakes slowly.

**TO STERILIZE & SEAL
JARS:** Boil canning jars 10
minutes in deep water. Scald
2-piece lids separately 5
minutes. Fill drained jars,
leaving ¼-inch headspace.
Wipe rims; put disk portions
of lids in place; screw on
rims. When cold, tap lids
with a teaspoon; a clear ring
indicates a good seal. An
unsealed lid will sound dull;
refrigerate any unsealed jar
for storage.

Makes about 5 cups

*Peel of 2 or 3 bright-
skinned oranges*
*4 cups frozen concentrated
orange juice recon-
stituted with 2 cans
of added water, not 3; or
4 cups fresh orange juice*
Juice of 1 lemon, strained
5 cups granulated sugar

CHUNKY ORANGE SYRUP OR SAUCE

ichly textured but pourable, this double-
orange syrup or sauce is meant for ice
cream, waffles, pancakes, French toast,
pudding, or other goodies that need a zesty sweet
topping. It will keep for months in the refrigerator,
longer if bottled and sealed, so the recipe makes a
generous amount. It's one of the best uses I know
for the smooth, brilliant peels of winter oranges.

For a spirituous touch when the sauce goes
over a dessert, stir in a little orange liqueur—Triple
Sec, Grand Marnier, or Cointreau—at serving time.

Kitchen adventurers will find that this syrup/
sauce rewards experimentation. Add the rind of half
a lemon to the orange peel, and/or include 3 or 4
tablespoons of finely shredded pineapple when it's
time for the final cooking.

Soak the peel in water to cover for 12 to 24 hours.
Simmer the peel, covered, in soaking water until very
tender, 30 to 40 minutes. Cool. Reserve the liquid.

Scrape most of the pulp layer from the inner side of
the peel, using the edge of a small spoon. Discard the pulp
and chop or shred the peel.

Combine 1 cup of the cooking liquid with the peel,
orange juice, and lemon juice in a large pot. Stir in the
sugar until dissolved, then boil the mixture, stirring often,
for 10 minutes, or until the syrup has thickened notice-
ably when a spoonful is poured back into the pot. (It will
thicken further upon cooling.)

Off the heat, cool the syrup, stirring it occasionally,
for 5 minutes (this keeps the bits of peel from floating).
Pour into a storage container, cool completely, and refrigerate; or seal while still very hot in sterilized canning jars,
using sterilized lids (see To Sterilize & Seal Jars, on the
left).

The syrup keeps for months under refrigeration.
Sealed jars will keep indefinitely at room temperature.

SUNDAY SUSTENANCE

Individual casseroles of Finnan Haddie in Cream (below), or Dad's Brainy Dish (below), optionally accompanied by broiled bacon or ham

Crisp rye toast, or "Barbecued" or Pulled Bread (page 51)

Sliced fresh peaches with sugar and a sprinkling of peach schnapps, or a bowl of cut-up seasonal fruits

To drink: *Coffee, tea, or other breakfast beverage*

T he dishes in both Column A and Column B (so to speak) of this menu are guaranteed to induce contentment lasting long enough to polish off the bulkiest Sunday newspaper, with energy left over for—oh, TV football-watching, or even a bracing walk. Neither dish marches in the vanguard of chic cuisine right now, but both are esteemed by breakfasters who know what's what.

You needn't be Scotch to delight in finnan haddie, here simply baked with cream and crumbs. When buying it look for the real thing—lightly cured and lightly smoked fish—not a "nowadays" version flavored by chemical shortcutting.

When I was young in California, one of the star turns in my father's breakfast performances was a dish of calves' brains scrambled with eggs, light-textured and most delicate to taste. (Out in the world, I later met versions of this dish in several cuisines.) The only problem in reproducing it is locating the raw material, which, like equally perishable sweetbreads, must be fresh and used promptly.

FINNAN HADDIE IN CREAM

It is kindly ordered that happiness should be the result of very simple arrangements, and not of gigantic efforts.

—E. S. DALLAS, WRITING OF FINNAN HADDIE IN

KETTNER'S BOOK OF THE TABLE.

innan haddie—which is smoked haddock (or now sometimes cod masquerading as haddock)—is generally lightly smoked these days, unlike some versions of the Scottish original. It's also rather lightly salted, so it requires very little soaking before it's cooked.

For warm and rich, smoky-flavored breakfast comfort, there are few things better. This is a dish I especially like. Good for supper, too.

SMOKING OUT THE REAL THING: When shopping for finnan haddie, it helps to know that all finnan haddie isn't created equal. (It isn't always haddock, either, but if honestly cured, "finnan cod" can be fine.)

The problem is that the smoky flavor and golden color of the genuine article can be thriftily approximated by using coloring and smoke flavoring; so, if in doubt, ask your fishmonger which kind he sells.

Serves 6

2 pounds finnan haddie
Butter for coating
    casseroles
1 cup, or as needed, cream
1 cup, or as needed, milk
3 tablespoons unsalted
    butter
⅔ cup coarse fresh bread
    crumbs
Garnish: *Lemon wedges*

Cover the finnan haddie with plenty of warm water and soak it for 30 minutes. Drain well.

Preheat the oven to 350°.

Divide the fish into 6 portions; arrange the portions in well-buttered individual casseroles or gratin dishes just large enough to hold them comfortably. (Alternatively, use a large shallow baking dish.)

Mix the cream and milk and pour enough over the fish to cover it lightly; if more liquid is needed, either milk, cream, or a mixture can be used.

Set the individual dishes on a baking sheet (not needed for a large single dish) and bake the fish 20 minutes.

Meanwhile, melt the butter and mix it into the crumbs. Strew the fish with the buttered crumbs and continue baking until the crumbs are crisp, perhaps another 10 minutes.

Serve hot. Wedges of lemon and a pepper mill should be on the table.

DAD'S BRAINY DISH

hen my father cooked this dish, which he did once in a while, my early interest in kitchen goings-on led me to learn the intricacies (there aren't many of them) of preparing brains for cooking, as well as Dad's favorite fashion of fixing them for Sunday-morning consumption by his family.

Later came the discovery, in a French restaurant of the type that used to be on every Manhattan block, of classic brains with black butter and capers. Then, in a trattoria in Florence one May, I tasted *cervella e carciofi*, a delicate mixed fry of calves' brains and tiny tender artichokes; and I so admired the nutty-tasting artichoke morsels and the creamy, almost ethereal nuggets of meat, in what had to be the perfect place and season for such food, that I enjoyed them several times more before leaving Italy. Each version was delectable, with only tiny differences from the last fritto misto.

If you'd like to try reproducing the Italian combination of brains and artichokes, see the outline of the how-to's on the following page.

Serves 6 or more

2 sets (about 1½ pounds) calves' brains, cleaned, blanched, and cooled (see Preparation, page 20)

6 tablespoons (¾ stick), or more, unsalted butter

8 large eggs

Salt and pepper, to taste

Minced parsley and/or snipped chives, to taste

Divide the brains into 1-inch chunks. Melt the butter in a wide skillet over medium heat just until it's foamy. (Dad would have used clear bacon fat, which is also good.) Sauté the brains just until golden-tinged and hot, turning the pieces gently.

Meanwhile, beat the eggs with salt and pepper. Pour the eggs over the brains and sprinkle the herbs over all. Lower the heat and let the eggs cook, without stirring, until partially set, then slowly and repeatedly draw the mixture in large curds from the sides toward the center. Stop the cooking while the eggs are still soft—they will continue to cook and become firmer from their own heat.

Serve the dish without delay.

THINKING ABOUT BRAINS:
Shopping: Veal, beef, pork, and lamb brains are all good; they differ principally in size, not quality. Calves' brains, due to the veal mystique, are most prestigious; a set usually weighs between 12 and 16 ounces. Pork brains are similar in size; lamb brains are expectably smaller, beef brains bigger.

Storing: Fresh brains can be frozen for later use. Otherwise brains must either be cooked the day they're purchased, or blanched and refrigerated for use within 2 days.

Preparation: Please pay *no* attention to directions (intended to save time, I suppose) for cooking brains more or less as they come from the market. Brains are encased in a membrane that isn't pleasant in terms of "mouth feel" if it's left in place, and they look better and are easier to handle after they are cleaned and blanched. *Cleaning:* Soak the brains in salted cold water for an hour, then pluck and pull off the encasing membrane. This is most easily done under a trickling tap.
Blanching: Boil a pot of water with a teaspoonful of salt and a tablespoonful of mild vinegar added to each quart. Add the brains and poach them at a bare simmer for 15 minutes. Cool them in the liquid, or drop them into ice water for a fast cool-down. If final cooking won't follow at once, drain and refrigerate.

SOMETHING EXTRA: A FRITTO MISTO OF BRAINS & ARTICHOKES: This Italian dish isn't always easy to reproduce—tiny artichokes suitable for frying are hard to find, and so are brains, as butcher shops become scarce. However, frozen artichoke hearts will do (see below), if you can get the brains—a culinary Catch-22. Here's a sketch of the dish, which makes a lovely lunch.

The poached brains (see Preparation on the left) are sliced, or divided into bits, dried on a cloth, floured lightly, and dropped a few pieces at a time into deep, sizzling-hot olive oil together with sections of quartered and floured baby artichokes. When golden, the "mixed fry" goes onto a warm plate; lemon wedges are added and the lunch is rounded out with a chunk of crusty, wonderful Italian country bread and a glass of white wine.

Substitutions: Baby artichokes aren't unknown this side of the water, but they aren't your everyday greengrocery item, either. Frozen artichoke hearts, a fair substitute, should be thawed, then dried well on a cloth before they're floured and fried. (The canned hearts taste canned, and aren't recommended.) There's no substitute for the olive oil, though; its flavor is essential to the dish. You needn't buy the most expensive kind, as long as it actually tastes of olives; a moderately full-flavored oil would be my choice.

FROM THE CORNFIELDS

Juice or fresh fruit

*Pennsylvania Dutch Scrapple (below), with optional eggs,
"over lightly" or otherwise*

Pancake Syrup à la Dad (below), any version

Alternatives: Instead of scrapple, serve
Corn Oysters (below)
and *Updated Home-Style Sausage (page 30),*
or thick-cut bacon
and one of the syrups below

To drink: *Tea, coffee, or other breakfast beverage*

The choice here is between two good and very American things. One, a meaty and herbal Pennsylvania Dutch Scrapple, is made with cornmeal; the Corn Oysters are fritters based on whole kernels of corn and served with my favorite home-style breakfast sausage. The sausage has been updated with directions for making it in a way that cuts down on the fat without a loss of porky character.

With either breakfast, enjoy one of the three versions of Pancake Syrup à la Dad. All three syrups are quick to make and somehow more down-to-earth in taste than most commercial kinds.

SCRAPPLE SEASONINGS:
I use savory in place of the sage preferred by many traditional cooks, and sometimes I include a few leaves of sweet marjoram, too. I hope you'll feel free to fiddle with the seasonings, preferably after you've tried the scrapple my way.

PENNSYLVANIA DUTCH SCRAPPLE

ankee cornmeal mush or Yankee hasty pudding, Italian polenta, Roman gnocchi, Rumanian mamaliga, Pennsylvania Dutch scrapple—only a few of the maize dishes the world has grown up on since New World foods first traveled from their native corner of the hemisphere. Scrapple, clearly, is a kind of polenta in which meat is cooked *with* cornmeal, not in a sauce to go on top. Like polenta and mamaliga and other "ethnic" corn dishes, but unlike some other old American foods that have been lost, scrapple is a survivor—in brick form, it's widely sold to modern Americans from butchers' cold cases.

Scrapple can be made country style or Philadelphia style, but the differences needn't detain us. This is the way I learned to make it from my mother, whose people on both sides had been established for many generations in the Delaware Water Gap country of New Jersey, just across the river from areas of "Dutch" settlement in northeastern Pennsylvania. No doubt because of that propinquity, some of her (non-German) family's recipes, including many of the handwritten ones later given me by my Great-aunt Minnie, who lived in the Water Gap country most of her life, are unmistakably "Pennsylvania Dutch" in ingredients, seasoning, and method. And also very good. (Like the best dishes of the Shakers—who are, unlike the "Dutch," a vanishing group in our society—really good examples of Dutch food seem to me to be especially honest. While pretending to no elegance whatsoever, they taste of "what they are," a great merit in a world of disguised edibles.)

This excellent version of scrapple makes a hearty breakfast or informal supper. The recipe makes two loaves, but it's easily halved if you like.

Makes 2 loaves, each serving 4 to 6

2 pounds boneless pork shoulder, or 3½ to 4 pounds pork neck bones
1 medium onion, sliced
1 teaspoon, or as needed, salt
1 teaspoon crumbled dried summer savory (or use sage)
½ teaspoon crumbled dried thyme
¼ teaspoon crumbled dried sweet marjoram, optional
2 cups yellow cornmeal, preferably coarse stone-ground meal
¼ teaspoon, or to taste, black pepper
All-purpose flour for dredging
Unsalted butter, or bacon or sausage drippings for browning
Accompaniment: Pancake Syrup à la Dad, below

Simmer the pork and the onion in water to cover, with 1 teaspoon salt, until very tender. Remove the meat. Skim off any excess fat and measure the broth; if necessary, add water or stock to make 4 cups.

Chop the meat fine, discarding any bones, and return it to the broth. Add the savory or sage, thyme, and the marjoram, if used. Heat to boiling.

Stir the cornmeal with enough cold water (about 1 cup) to dampen it well. Stir the wet meal gradually into the boiling broth and cook over medium heat, stirring often, until the mush is very thick and ploppy, about 20 minutes. Season with the pepper and taste critically; it may need more salt, more pepper, and more herb(s).

Spoon the scrapple into 2 medium-size loaf pans rinsed out with cold water. Cool, cover with plastic or foil, and refrigerate. When firm, remove the loaves from the pans and wrap them for storage. They'll keep for 2 weeks refrigerated, for months if frozen.

To prepare for serving: Slice the scrapple (thawed in its wrappings if frozen) ½ inch thick with a serrated knife. Flour the slices and brown them on both sides in a skillet filmed with butter, bacon or sausage drippings, or other fat. Serve with syrup.

PANCAKE SYRUP À LA DAD

hen Dad was baking Sunday-morning pancakes on his cast-iron griddle back home in California, grocery-store syrup wasn't on the table; Dad made pancakes *his* way, with a sourdough batter, and he made syrup by melting and caramelizing sugar to a deep gold, then boiling it with water. The flavor was so pleasing that Dad often skipped the maple flavoring, and sometimes he melted butter in the hot syrup and served the mixture in a pitcher. For a tableful of children, this eliminated many requests to "pass the butter," and it did (and does) taste good.

CAUTION: Melted sugar can be tricky—it spits and sputters—so proceed with care.

Makes 2 cups

2¼ cups granulated sugar
1½ cups water
¼ cup light corn syrup
Pinch of salt
1 teaspoon Mapleine or
    other maple flavoring, or
    to taste, optional

FOR BUTTERED SYRUP:
    Unsalted butter

POWDERED MAPLE:
Powdered maple has come on the scene fairly recently; it's a delicious addition to the pantry shelf. Dad would have loved it, if technology had then existed for dehydrating maple syrup to a light powder. It keeps indefinitely, whereas syrup, once opened, will develop mold unless it's refrigerated (okay for a month or two) or frozen (okay indefinitely).
Making syrup from maple powder takes only moments; directions are on the package. We get ours by mail order from Vermont.

PANCAKE SYRUP À LA DAD (CONTINUED)

If we had "maple" syrup, it was made by adding to the syrup a concentrated flavoring called Mapleine. (It's said to be still on the market, though I haven't seen it for years.) Dad's Mapleine syrup was richer in flavor than Grade-A real maple, which to my taste, to this day, is wishy-washy. I prefer dark (Grade B) syrup when I can find it, surely because of all those Sundays' worth of pancakes and syrup. These syrups aren't for pancakes only, as the pairings in this menu demonstrate.

Stir the sugar and ¼ cup of the water in a large, heavy saucepan or cast-iron Dutch oven over low heat, using a wooden spoon or spatula. As the sugar heats, watch it like a hawk and stir it often. When pale-brown streaks appear and melting starts, stir constantly until the mixture, which will bubble wildly, becomes just golden brown, about the color of an unblanched almond; depending on the heat of the burner, this will take at least 5 minutes. Don't let it overbrown or it will be bitter.

At that point, stand back and add the remaining water—a lot of sputtering will follow, so keep out of range. Cook and stir the syrup until the hardened caramel dissolves and the syrup thickens a little, a matter of 2 or 3 minutes. (It will thicken more as it cools.)

Stir in the corn syrup and salt. Cool slightly, then add the flavoring if you're using it.

Serve warm. Refrigerate leftovers.

For buttered syrup: Melt 2 or 3 tablespoons of unsalted butter in each cup of hot syrup.

———

BROWN-SUGAR SYRUP: To make about a pint of brown-sugar syrup without caramelizing the sugar, combine 1 pound (1 box) of light-brown sugar with 1½ cups water and ½ cup light corn syrup in a saucepan. Boil, stirring often, until syrup thickens a bit, perhaps 5 minutes. Add a pinch of salt and, if you like, 1 teaspoon (or more, after tasting) of maple flavoring.

CORN OYSTERS

amed for the fried oysters they're supposed to resemble, these small fritters of the tenderest corn are held together by a bare minimum of egg batter. They're great for breakfast or brunch with a splash of Pancake Syrup à la Dad (any version) or store-bought maple syrup. For dinner, Corn Oysters make beautiful music with fried chicken and gravy.

Makes about 2 dozen fritters

2½ cups fresh sweet corn kernels and pulp (you'll need 4 to 6 ears; see Cutting Kernels, below)
3 large eggs, separated
3 tablespoons all-purpose flour
½ teaspoon salt
Large pinch of freshly ground pepper
Very small pinch of freshly grated nutmeg, optional
¼ cup, or more as needed, corn oil
2 tablespoons, or more as needed, unsalted butter

Cut and measure the fresh corn; if the kernels are very large, chop them a bit if you wish.

Whisk the egg yolks, flour, salt, pepper, and optional nutmeg together; stir in the corn.

Beat the egg whites to soft peaks. Stir one-fourth thoroughly into the batter, then fold the rest in gently.

Heat half each of the oil and butter in a heavy skillet over medium heat. When the butter stops foaming, drop heaping tablespoonfuls of batter into the skillet and cook the "oysters" rather slowly, 3 or 4 minutes on each side, until they're delicately firm and browned. As they're finished, keep them warm in a low oven (200°) on a platter lined with paper toweling. Using the remaining oil and butter as needed, cook the remaining fritters. Serve hot.

CARNIVORES' CORN FRITTERS: If a tempting amount of meat still lingers on a smoky ham bone in the refrigerator, you might consider modifying this menu in favor of including some of it in the Corn Oysters.

The idea would be to omit the sausage or bacon from the bill of fare and fold a generous portion of chopped or ground ham—up to ¾ cup—into the batter for the fritters. The quantity of corn should be reduced by ½ cup or a little more, and the salt will need to be reduced by half (or more, if the ham is quite salty—taste it before proceeding).

CUTTING KERNELS: To remove kernels from an ear of corn, stand the ear on end and slice down with a sharp knife, cutting off the upper half or two-thirds of a few rows of kernels; repeat around the ear. To finish, scrape down the cob with the back of the blade, pressing out all the tender pulp.

CURRYING FLAVOR

Tomato juice enlivened with hot pepper sauce, lemon juice, and Worcestershire sauce; or Bloody Marys

Eggs à la Hotrod (below)

Broiled or sautéed thin-sliced Canadian-style bacon or ham

Butter-Poached Apples (below)

Toasted English muffins
Ginger marmalade

To drink: *Tea, coffee, or other breakfast beverage*

Talking about way-back-when, who else remembers Eggs à la Goldenrod, a nourishing dish that used to be taught to girls in Home Ec classes? Musing about that fancily named dish—I was looking back on this cook's beginnings with some amusement, while stirring a potful of something—I decided to rejigger its near-terminal blandness into a breakfast dish that might be more interesting to the palate of anyone over three years of age. The results are here—a lightly curried dish I've dubbed "Eggs à la Hotrod."

For close harmony, the eggs are accompanied by Butter-Poached Apples, and ginger marmalade is suggested for the muffins.

EGGS À LA HOTROD

This is a fast forward from the Eggs à la Goldenrod of Home Ec class to something more venturesome, just for the fun of seeing if it can be done. Drastic revision of the classic formula has resulted in eggs in a sauce with "devil" seasonings, topped with what the French—who don't have our native goldenrod—would call a "mimosa" of sieved egg yolks hotted up with a little curry powder. It's a zesty breakfast-lunch dish, "retro" only in its origins.

Cover the eggs with hot tap water in a saucepan and simmer 10 minutes. Set under the running cold tap to cool slightly, then shell.

While the eggs cook, melt the butter over medium heat in a shallow fireproof casserole that can go to the table; add the flour and cook, stirring, for a minute or two. Gradually whisk in the broth, then the milk, and bring to a boil; add the bay leaf and boil gently, stirring, for 3 minutes. Taste; season with salt, pepper, mustard, the Worcestershire, and a few drops of Tabasco; the flavor should be lively. Remove the bay leaf.

Chop the egg whites coarsely and fold them into the sauce. Mash the yolks well with the curry powder, starting with 1 teaspoon; taste for spiciness before adding more.

Rewarm the sauced eggs until piping hot, place in a serving dish, then press the curried yolks through a sieve over the top. Serve hot with (or over) toast or muffins.

EGGS À LA GOLDENROD, THEN: The dish started with a carefully constructed "cream" sauce—really a white sauce—seasoned with a pinch of salt (I don't remember pepper). Diced whites of hard-boiled eggs were added to the sauce, which was spooned over toast. The yolks were pushed through a sieve to make "goldenrod" flowers over the top. We didn't notice that the eggs were pretty bland—we had cooked! Artful seasoning was yet to come...

WHITE SAUCE NOTE:

These proportions of butter, flour, and liquid make a sauce on the light side. For denser sauce increase the butter and flour to 8 tablespoons each (1 stick butter, ½ cup flour). Either version can be thinned, after cooking, with more broth or milk.

Serves 6

10 large eggs
6 tablespoons (¾ stick) unsalted butter (see White Sauce Note, above)
6 tablespoons all-purpose flour (see White Sauce Note, above)
2 cups chicken broth
2 cups milk, or 1 cup each light cream and milk
Medium bay leaf, optional
Salt and pepper, to taste
1 teaspoon, or to taste, Dijon-style mustard
½ teaspoon, or to taste, Worcestershire sauce
Few drops Tabasco or other hot pepper sauce
1 to 2 teaspooons curry powder, depending on strength
6 slices buttered crisp toast, halved, or 6 halved, toasted, and buttered English muffins

BUTTER-POACHED APPLES

ore delicate in both texture and looks than fried apples, these poached slices are particularly good with the curry-touched Eggs à la Hotrod. They're also dandy as an accompaniment for ham or sausage, or as a hot fruit topping for waffles.

With the optional drops of vanilla and a little cream, the apples make a pleasant small dessert.

Melt the butter in a large skillet. Add the apples; sprinkle with ¼ cup sugar, 1 tablespoon lemon juice, and, if you like, the vanilla.

Cook the apples gently, partly covered, over low heat until they are translucent, turning once or twice. Cooking takes 15 minutes or so, depending on the firmness of the fruit.

Taste; add more sugar and lemon, if needed. Serve warm.

————

APPLE "PIE" FOR THE CHILDREN: Talk about nursery food—apples cooked along these lines are remembered from childhood, piled warm on whole-wheat bread. The motherly rationale must have been that this simple sweet was better for young stomachs than apples in pie crust, but it was nevertheless delicious. Cinnamon went on top.

Serves 6

4 tablespoons (½ stick) unsalted butter

2 pounds firm sweet apples, peeled, cored, and cut into ½-inch wedges

¼ cup, or as needed, granulated sugar

1 tablespoon, or as needed, fresh lemon juice

½ teaspoon vanilla, optional

FOR A HUNGRY MORNING

---

*Patties of Updated Home-Style Sausage (below), or the
original sausage following the recipe*

*Cored and sliced tart apples pan-browned in a little of the
sausage fat*

Curdled Eggs (below)

*Hot Biscuits or Buttermilk Biscuits (below), or the Blueberry
Version (page 217) of Cinnamon-Cupped Apple Muffins
Jam or marmalade*

To drink: Coffee, tea, or other breakfast beverage

Good, even great, appetites will be perfectly happy with the updated version of breakfast sausage in this menu, even though it's considerably reduced in fat content. For any unreconstructed traditionalists out there, the recipe for the full-fat original is also included.

To go with the sausage, you might have eggs prepared in the uncommon but not particularly far-out way below (or just scramble some eggs). And I hope you'll make some fast and delicious, *real* hot biscuits, just to strike a blow for real food and simultaneously thumb a nose at boxed biscuit mixes, which aren't all *that* much easier to use.

UPDATED HOME-STYLE SAUSAGE

Traditional breakfast sausage is one of the easiest meat specialties to make, now that the food processor has replaced the meat grinder. But, alas, sausage is under fire from the cholesterol police because of its high fat content. What to do?

After making sausage occasionally over the years I'd hate to erase it from my repertory, so I've worked out this lower-fat version of my best recipe that's hard to tell from the cholesterol- and calorie-laden original. (For the key to fat reduction I'm indebted to Carl Sontheimer, the introducer of the food processor to this country, who publicized the use of rice—an inspiration of the Jones sausage people—as a not-so-secret sausage ingredient.)

If you'd like to try the cholesterol-be-damned original of my modified formula, it follows the main recipe. That classic type is preferable for making cassoulet and similar dishes because of its shape-holding ability and its fat lusciousness.

Either version of the sausage is less salty, by design, than most store-bought sausage, and, of course, neither recipe here contains nitrites.

Food-processor method: Put into the processor bowl the salt, sage, thyme, hot peppers, peppercorns, bay leaves, and, if used, marjoram; pulse the machine until the seasonings are ground. Remove and reserve.

Chop the meat and fat coarsely by pulsing the machine on and off, being careful not to overgrind it. Add the rice or bread crumbs; pulse briefly twice; add the ground seasonings and ½ cup ice water and pulse briefly, just to mix. (If your machine can't do all the chopping and mixing in one batch, divide the meat and rice for chopping, then mix the seasonings in by hand.) The final

Makes about 2½ pounds

2 to 2½ teaspoons coarse
    (kosher) salt
1½ teaspoons crumbled
    dried sage leaves or
    ground sage
1½ teaspoons crumbled
    dried thyme leaves
2 or 3 small dried hot red

peppers, seeds removed,
or ¼ teaspoon ground
hot red pepper, or ½
teaspoon red pepper
flakes
½ teaspoon whole white
peppercorns
2 medium bay leaves,
stems removed, broken
up
¼ teaspoon crumbled
dried sweet marjoram,
optional
2 pounds trimmed chilled
pork shoulder, no more
than 10 percent fat,
cubed coarsely
⅔ cup soft-cooked rice
(short-grain works best),
chilled (or substitute ¾
cup coarse, soft bread
crumbs)
½ to ⅔ cup, or as needed,
ice water
Oil or shortening for skillet

texture should be light; if not, work in a little more ice water, adding it gradually to avoid overdoing it.

Meat-grinder method: Grind the seasonings in a spice mill, blender, or mortar. Cut the meat into strips 1 inch wide; mix with the seasonings, then grind through a plate with medium holes. Pass rice through the grinder, then mix the meat, rice, and ice water with a spoon or spatula. If the texture isn't light, beat in a little more ice water, adding a small amount at a time.

To check seasoning, cook a small sample in a lightly greased skillet over low heat until thoroughly done. (Raw pork should *never* be tasted.) Add more seasonings if they're needed, remembering that the flavor of the sausage will deepen further as it mellows.

Wrap the sausage in plastic or foil and refrigerate it for at least 12 hours, or for up to 4 days, before using. If it's to be stored longer, freeze as outlined in Storing Sausage (below).

Cooking: Make patties about ⅓ inch thick; place in a cold, lightly greased heavy skillet, add ¼ inch water, set over low heat, cover, and cook, turning often, until the patties are cooked through, at least 10 minutes. Uncover; evaporate the liquid and let the patties brown *lightly.* Avoid overbrowning the sausage, which would tend to make it dry.

THE ORIGINAL SAUSAGE: Omit rice and ice water; use 2¼ to 2½ pounds of pork and fat—3 parts lean meat to 1 part fat. Judge proportions by eye, or weigh the meat and fat separately. Use the set of seasonings you prefer, and assemble the sausage in the same way.

SEASONING TO TASTE: Salt and pepper are the basic sausage seasonings; beyond that, sausagemakers suit themselves. The seasonings in my recipe aren't cast in concrete. If sage is your pleasure, increase the quantity to 3 teaspoons, omit the thyme, marjoram, and bay leaves, but include the salt, hot peppers, and white pepper.

Another combination: Try 1 teaspoon dried summer savory, 1 to 2 teaspoons sage, and 2 bay leaves, plus the salt, hot pepper and peppercorns; omit the thyme and marjoram.

STORING SAUSAGE: Stored in the coldest part of the refrigerator, uncooked sausage can be kept for 4 days from its making. For longer storage, shape patties, freeze them on a baking sheet, then seal them airtight; they'll keep in the freezer for 2 months. Cooked sausage patties may be refrigerated for 2 days or so before use; or freeze them like raw sausage.

CURDLED EGGS

he original of this Victorian-era dish, discovered in *I Go A-Marketing*, by a Boston lady named Henrietta Sowle, was made with quantities of heavy cream; it is a delicious thing, but its calorie count is off the scale. A little fiddling resulted in a dish of eggs that look and taste creamy without the surtax of butterfat.

Eggs prepared this way are dandy for keeping warm on a breakfast buffet, as they hold their creamy texture well instead of turning into concrete before they're all eaten up.

Serves 6

2 cups milk
3 to 4 tablespoons
  unsalted butter
2 tablespoons cornstarch
Salt and white pepper, to
  taste
Pinch of freshly grated
  nutmeg
10 large eggs, beaten just
  to mix
A little grated Swiss
  cheese, optional

Heat all but 3 tablespoons of the milk with the butter in a skillet that can go to the table. Meanwhile, stir the reserved milk with the cornstarch.

When the butter has melted in the hot milk, stir in the cornstarch mixture and cook over low heat until the sauce has thickened, stirring constantly; this usually takes 2 or 3 minutes. Season with salt, pepper, and nutmeg.

Pour the eggs slowly into the simmering sauce in a spiral pattern. Cover; cook over the lowest heat until the edges have set, then pull the set portion to the center with a few spatula strokes; cook just until the eggs have become soft curds in the creamy sauce. Serve hot.

Optionally, a minute or two before the eggs are done, sprinkle the cheese over them and brown the top lightly under the broiler.

THE ORIGINAL EGGS, RUNNING AWAY FROM THE CHOLESTEROL POLICE: Mrs. Sowle used heavy cream, alone, for the liquid in which her eggs were "curdled." Anyone who would like to approach the original should avoid using ultrapasteurized cream.

If you can get ordinary heavy cream, omit the butter and cornstarch; just heat the cream to simmering, season it, and proceed to cook the eggs. ("Henriette" always included the cheese topping.)

The finished dish will still be lighter in fat than the original, which was devised in the days when heavy cream was *heavy*.

BISCUIT FLOUR: Not for nothing are Southern cooks famous for their hot breads. The best Southern biscuits are made with soft-wheat flour (White Lily is a well-known brand), which is much lower in gluten than the all-purpose flours found over most of the country, and much, much lower in gluten than bread flour. In this recipe, pastry and all-purpose flours are combined to lower the gluten content if soft-wheat flour is beyond reach.

HOT BISCUITS

ot biscuits that are truly wonderful, if you ask me, just can't be made from store-bought mixes. A pity, because mixes are time-savers; but they're also overloaded with ingredients that range from too much salt to too many chemicals included to prevent shelf spoilage. Good scratch biscuits *can* be put together by the veriest beginner while the oven is heating, and they'll be ready to serve 10 to 12 minutes after they go in. Guaranteed.

For do-it-ahead cooks, slightly underbaked biscuits can be frozen for quick reheating in a conventional or microwave oven. Just stop the first baking when they're firm but still a little pale, cool, wrap or bag, and freeze.

Preheat the oven to 450°.

Sift the 1 cup each all-purpose and pastry flour, the baking powder, salt, and sugar (if included) together twice, or whisk them vigorously; thorough mixing is important. Cut in the shortening with a pastry blender, two knives, or your fingers until mixture is mealy. Make a small hollow in the center.

Add the milk and stir from center outward to make a soft dough. Turn the dough onto a lightly floured surface and knead it half a dozen strokes, no more.

Pat or roll the dough out ½ inch thick (⅜ inch if you want thin biscuits) and cut rounds with a biscuit cutter. Place on a (preferably) dark-surfaced baking sheet, close together for soft sides, an inch apart for crisp sides. Brush tops with a little milk or cream.

Bake 10 to 12 minutes, until well browned. Serve the biscuits hot.

Makes about 1 dozen large biscuits

1 cup all-purpose flour, plus additional as needed
1 cup pastry flour (see Biscuit Flour, above)
2 teaspoons baking powder
½ teaspoon salt
1 teaspoon granulated sugar, optional (it helps browning)
6 tablespoons vegetable shortening, or 3 tablespoons each shortening and lard
¾ cup milk
A little milk or cream, for brushing tops

BUTTERMILK BISCUITS: Add ¼ teaspoon baking soda when sifting dry ingredients. Substitute commercial buttermilk (or regular milk stirred with a scant tablespoonful of white vinegar) for the regular milk.

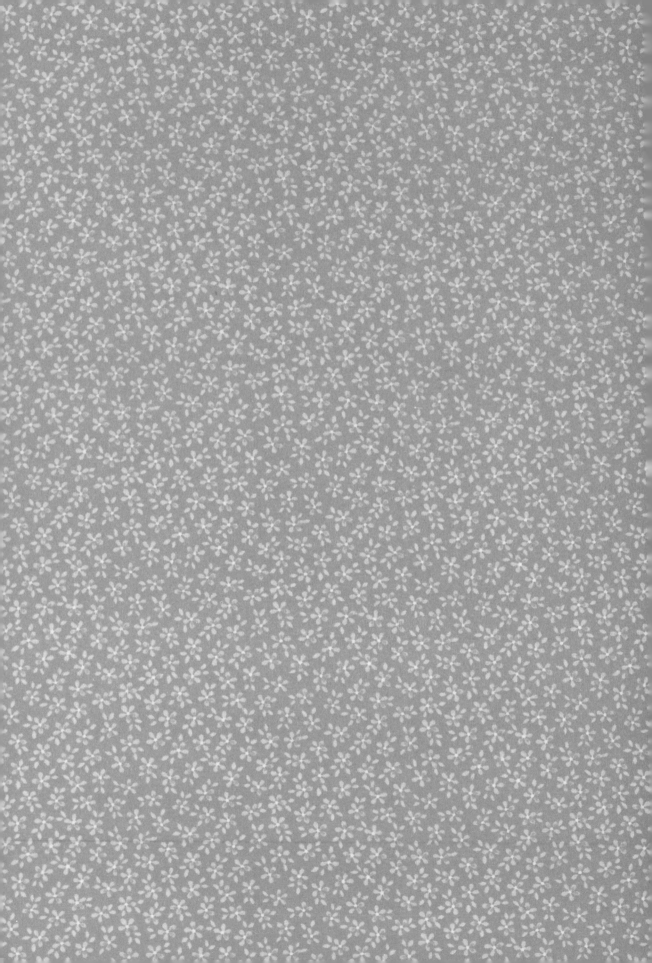

THE LUNCH, PICNIC & COOKOUT CONTINUUM

Then out with their watches, and "Isn't it time to lunch?" So there they have been lunching ... They brought themselves a pick-nick lunch, with Madeira and Champagne to wash it down.
—MARIA EDGEWORTH, *THE ABSENTEE*, 1812,
QUOTED IN ARNOLD PALMER, *MOVABLE FEASTS*

When we say "lunch" nowadays, we often mean a time of day as much as a specific meal, although the word didn't even exist in Britain, where most American food patterns got their start, until the early nineteenth century. "Lunch" came into being back then, historians tell us, only because dinner—the main meal—was being served later and later in the day (though not nearly so late as now), leaving a lengthening midday period in which people stayed their stomachs with snacks consumed as opportunity offered. Those repasts needed a name, and "lunch," derived from "nunch," a countryman's term for a bite to eat, crept into existence on hungry little feet.

Ever since, "lunch" has meant what you wish: a sandwich from a paper bag, an opulent interlude in a white-tablecloth restaurant, something purchased from a vendor's cart or reheated in the office microwave, or—best of all, and usually encountered on weekends, when there's time—a more or less special meal for the whole family and, often, guests.

Speaking for my own household, we find that such festive but unfussy occasions are often more acceptable entertainments than dinner, especially when our guests don't live close by. And, of course, in the warm seasons, guest lunches often take the form of a cookout or picnic. (Trivia item: The picnic acquired its English name at about the same time as lunch.)

The chapter that follows has tastes of all three kinds of lunch, ranging from one of perfect tomato sandwiches and corn on the cob to a pretty fancy feast of lobsters.

FINDING LUNCH IN OTHER CHAPTERS

The lunch possibilities aren't all in the menus that follow. In other sections you'll find many dishes that make a good lunch: Linguine with Clams & Pancetta; hot and cold Lobster Rolls; baked ham and a special salad; a *fritto misto* of calves' brains and baby artichokes; Herb-broiled Chickens, cooled to room temperature; Yankee-Mex Beans; Orzo Risotto with added cheese; Tacos; Pretty Good Chili con Carne; Tomato Aspic with Avocado; hot open sandwiches of leftover Pristine Pot Roast; and many soups and pottages—Lobster Stew, Beef & Okra Soup, Wild Rice & Porcini Soup, Sorrel Egg-Flower Soup, Oyster Stew, and Six-Seafood Chowder among them. For the recipes, and for desserts that might go along, check the Index. (And see the Seasonal Recipe Lists, too.)

DINNER AT NOON

*Steamed & Chilled Clams with Lime, Chive & Mustard
Mayonnaise (below)*

*Classic Chicken Salad (below) or Classic Lobster Salad
(below), either salad garnished with diced, salted, and drained
ripe tomatoes tossed with torn fresh basil*

Fresh Corn Popovers (below)

*Blueberry & Pound Cake Summer Pudding (below) or sliced
and sugared peaches or nectarines, with bakery cookies*

*To drink: A white wine—a Chardonnay, Sauvignon Blanc,
Pinot Blanc, or Fumé Blanc, or a dry white Zinfandel*

The main-dish choice in this three-course meal—it's really a midday dinner—is between creatures from the sea and those from the farmyard, with an offering of steamed clams as an opener to precede either. Fresh Corn Popovers and a blueberry dessert round out the feast. (These two, as noted, can be made in seasons other than summer, thanks to the freezer.) Now that clams and lobsters are within reach of most of us, thanks to air shipment and better-stocked ''gourmet'' fishmongers' shops, this meal is as feasible inland as at the shore, although it may take a bit more planning if you live far away from the crashing waves.

Whether chicken or lobster is the base of the hearty salad, a Sunday ''dinner'' along these lines will make only a light supper necessary, come evening.

STEAMED & CHILLED CLAMS WITH LIME, CHIVE & MUSTARD MAYONNAISE

teamer (or soft-shell) clams are naturally tender enough to be cooked, chilled, and sauced for a vivid and satisfying first course. The sauce here is no kin whatever to the ketchupy stuff that too often swamps cold seafood; it's a good bet with cold shrimp or crabmeat, too.

Small quahogs (on the East Coast) or Manila or other local hard clams (West Coast) may be substituted for steamers. Because their shelled-out meats are firmer and their necks needn't be skinned, they tend to be neater morsels than the raggedy soft-shells, but steamers hold the edge for flavor. Be sure to steam hard clams just until they begin to open; they can toughen in a flash if over-cooked.

Boil half an inch of water in a large pot. Add the well-scrubbed clams (see Storing & Cleaning Clams, below), cover, and bring to a boil over high heat. Uncover (to prevent boiling over) and cook, shaking the pot or stirring the shellfish whenever the foam boils high, for 2 or 3 minutes, or just until all the clams have opened.

Pour the potful into a colander set over a big bowl; reserve the broth. When the clams have cooled, shuck them, pulling off and discarding the rubbery ring of membrane encircling the bodies as well as the loose, dark skin covering the "neck," or siphon. Place in a big bowl.

Strain the broth onto the clams through cheesecloth in a sieve; stop pouring before any sand appears.

Stir and swish the clams through the broth to further

Serves 6

2 quarts (about 3 pounds) medium steamer clams
Lime, Chive & Mustard Mayonnaise (below)
Garnish: *Parsley, coriander, watercress, or baby lettuce*

de-sand them (some grains always survive the earlier steps.) Lift out the clams with a slotted spoon and set them aside. Let the broth settle, strain it again, and repeat the clam rinsing and draining, twice if it seems a good idea.

Chill the clams. Refrigerate or freeze the broth for a future chowder or sauce.

No more than 3 hours before serving, drain the clams again and fold them into about half of the mayonnaise. Refrigerate.

To serve, divide the sauced clams among seafood cocktail glasses or small glass bowls. Top with more mayonnaise; garnish with a leaf or two of green stuff—parsley, coriander, watercress, or baby lettuce.

LIME, CHIVE & MUSTARD MAYONNAISE

Makes about 1¼ cups

1 large egg yolk
1 tablespoon fresh lime juice
1½ teaspoons Dijon-style mustard
¾ cup corn, peanut, or other mild vegetable oil (not olive)
½ teaspoon, or to taste, salt
Big pinch freshly ground white pepper
2 teaspoons finely snipped fresh chives or frozen chives
¼ teaspoon finely grated lime zest (colored rind only, no pith)
Few drops of Tabasco or other hot pepper sauce

Whisk together the egg yolk, lime juice, and mustard. Whisking hard, begin adding oil a few drops at a time, beating in each addition completely before adding more. After the mixture has thickened, add the remaining oil in a thin stream while beating rapidly.

Season with salt, pepper, chives, lime zest, and Tabasco. Taste carefully; the mayonnaise should be highly seasoned, so add more lime juice, mustard, pepper, and/or Tabasco if needed, but be cautious about salt; the clams will supply enough brininess for most tastes.

Refrigerate until needed.

***

STORING & CLEANING CLAMS: Whether we dig our own clams in a near-by Long Island "creek"—actually, a most beautiful bay—or break down and visit the seafood shop, we take care to clean the catch carefully (below) and to rinse the shucked clams in their own juice (see the recipe for the Witty method) to avoid tooth-grating sprinklings of sand in our food. Whatever you do, don't rinse clams in water once they're out of the shell—it robs them of their briny flavor.

Store fresh clams in the refrigerator with a light covering, not airtight. Clean them as close to cooking time as possible. To clean, scrub the shells under the running cold tap with a vegetable or potato brush; give special

THE CHICKEN CANON: To identify the bird we want for chicken salad, consider the pecking order noted by E.S. Dallas in his Victorian-era *Kettner's Book of the Table:*

There is the infant—the spring chicken, or poulet à la Reine; *the boy pullet, or* poulet de grain; *the young gentleman, or* coq vierge; *the young lady, or* poulard; *the capon, the hen, and the old cock.*

attention to the hinges. Cover with fresh water and soak for an hour or so, stirring them about once or twice. Lift them out of the soaking water to leave behind the sand they will have shed.

THE CORNMEAL QUESTION: *ARE YOUR CLAMS HUNGRY?* Some folk wisdom calls for stirring cornmeal into the soaking water to force clams to "feed," which is supposed to make them eliminate any sand in their innards. Does this work? Impossible to decide, though we've put many clams to the cornmeal test. On the whole we prefer the scrub, the soak, and the final rinsing of the meats in their own juice. By the way, shucked raw clams should be rinsed, if at all, only in the juice they yield when they're opened.

CLASSIC CHICKEN SALAD(S)

or a salad rejoicing in the deepest, most chickeny flavor, first catch your *hen*— what used to be called a boiling fowl, now scarcer than the kiwi bird and hardly to be hoped for unless you are within striking distance of a poultry farmer. A well-developed roasting chicken will do very well, and smaller birds will do fairly well, so long as they aren't too young.

Whatever the age of the chicken(s) you obtain, the careful poaching described in the recipe is the key to tender, moist meat and a bonus of chicken broth for another use. (You can of course make salad with leftover roast chicken if you're not doing the whole project "on purpose.")

The dressing for this salad is mayonnaise; in generations past, a "boiled dressing"—which some old cookbooks quaintly confused with genuine mayonnaise—was used. Such a cooked dressing is still excellent for chicken salad; big general cookbooks such as *Joy of Cooking* have reliable recipes.

Serves 6 generously

*About 5 pounds chicken
    (one or two birds), whole*

FOR COOKING THE
    CHICKEN:
*Big handful celery tops
1 carrot, scrubbed and
    quartered
Half an onion
1 clove garlic, slightly
    flattened but unpeeled
8 to 10 peppercorns
1 bay leaf
Pinch of dried thyme
Salt, as needed*

FOR THE SALAD:
*1 to 2 cups chopped very
    tender celery, more if you
    wish*

OPTIONAL EXTRAS,
    CHOICE OF:
*1 to 2 tablespoons drained
    tiny capers
2 to 3 tablespoons finely
    diced sweet red peppers
2 to 3 tablespoons sliced
    pimiento-stuffed green
    olives
About 1½ cups
    mayonnaise, homemade
    (page 272) or the best
    you can buy
Salt and pepper, to taste
A little ground hot red
    pepper
Strained fresh lemon juice,
    if needed*

Rinse the chicken(s) inside and out and set aside to drain.

The poaching: Choose a large pot; run in enough water to cover the bird(s)—more can be added later if your estimate is wrong—and bring it to a boil with the seasonings listed for cooking the chicken, plus a very little salt.

Place the chicken (and the neck, heart, and gizzard, but *not* the liver) in the pot; bring to a boil over high heat, removing any scum as it rises, then lower the heat, cover the pot, and cook the chicken at a simmer. (If the liquid doesn't cover the chicken, add boiling water.)

Cook (poach) the chicken very gently for 30 minutes (for 2 chickens totaling 5 to 6 pounds) or 45 minutes (for 1 large bird). Turn off the heat and leave the chicken in the covered pot for 30 minutes, then uncover and let the chicken cool to lukewarm in the broth.

Drain the chicken(s), saving the broth. Pull off the skin and return it to the broth; remove the chicken from the bones in good-sized chunks; return the bones to the pot, where the giblets have been left. (The plan is to have a pot of wonderful stock for another use.)

Re-cook the broth, bones, and giblets, simmering the pot uncovered until you think the stock has developed maximum flavor. Strain the broth from the debris, cool it, and freeze or refrigerate it for soup or sauces.

Back to our chicken: The salad will be most succulent if it isn't necessary to refrigerate the chicken before the dish is assembled, but don't hold the meat unrefrigerated for more than an hour or two.

To assemble the salad, toss the chicken meat, celery, and any optional extras lightly together. Whisk the mayonnaise to lighten it and fold it into the salad. Taste for seasonings and add salt, pepper, hot pepper, lemon juice, or other seasonings as desired. Serve in a glass or pottery bowl or on individual plates, garnished with a little more mayonnaise if you like.

———

FRUITED CHICKEN SALAD: For a salad of chicken happily matched with fruit, use the same ingredients until you reach the optional extras; then skip the capers and olives, but you may want to include the red peppers (I would). Add 2 to 3 cups of fruit, which can be fresh, cooked, canned, or dried, either one kind or a combination. A few walnut halves or sliced almonds would not come amiss, either.

Suggested fruits: Raisins (soak them in warm water if they are at all dry); halved seedless or seeded grapes; cubed ripe papaya or mango; firm-fleshed apples, with or without skin; diced ripe pineapple or drained chunks of canned pineapple; skinless and sliced segments of orange or grapefruit.

Add a good slug of orange or pineapple juice, or a little lemon or lime juice, to the dressing and taste it thoughtfully to see whether any other adjustment is needed.

A SUPPLE SALAD: Chicken salad is a versatile dish that can be encouraged in various directions. Sometimes I put some chutney or a sprinkling of curry powder into the mayonnaise (these touches are also good for the fruited version). One or two diced cornichons add a tart note, and for more tooth-resistance try a handful of such crisp things as diced jicama or raw Jerusalem artichokes. Almonds or walnuts are excellent in either fruited or savory salad.

CLASSIC LOBSTER SALAD

t follows a traditional pattern, this recipe, and it's as excellent as ever it was. The proceedings begin with cooked and shelled lobster—the how-to's are in Basic Lobster (page 60). For a party of 6, the meat of 3 medium-size lobsters—1½ to 2 pounds each—should be sufficient.

Serves 6 as a main dish

Meat of 3 cooked medium-sized lobsters (about 6 cups), diced; reserve a few claw tips for garnish
1 to 2 cups diced innermost hearts of tender celery, including a few leaves

Toss the lobster, celery, and capers lightly together.

Whisk together the mayonnaise, yogurt or buttermilk, sieved egg yolks, and onion; toss with the lobster. Taste carefully, and season with salt, pepper, hot pepper, and lemon juice.

Scrape into a serving dish and garnish with a few small tender lettuce leaves and the reserved lobster claws. Allow to rest in a cool spot for half an hour or so; refrigerate the salad only if it must be held longer. Its flavor is best at room temperature.

2 tablespoons drained
capers, coarsely chopped
About 1½ cups
mayonnaise, homemade
(page 272) or the best
you can buy, more if
needed
2 or 3 tablespoons yogurt
or buttermilk
Yolks of 3 hard-cooked
large eggs, sieved
A small amount—no more
than a teaspoonful—of
mild onion, minced or
pushed through a garlic
press
Salt and white pepper, to
taste
Ground hot red pepper, to
taste
Fresh lemon juice, as
needed
Garnish: Lettuce leaves

LOBSTER SALAD IN TOMATO CASES: In ripe-tomato season, skin, core, salt inside, and drain upside down a large tomato for each person. Set each tomato on greens on a serving plate; cut down and spread the sides to make "petals"; heap lobster salad in the center. This shouldn't be refrigerated if you can help it.

LOBSTER ROLLS: Luxurious deck or patio picnic fare. Use high-quality longish frankfurter buns; slit open their tops lengthwise. Brush the insides with softened butter or mayonnaise, then fill the rolls to heaping with lobster salad. Serve with plenty of napkins and a dish of cornichons, your own or store-bought, or have some Swedish Cucumbers (see page 281).

FRESH CORN POPOVERS

 versize popovers crunchy with fresh sweet corn were an invention of mine one summer at the start of the eighties when farm stands were overflowing and I experimented with corn every which way but raw. The big golden balloons were a decided success, so I included the popovers in an article commissioned by a food magazine. Unfortunately it was erroneously captioned "traditional" by somebody or other before it hit print. Perhaps because of the caption the recipe has, alas, been "borrowed" twice for republication elsewhere.

Well, corn popovers *aren't* traditional; they are (or were) mine, and now they're yours. Decide for yourself whether they should enter the corn hall of fame.

High-quality whole-kernel canned or frozen corn can be used with good results when the real thing is out of season, or when you doubt the quality of the only fresh corn obtainable.

Makes 6 to 8

*Vegetable oil for coating
  pans
⅓ cup (lightly packed)
  fresh sweet corn kernels
  (see Choosing & Cutting
  Corn, below)
⅓ cup water
3 large eggs
½ cup milk
1 tablespoon corn oil or
  melted unsalted butter
1 teaspoon granulated
  sugar, optional
¾ teaspoon salt
⅛ teaspoon freshly ground
  white pepper
1 cup sifted all-purpose
  flour*

**CHOOSING & CUTTING
CORN:** Anything made with
corn, including these
popovers, is going to be good
only if the corn is good.
Luckily, whole-kernel corn of
excellent quality is vacuum-
packed in cans (get the kind
with very little liquid) and is
also to be found in the
grocer's freezer. As always,
fresh corn is the first choice
if you can get it—to choose
perfect ears, see the remarks
on page 55. If you need a
brush-up on getting the
kernels off the cob, see page
25.

FRESH CORN POPOVERS (CONTINUED)

Preheat oven to 425°.

Oil 6 to 8 heavy ceramic custard cups, or the cups
(usually 7) of a popover pan. Set custard cups, if used, on a
baking sheet. (Alternatively, the well-oiled cups—which
are smaller—of a muffin pan can be used; count on
making about 10 popovers of that size.)

Chop the corn with the water until medium-coarse,
using a blender or food processor.

Drain well in a sieve over a bowl; reserve both corn
and liquid.

Add water to the liquid to make ½ cup. Whisk
together (or blend in a blender) the corn liquid, eggs, milk,
oil, sugar, salt, and pepper. Add the flour; whisk (or blend
in on–off bursts) just until the batter is smooth; stir in the
corn. (The batter may rest at room temperature for 1 to 2
hours at this point.)

Place the sheet of custard cups, or the popover pan,
in the oven to heat for 5 minutes. (The muffin pan should
heat for only 2 minutes or so.)

Stir the batter briefly, then quickly remove the sheet
or pan from the oven, closing the door fast. Fill the cups
halfway with batter and return them to the oven.

Bake the popovers 15 minutes (do not open the oven
until they're almost done), then reset the oven to 400° and
continue baking until the popovers are firm and well
browned, about 20 minutes more.

Remove the popovers from the oven and their cups
and serve them promptly. If you'd like extra-crisp popovers, leave the oven heat on; pierce each popover just
above the cup rim with a knife blade; remove them from
the cups, open the slashes a little, lay them over the cups,
and return them to the oven for 3 to 5 minutes.

BLUEBERRY & POUND CAKE SUMMER PUDDING

 reater than the sum of its parts. Long ago some suave Yankee substituted native blueberries for the traditional English fruits in summer pudding, a confection built on a foundation of lavishly buttered bread, and people have been doing it ever since. (Directions follow the main recipe.) My version of this dessert uses pound cake in lieu of bread and butter; any other plain cake would do as well.

Simmer the blueberries, sugar, water, and cinnamon together until the berries have popped and the mixture has thickened a little, 8 to 10 minutes. Pick out and discard the cinnamon. Taste the berries; add lemon juice and more sugar, if needed, remembering that the pound cake is sweet.

Lightly butter a 6-cup bowl with a round bottom. Trim the crusts from the cake and reserve the scraps; cut the loaf into ¼-inch-thick slices. Line the bowl with cake slices, cutting them as necessary to make them fit together snugly.

Pour in half of the berry filling; top with cake trimmings, plus some of the sliced cake if it is needed to cover the filling well. Pour in the rest of the berries; cover the top snugly with the remaining cake slices, fitting them closely together.

Lay plastic wrap over the top, then add a small plate that just covers the pudding inside the bowl. Weight the plate lightly (try a 1-pound can of food). Refrigerate the pudding for at least 24 hours before serving it; it will keep for 3 days.

To serve, loosen the sides of the pudding with a knife blade, then turn it carefully onto a pretty plate. Garnish with a ring of fresh blueberries (or other fruit) or a garland of mint leaves. Serve with whipped or plain cream or other topping.

Serves 6 to 8 generously

2 pint baskets (about 6 cups) blueberries, sorted and rinsed (see Frozen Blueberries in Place of Fresh, next page)
⅔ cup, or as needed, granulated sugar
½ cup water
1 stick (3 inches) cinnamon, broken coarsely
Fresh lemon juice, optional
Butter for coating bowl
A 7-inch loaf of pound cake (a baker's 12-ounce loaf)
Garnish: Extra blueberries, or mint leaves
Accompaniment: Lightly whipped or plain heavy cream, or soft yogurt, or dairy sour cream

BREAD & BUTTER PUDDING WITH BERRIES: Use about 12 slices of thin-sliced firm white bread, crusts trimmed off, to line the bowl, first spreading both sides with soft unsalted butter—about 6 tablespoons should do it—and increase the sweetening of the berries a little. Put a slice or two of the buttered bread in the center of the pudding where cake scraps are called for in the pound-cake version. Finish as directed.

FROZEN BLUBERRIES IN PLACE OF FRESH: Frozen berries will work perfectly well. While commercially frozen berries are ready to use without rinsing, home-frozen berries hold best if they haven't been washed before freezing. If I've been forehanded in July, there are usually pint boxes of blueberries, overwrapped in plastic and frozen as is, in my freezer. Before use the berries are tossed, loose but still frozen, into a colander, rinsed with quite warm water (the warmth keeps them from refreezing into a block), then sorted; they're then ready to blot dry (if necessary—it's not, for this recipe) for use.

OTHER CHOICES: Nowhere is it written that berries other than blueberries can't be used; wild blueberries are heavenly, and blackberries, if you can find them, are a happy choice.

NOT YOUR EVERYDAY COOKOUT

With the cocktails, beer, or other drinks: *Crisp Garlic Garbanzos (below)*

Citrus-Glazed Pork Ribs (below)

Foil-wrapped sweet potatoes in their skins, roasted over charcoal (allow about an hour)

Corn Grilled in the Husk (page 56), with butter creamed with black pepper and a little lime juice

A bowl of coleslaw (see Index)—and/or a farmstyle salad platter: sliced, salted and peppered tomatoes; rings of red onion; sliced cucumbers

"Barbecued" or Pulled Bread (below)

Nectarine & Almond Custard Pie (below) or Hazelnut Cheese Tart (page 151)

To drink: *Beer, or jug wine, or a lemony soft drink*

From the garlicky garbanzos with the drinks through the citrusy barbecued ribs, to a dessert that makes a match between summer fruit, almonds, and custard, this isn't your standard patio cookout but it does include some beloved basics.

CRISP GARLIC GARBANZOS

evised on a summer weekend when swarms of people were expected on the deck for cocktails, this treatment of garbanzos—also known as chick-peas—is now much in request. The nutty little legumes are especially good with a glass of dry sherry or white wine; their texture is a pleasant contrast to the smooshier types of cocktail food.

Like fava beans, garbanzos have an extra coat of skin, and they're more pleasant to eat without it; so, if time permits, I pinch off their outer coats after they've been soaked. The skinning isn't essential, and neither is starting from scratch; canned garbanzos do quite well when time is short.

Garlic garbanzos are a dandy side dish with chili, too; how-to's follow the main recipe.

About 3 cups

*2 cups dried garbanzos
    (chick-peas) or 2 cans
    (19-ounce size) canned
    garbanzos
Salt, as needed
½ cup, more if needed,
    full-flavored olive oil
4 or more large cloves
    garlic, peeled and
    chopped*

Starting from scratch: Soak dried garbanzos 6 hours or overnight in ample water. Drain. If you wish, pinch off the outer coats. (They can be a bit tough.)

Cover well with fresh water and simmer, partly covered, until tender-firm, not mushy, 1 to 2 hours depending on how long the garbanzos have been stored. Add salt to taste toward the end of cooking.

Drain; spread out to cool and dry off. If necessary, pat with paper towels.

If using canned garbanzos; Drain, rinse well under running water, and pat dry with paper towels.

Heat the oil in a large skillet or wok. Add the garlic and garbanzos and toss-fry over medium-high heat, scooping and tossing them constantly, until they are crisp and deep gold in color, about 8 minutes. Salt lightly and serve warm or at room temperature.

Refrigerate leftovers. They'll soften in storage but can be recrisped by a few minutes' tossing in a skillet.

GARLIC GARBANZOS TO GO WITH CHILI: Garlic Garbanzos that have been sautéed a shorter time, without becoming crisp, are a pleasure with my West Coast version of Chili con Carne (see page 148), or with any other version of chili. To serve 6 as a side dish, I'd double the recipe above.

COUNTRY-STYLE PORK RIBS TWO WAYS

he ribs called "country-style" come from the blade end of the loin, near the shoulder, a succulent part of the pig that's valued by home sausage-makers. (Our home-style sausage on page 30 is made from the shoulder cut.)

Unlike a rack of garden-variety spareribs, which looks like a hungry xylophone more than anything else, these meaty morsels are cut apart for sale and resemble mini-chops, though they're a good deal smaller and narrower than any chops I've met with. Each has a bone surrounded by several generous bites of meat, and there is enough of the succulent piggy fat here and there to keep the meat well basted as it cooks.

When they have been slow-baked in the oven until they are ready to leave the bone, with a seasoning of salt and pepper only, the ribs are delicious just as is. (Elsewhere in these pages you'll find a dinner menu designed around that simon-pure version.)

For a cookout, we're glazing the ribs with the citrusy sauce in the second recipe of the set on the following page. (This would also be good if you'd like a touch of barbecue-style eating indoors.)

Ribs that are to be glazed as a final step may be prebaked a day ahead of time and refrigerated to await their final baptism of sauce and fire.

A LITTLE-KNOWN PIGGY PART: Country-style ribs have surely been enjoyed by country folk since the time of Charles Lamb's mythical discoverer of roast pig, but this cut is seldom dealt with in treatises on meat. Out of a half-shelf's worth of cook's books on the subject, only Merle Ellis's dandy *Cutting-Up in the Kitchen* (San Francisco, Chronicle Books, 1975) discusses this flavorful cut from the blade (cheap) end of the pork loin.

SLOW-BAKED MINIMALIST PORK RIBS

Serves 6 generously

5 pounds country-style
  pork ribs, or 2 meaty
  ribs per person
Salt and pepper, to taste

Preheat the oven to 325°.

Trim surplus outside fat from the ribs, then rub them generously with salt and pepper. (Chopped garlic, onion, or herbs may be added, but I don't use them.)

Lay the ribs on their sides and close together on a rack in a shallow baking pan; put ½ inch of water in pan. Cover with aluminum foil, ballooning it a little and crimping it to the pan to seal all around.

Bake the ribs in the preheated oven for 2 hours, then check; only small ones will be approaching doneness, but you'll want to have an idea how things are going; big ribs can take up to 3 hours. The ribs are ready when they're meltingly tender and lightly browned. If you continue cooking, reseal the foil cover. If the meat is done but looks pallid, remove the foil covering and bake a few minutes longer.

The finished ribs can wait, covered, in the turned-off oven with its door open for half an hour or so. Serve them hot.

If ribs are to be glazed, proceed as described below. If glazed ribs are to be on tomorrow's menu, cool the plain baked ribs uncovered, then wrap and refrigerate them, being sure to save the pan juices for the glazing sauce.

Citrus-Glazed Pork Ribs

Serves 6

Slow-Baked Minimalist
  Pork Ribs (below) and
  their pan juices
2 tablespoons minced
  sweet or very mild onion
2 tablespoons grated fresh
  orange zest (colored rind
  only, no pith) or briefly

If the ribs have been cooked ahead and refrigerated, reheat them slowly, wrapped in foil, in a slow oven or on the barbecue grill, then proceed with the directions below.

Remove the fat from the pan juices, pour the juices into a saucepan, and add all the remaining ingredients except the salt and pepper.

Cook the sauce over medium heat, stirring it occasionally, until it has reached good brushing consistency, about 10 minutes; it should be thick enough to cling to the ribs.

*soaked and minced Dried
Peel (page 271)*
*3 tablespoons fresh or
bottled lime juice
(sweetened juice will be
fine)*
*3 tablespoons cider or
white wine vinegar*
3 tablespoons honey
*3 tablespoons tomato
ketchup*
*2 or 3 dashes Tabasco or
other hot pepper sauce*
Salt and pepper, to taste

Purée the sauce in a blender or food processor until it is quite smooth. Taste; add salt and pepper and, if needed, more hot sauce, vinegar or citrus juice, or honey.

Brush the sauce over the hot ribs and proceed to glaze them. This can be done on a broiling pan and rack placed several inches from the preheated broiler element, or on a barbecue grill. If you're grilling over charcoal, place the ribs to one side of (not directly over) coals that are only medium-hot—they should be coated with white ash.

However you're cooking them, turn the ribs and brush them with more sauce every few minutes until they're glazed to suit. And whether you're cooking indoors or out, watch and baste—don't stroll away during the glazing, if you don't want to risk scorching or drying out a meat that should be delightfully succulent when served.

"BARBECUED" OR PULLED BREAD

THE GARLIC VERSION:
Fold a square of foil around several large cloves of garlic sprinkled with olive oil; wrap; bake on the grill, near but not directly over the coals, until the garlic is soft and fragrant. Mash the garlic, adding more oil if you like, and brush the pulp over the pulled-apart bread, adding more oil if you like, then "barbecue" it.

hile the barbecue grill is firing up for a cookout, or while the main course is over the coals, I sometimes prepare golden, dry-crisp, and appetizing chunks of bread this way. "Pulled bread" dates back to Victorian days.

Just pull a loaf of French, Italian, or Western-style sourdough bread apart into rough peaky chunks, not too small, and grill them to one side of the bed of coals until they are done; turn the pieces now and again.

The crisp, light texture of the bread is irresistible with steak, hot lobster, barbecued chicken, or a pot of chowder. It's not for cookouts only; a slow oven does a fine job indoors. Any left-over barbecued bread keeps well in a canister, and it makes especially good crumbs.

NECTARINE & ALMOND CUSTARD PIE

he disc of fruit-studded almond custard that beams out from this open pie conceals a layer of almond crunch. This is a soothing finale for a summer fiesta.

Pastry: Roll out the chilled pastry and line a 9-inch pie pan; trim excess pastry, leaving 1 inch extra beyond the rim of the pan. Fold the extension under and flute the pastry into an upstanding edge. Chill the shell until it's needed.

Preheat the oven to 425°.

Almond crunch layer: Mix the nuts, sugar, egg yolk, butter, and almond extract; crumble into the pie shell.

Bake in the center of the oven until the pastry has set and just begun to brown slightly, about 12 minutes. Remove the shell from the oven; press down the almond crunch if there are billows. Reset the oven to 325°. Cool the shell.

Fruit: While the shell bakes, boil the water and sugar; add the fruit; poach the fruit at a simmer for 5 minutes. Drain well (keep the syrup for fruit salad). Measure the fruit; you need 1 cup.

Custard: Beat the egg and egg yolks together to mix well; beat in the sugar, salt, milk, cream, and almond extract.

Assembling the pie: Set the pie pan on a baking sheet; distribute the fruit over the almond crunch. Put the baking sheet on a pulled-out shelf in the lower third of oven; pour the custard (through a strainer, for best texture) into the pie. Push the sheet gently into the oven and bake the pie about 30 minutes, or until the custard has just set—it should still jiggle a little when nudged. Cool the pie on a rack.

To serve: Serve at room temperature if the pie is consumed within an hour or two of complete cooling; if held longer, refrigerate. Leftovers should be refrigerated.

Makes a 9-inch pie

*Tender Pie Pastry
(page 278)*

ALMOND CRUNCH LAYER:
*½ cup chopped toasted
   natural almonds (see
   page 276)
⅓ cup granulated sugar
1 large egg yolk
2 teaspoons melted
   unsalted butter
3 or 4 drops almond
   extract*

FRUIT:
*½ cup water
¼ cup granulated sugar
2 pounds (1½ cups peeled
   and diced) nectarines or
   peaches (about ¾-inch
   dice)*

CUSTARD:
*1 large egg plus 2 egg
   yolks
⅓ cup granulated sugar
Pinch of salt
1 cup milk
¼ cup heavy cream
¼ teaspoon almond
   extract*

OLD-FANGLED FIXINGS

Tomato Sandwiches (below)

Corn on the Cob: The Perfect Ear (below) with pats of sweet butter creamed with salt and pepper

Blueberry version of Cherry, Blueberry, or Plum Picnic Cake (below), or ice cream or sherbet and purchased or home-baked cookies (see the Index for recipes)

To drink: Lemonade or Limeade, made from Lemonade or Limeade Base (below)

A lot of us grew up on wonderful summer sandwiches of dead-ripe tomatoes back when the flavor of tomatoes had a fine edge of acidity that set off their sweetness—an edge, alas, now "improved" out of them. Those were fragrant tomatoes, zesty enough to eat like an apple, with a little salt if it was handy. There still aren't many better ways to enjoy this fruit than "just plain," if the farmer has planted a decent tomato variety to begin with (that's a considerable "if"), and if the fruits have been allowed to ripen on the vine, not in a gas chamber.

If you can find relatively good tomatoes—the wise person who has a garden patch grows them at home—what could be better than old-fangled tomato sandwiches and corn on the cob for an August lunch or supper? Add a simple cake enriched with seasonal fruit and some from-scratch lemonade or limeade, and there you are.

OFF WITH THEIR PEELS:
Some finer spirits prefer their tomatoes sans skin, whereas some fine cooks don't like to scald tomatoes in order to peel them if they will be served raw—some "cooking" is inevitable.

Solution: To remove skin from a ripe tomato, rub it firmly, all over, with the back edge of a knife blade. This bruises the underlayer just enough to permit the skin to be stripped off with ease.

TOMATO SANDWICHES

e were talking sandwiches. You need big, dead-ripe tomatoes of the type called "beefsteak," and firm, thick-cut white bread (or really good hamburger buns—I like to use hamburger-size Angel Rolls or Biscuits, page 266).

Slice the tomatoes at least half an inch thick and spread the bread generously with butter or mayonnaise (it helps keep some of the juice where it belongs). Cover a slice or a bun half, border to border, with tomato; sprinkle on a little lemon juice if you're nostalgic for tomatoes with temperament; add salt and pepper.

Cover, clutch, eat. Let the juice drip where it may. (Where are those silly lobster bibs when they're really needed?)

A HERBAL TOUCH: Back then, "basil" meant Mr. Rathbone. Now that the soulmate herb for tomatoes is in every summer market, sometimes it's meritorious to lay sliced tomatoes on (or cover them with) torn, not cut, basil leaves; let the fruit imbibe the fragrance for half an hour or so before the sandwiches are made. Don't put in the basil leaves—they've done their job.

TOMATO JAM: In a good tomato summer, try this slightly offbeat preserve to enjoy on toast or muffins.

Skin meaty, ripe red tomatoes (scald 1 minute, then strip off the skins). Cut crosswise and squeeze out the seeds and surplus juice; cut out hard cores. Dice or chop.

Measure the tomatoes into a saucepan. To each 4 cups (from about 3 pounds fruit) add the juice of 1½ lemons and 1 teaspoon of grated lemon zest. If you like, add 2 teaspoons (or more) of fresh ginger, grated.

Simmer all this until the tomatoes are tender, stirring often. Add a big pinch of salt and 2½ cups sugar; continue cooking over medium heat, stirring even more frequently, until the jam is thick and translucent; a thermometer will read 220°.

Ladle the jam into a jar, cool it, then refrigerate it for a few weeks' storage.

HOW TO CHOOSE GOOD CORN: Besides stripping back the husks (frowned upon by corn sellers), there are other ways to judge an ear. Husks should be green and fresh looking, not pale and dry; the cut end of the stem shouldn't be whitish and dry unless the ear has been too long out of the field. The silk should look fresh and moist where it emerges from the tip of the ear, although the ends of the silk will (and should) be brown. (Suspect any ear whose silk has been trimmed off.) If it's possible to test a kernel with a fingernail without incurring the seller's wrath, it should be tender and spurt milky juice when pierced; if there's no juice, the ear is too ancient. In the matter of size, some varieties normally produce larger ears than others, but within a batch of the same variety, the fatter and heavier ears are the more mature ones, with relatively coarse kernels; if pearly young kernels are wanted, choose the slimmer ears. What about color? The golden varieties are old-fashioned favorites, but for sweetness I'd choose silver or white corn, with second place going to ears with mixed gold and white kernels.

CORN ON THE COB: THE PERFECT EAR

 oming from a line of people who were brought up to pick sweet corn at the last possible moment before a meal, I learned in youth how to tell a good ear from something that looks like corn but turns out to be starchy, dull, and tough to eat. During corn season I do indeed remember tearing out to the back of my family's garden to gather the ears when, yes, the pot *was* on the stove and the water was coming to a boil. Something of a stunt, perhaps, this last-minute dash, but still the best way to insure crisp kernels that burst under the tooth with sweet juice. The next best way is to live near a farmstand.

CORN GRILLED IN THE HUSK

Oh my, how good corn can be this way. First catch your corn, choosing it in the way we've just been discussing. If you're picnicking on an ocean or bay beach, plan to soak the corn, in its husks, in a pail of sea water for a while before it goes on the fire—this adds a salty savor to the smoky effect. Away from salt water, you can skip the soak, or use plain water.

Strip back the husks, but don't tear them off; rub and pull off the silk; smooth the husks back into position and tie the tips of the husks together, using a strip torn from an outer husk.

Roast the corn over hot but not flaming coals of driftwood or charcoal (you can even roast corn over fireplace coals), resting the ears on a grill 6 inches or so above the heat. Turn the ears often as they roast; the corn is done when it's irresistibly aromatic, the husks are deeply browned and charred here and there, and the kernels are done to your taste—either moist and steaming, or slightly

CORN COUNSEL: Anyone who doesn't have a garden patch or who doesn't live in corn country will do better to use frozen or canned whole-kernel corn—both can be very good—in corn pudding, fritters, oysters, or succotash instead of risking the disappointment of poor corn on the cob. I want to weep when I see the dreadful ears in supermarkets, "fresh corn" that hasn't been fresh for several days.

caramelized, or actually browned inside the husks.

Allow half an hour, give or take; the time depends on the heat of the embers and how far above the coals the corn is placed.

Buttering the corn is facilitated by mixing coarse salt and fresh pepper into butter beforehand and packing it into a picnic container; small plastic knives are handy for spreading.

COOKING THE PERFECT EAR

If corn is not to be cooked at once, refrigerate it without husking. Shuck the ears just before cooking.

Don't heat a big potful of water, which takes time and fuel and overheats the kitchen; boil a few inches of water in a wide pot, add the corn, sprinkle on a little sugar—1 or 2 tablespoons—clap on the lid, bring the water just back to a boil, turn off the heat, and leave the corn for 8 to 10 minutes, when it will be ready. Serve one round of ears at a time; the rest will come to no harm if left in the water for as long as half an hour.

Some cooks salt the cooking water—I don't, because it toughens the corn; some swear by a cupful of milk in the water; and some use milk plus salt or sugar. Whichever way seems best to you, just don't cook corn to death, as was once considered necessary; half an hour's boiling was a common direction in cookbooks gone by.

LEMONADE OR LIMEADE BASE

ust thinking about the fake "fruit" drinks that are supposed to be fit for human consumption sets up a thirst for real, live lemonade made from genuine lemons.

As kids with sidewalk stands know (or used to know—perhaps now they just dilute some canned concentrate from the family fridge), making real lemonade is as simple as cutting, squeezing, stirring in sugar, and adding water and ice. However, making a syrup for sweetening is worth the few minutes it takes—the payoff is a smoother glassful.

Here's how to make a supply of lemonade base to keep on ice or in the freezer. Limeade base is made the same way, but use less of the intensely aromatic lime peel, perhaps only one lime's worth.

Makes enough base for about 12 servings

1 cup granulated sugar
2 cups water
Peel from 2 lemons, cut in strips
1 cup lemon juice (from about 8 big lemons), including the pulp but without the seeds

Boil the sugar and water for 3 or 4 minutes; cool. (This syrup keeps indefinitely in the refrigerator, handy for smooth sweetening of fruit dishes as well as beverages, so it's not a bad idea to make a double or triple amount while you're about it.)

Twist each strip of peel over a pitcher or storage jar to release the flavorful oil; drop the strips into the pitcher. Stir in the lemon juice and cooled syrup.

Refrigerated, the base keeps for days; or strain and freeze it in an ice-cube tray, turn out the cubes, and seal them for storage in a freezer bag.

To serve: For each glassful of lemonade or limeade, use ¼ to ⅓ cup of base or the equivalent in frozen cubes; add ice; fill with club soda or water.

CHERRY, BLUEBERRY, OR PLUM PICNIC CAKE

From cherry time in early summer to blue-plum time in autumn, this dessert travels with the seasons. It's sized for a gathering—a picnic, a cookout, or a covered-dish party—and it can be moved around without fuss, right in its baking pan.

For a cake big enough to serve 6 to 8, halve the ingredients and use an 8-inch square pan; baking time will be about 50 minutes.

Preheat oven to 350°. Grease a 13 × 9-inch baking pan.

The topping: Blend the brown sugar and butter with a fork; add the flour and cinnamon and mash to make coarse crumbs. Reserve.

The cake: Sift the flour, sugar, baking powder, salt, and mace into a mixing bowl; stir in the lemon zest. Cut in the butter with a pastry blender to make a mealy mixture.

Beat the eggs to mix; stir in the milk and flavoring. Mix the liquid lightly into the dry ingredients, just until moistened; do not overmix.

Pour the batter into the prepared pan and smooth the top. Drain any liquid from the fruit, then scatter it over the batter and press the pieces just under the surface. Distribute the topping over the cake in a more or less even layer.

Bake the cake in the center of the oven for 1 hour to 1 hour 10 minutes, until a cake tester emerges dry from the center and the edges have shrunk slightly from the pan.

Cool the cake, in its pan, on a rack. Serve it warm or at room temperature. It's lovely with vanilla ice cream, if the occasion is a cake-and-ice cream one.

Storing: Store the cooled cake, covered with foil or plastic, at room temperature for up to 24 hours.

Refrigerate or freeze for longer keeping.

Leftovers: Leftovers keep well under the crumbly topping. Refresh the cake, wrapped in foil, in a 325° oven for 10 minutes if it has been refrigerated, or has been frozen and thawed (thaw it in its wrapper). Refreshing will take 20 to 30 minutes if the cake is still frozen.

Serves 12 to 16

Oil or shortening for coating the pan

TOPPING:
¾ cup (packed) light-brown sugar
6 tablespoons (¾ stick) unsalted butter
¾ cup all-purpose flour
1 teaspoon ground cinnamon

CAKE:
2½ cups all-purpose flour
1 cup granulated sugar
1½ teaspoons baking powder
½ teaspoon salt
¾ teaspoon ground mace
1½ teaspoons grated lemon zest (colored rind only, no pith)
1 stick plus 2 tablespoons cold unsalted butter
2 large eggs
1¼ cups milk
1 teaspoon vanilla extract, plus ¼ teaspoon almond extract for the cherry version

FRUIT:
4 to 5 cups blueberries, or pitted cherries (halved if large), or pitted blue plums (prune plums), cut into 4 to 6 wedges each

Optional accompaniment:
Vanilla ice cream

A CELEBRATION OF LOBSTER

Basic Lobster (below)

Individual dishes of melted butter
Wedges of lemon, or individual pipkins of fresh lemon juice

A country loaf, sourdough for choice, torn into rough chunks;
or "Barbecued" or Pulled Bread (page 51)

Fresh fruit, or Raspberry & White Wine Ice (page 92)

To drink: Dry white wine—a domestic wine such as
Johannisberg Riesling, or a French Muscadet or Sancerre

People who truly like lobster—not those who order it just because it's costly—think it's a crime to fuss too much with this sea creature. We want our lobster steamed or boiled; to us, broiled lobster seems as poor a notion of cookery as the Gay Nineties conceit of roasting the beast on a spit.

We also believe it's a pity to complicate its deep-sea flavor; it can be quite swamped in some dishes, especially in bouillabaisse, in which no right-thinking Frenchman would dream of drowning it.

So this menu calls for lobster hot from the steamer, and not much else. It's just the ticket when there's time to gather informally around a summer table and savor every succulent bite.

BASIC LOBSTER

The most succulent lobster is lobster hot from the steamer, served whole (or halved, if it's quite large), to be dug out of its shell bite by bite, dipped into melted butter cut with a few drops of lemon, and eaten with an occasional morsel of the best and crustiest bread to be found. (Opinionated? Me?)

Next best—and first choice for anyone who doesn't want to cope with lobster in the shell—is an individual casserole of hot Buttered Lobster; tying for third place are Lobster Stew, rich and rosy with lobster coral, and Lobster Salad, either formally arrayed on a garnished plate or heaped into a frankfurter roll split lengthwise down its top, an unpretentious feast that's the best of seashore lunches. (See the Index for those variations on the lobster theme.)

When I first began to spend summer time on the eastern tip of Long Island, which stretches more than a hundred miles eastward from Manhattan, lobsters cost less than a dollar a pound (seventy-nine cents comes to mind) at Mr. Emerson Taber's lobster pound on Three Mile Harbor; the price has doubled quite a few times since then. Nevertheless the deeply felt need for an occasional feast of Basic Lobster has survived the sticker shock of escalating prices.

You needn't bother with anything printed below if you come from lobster country; you don't need it. The detailed game plan is offered in the hope of making converts, not in order to preach to the converted.

Similarly, if your lobster has come by air express in a steamer pot, ready to cook, pay attention to the shipper's directions for cooking the beasts, not to the discussion below.

A LOBSTER PRIMER

"Lobster. A crustacean widely used in cooking."

— *Alexandre Dumas' Dictionary of Cuisine*, edited by Louis Colman.

"Lobsters are very belligerent, and when two or more get into a [lobsterman's] pot they fight."

—TOM STOBART, *The Cook's Encyclopedia.*

"In general, the Bretons practice only one method of preparing their lobsters . . . boiling them in seawater, which is fine if what you want to taste is lobster."

—A.J. LIEBLING.

Choosing a lobster—the size of it: It's not true that large lobsters—over 4 pounds, say—are sure to be tough. I've cooked succulent specimens weighing in the double digits, and I've been served dry, tough small lobsters; it's all in the cooking.

Larger lobsters are Best Buys compared to mediums and especially to chickens (the smallest size sold, about 1-¼ pounds, depending on state laws), which are really too young to be let out alone. Larger sizes yield more meat per pound, and it's also easier to extract that meat. A small lobster will yield about 1 cup of picked-out meat, sometimes more, depending on the skill of the operator.

Allow a whole lobster per person, unless the beast weighs at least 2½ pounds; that size will serve two, unless the two are Down Easters or members of my immediate circle.

Considering sex: If there's a choice, pick female lobsters; they are meatier than the males, and, as a bonus, they usually contain clumps of coral, or roe, which is delicious.

Considering condition: Choose the feistiest lobsters in the tank; if they seem limp or lazy, pass them by. Also pass up a lobster that's light for its size or has visibly damaged claws or shell. Single-clawed lobsters can be good buys if they're large enough to contain a good deal of body meat.

Storing: To keep them for a few hours, refrigerate lobsters-in-waiting in a paper bag; don't use a plastic bag or you'll suffocate them.

Cooking lobster: Some recipe timings appear to be survivals of Victorian days, when lobster was considered so indigestible that *very* long cooking (plus heavy seasoning) was needed, cooks believed, to make it easier on the stomach. The timings below, together with the recommended test for doneness, will yield fully cooked but still-succulent flesh.

Use a big pot with a tight lid; bring 2 inches of water to a boil over high heat; add a moderate quantity of salt, perhaps 2 tablespoons. (Use sea water if you're at the shore, or add a skein or two of fresh rockweed to the water; both add briny flavor.) Put a rack in the pot, if you wish.

Drop in the live lobsters, grasping each just behind the head (or you can use tongs), clap on the lid, and watch for steam to escape under the lid.

MAKING LOBSTER STOCK: THE SHELL GAME.

The lobster shells are rich in flavor, so it's a good idea to brew a delicious stock from them to use in other seafood dishes. Cover the shells with water, add a little celery and carrot, and simmer them for 20 minutes. Strain off the stock, cool it, and refrigerate it (for 2 or 3 days) or freeze it for months. Use the stock in sauces, soups, seafood stews, and chowders.

Start timing when steam begins to jet out. *Cooking time depends on the size of individual lobsters,* not the total weight of a potful.

Timing: Allow 10 minutes for lobsters weighing 1¼ pounds each (chicken size);

12 minutes for approximately 2-pound lobsters;
about 16 minutes for 2-plus to 3 pounds;
about 21 minutes for 3 to 5 pounds;
and so on, up to 35 minutes for giants (8 pounds).

If you find a lobster weighing more than 8 pounds, please invite me to dinner and I'll help cook.

Checking doneness: Tug on a feeler; it will pull out easily when the lobster is done. Lift out the lobsters, drain them briefly, claws down, and serve them at once.

Serving: Optionally, first crack the big claws—if you don't have claw-crackers, taps of a small hammer or a mallet will do the job. On the table, have individual dishes of melted butter, squeezed fresh lemon juice or wedges of lemon, and a pepper mill. Set out, if you have them, claw-crackers and/or lobster shears, picks, and small forks. Have plenty of napkins.

Dismantling a lobster: To extract the meat, twist off the tail section; cut the shell lengthwise down the underside with scissors (or halve the whole tail with a knife) and remove the tail meat. With a fork or a knife tip, find and remove the vein running through the tail, if you wish; often it can't be located, and it doesn't matter. A big lobster will yield a little meat from the roundish flappers at the end of the tail; they aren't worth the trouble if lobsters are small. Twist off the small claws, clip off the body end of each, crack the joint, and squeeze out the morsel of meat. (The teeth do this best.) Twist off the big claws and crack them if this hasn't been done in the kitchen. Pull the shell off the "thumb" and the main claw.

The body portion rewards a bit of rummaging unless the lobster is tiny. Break free the top (head) section so you can find and discard the inedible stomach, which is a small, irregular box of cartilage. Scoop out for consumption, if you wish, the green tomalley, or liver, tasty if unhandsome, and don't miss a scrap of the firm red coral found in hen lobsters. From the body, remove and discard the spongy "fingers," or lungs, then dig out, using a pick or small fork, the choice nuggets of meat in the side compartments of the shell. Scoop out the cream-colored fat lining the shell—it's rich in flavor.

Eating strategy: Consume the lobster meat bite by bite, dipping each morsel in butter and lemon; or accumulate a hoard of lobster before starting in. Either way, have a bite of crusty bread now and then as a palate-cleanser.

A GLORIOUS GRILLFUL

A Grillful of Sausages (below)

Sweet & Hot Orange Mustard (below), plus any other favorite mustards, from ballpark to tarragon

Eggy Potato & Bacon Salad (below) or Summer Potato Salad (page 74)

Relishes: *Chunk pickles; Prepared Horseradish (page 102); one or two fruit chutneys or relishes; strips of fresh cucumbers (or Swedish Cucumbers, page 281) and sweet red peppers*

Sliced French bread spread with garlic butter and grilled lightly, or the Garlic Version of "Barbecued" or Pulled Bread (page 51)

Summer Fruit Shortcake (below), made with peaches

To drink: *Beer is the classic accompaniment for these viands, but a robust white wine may be preferred*

For the main event of a cookout that doesn't depend on the usual suspects—hamburgers and hot dogs—I sometimes set out in search of interesting sausages. For me, the *wurst*-lover's paradise of Yorkville, in New York City, is within reach for a special occasion, and both in the city and closer to home there are shops selling (and some of them making) sausages from Central and Eastern Europe, Italy, France, the Orient, and the Hispanic countries. An expert has estimated that more than a hundred kinds of sausage are made in American communities, and many of them, especially the fresh and lightly smoked sorts, take kindly to grilling. If the party is large enough, it's a pleasure to choose several from the kinds suggested below.

With sausage goes, naturally, potato salad, your favorite or mine. And relishes, and condiments, and a glass of beer. For dessert I'd vote for a peach shortcake; the sweet tartness of peaches, set off by the soothing biscuity shortcake, is just right to round off a meal of challenging spiciness.

A GRILLFUL OF SAUSAGES

HOW DO I GRIND THEE? LET ME COUNT THE WAYS. There are scores of American and naturalized sausages—fresh, smoked, cooked, semidry, or dry—in the shops. Among them are bockwurst; braunschweiger, kalbsrouladen, and other liver sausages; cervelat; chorizos; blood sausages; andouilles; chaurice; Cajun *boudin;* luganega; fresh and smoked bratwurst; summer sausage; Chinese pork and liver sausages; frankfurters; longaniza; Vienna sausages; knockwurst; little breakfast links; country-style bulk sausage; garlic sausages of many kinds; Italian fennel or hot sausage links; coteghino; crepinettes; pepperoni; Portuguese linguiça and chourico; kielbasa; mettwurst; bologna— Lebanon, ham, or smoked; bauernwurst; kosher salami, and other salamis from Italy, Hungary, Denmark, Germany, and elsewhere; capocollo; *boudin blanc;* weisswurst; chipolatas; head sausage or headcheese; Lyon sausage; and specialties made with venison, seafood, crawfish, chicken, duck, rabbit, or turkey.

esides exploring exotic sources for lesser-known kinds of sausage, don't fail to check your best supermarket or delicatessen for such things as smoked or unsmoked knackwurst, kielbasa, chorizos, small Italian sweet or hot sausages with or without fennel, a chunk of good bologna, home-style bulk sausage for broiled patties (see page 30 if you'd like to make your own), bratwurst, bockwurst, and weisswurst. If you feel uncertain about unfamiliar kinds, ask the butcher's advice about grilling them. Most fresh or smoked sausages, except dry "keeping" kinds (salami, pepperoni, and so on) will be suitable.

How much to buy: Allow a sample of each of two or three kinds per eater, depending on your estimate of appetites; that will work out to about one-third to one-half pound of sausages per person, on the generous side. (Leftovers won't be a problem—you can always look forward to a next-day melange of sausages with lentils or cabbage to use up any that aren't consumed.)

Before your start grilling: Parboil (rather, poach for 10 minutes, in a large pot of boiling water with the heat turned off when the sausages are added) the kinds that are better if lightly precooked: kielbasa, bockwurst, weisswurst, small Italian sausages, and knackwurst, for example. Prick their skins first.

Split bologna and any other very thick sausage lengthwise and remove the casing, if synthetic. Prick the skins of sausages in natural (gut) casings. Form bulk sausage meat into not-too-thick patties.

Brush everything lightly with oil or melted butter.

Grilling: Grill the sausages rather slowly, several inches above charcoal (or below a grill element) that is only moderately hot. Turn them from time to time with tongs. The sausages are ready when patties are thoroughly cooked through and browned and sausages in casings are golden-brown all over and piping hot throughout.

A too-hot fire or too-long cooking can dry out sausages to dullness, so keep a sharp eye on the grill.

SWEET & HOT ORANGE MUSTARD

 nventive mustards like this one can be made quite easily from scratch, but scratch mustard needs to mellow for a while to lose some fire and gain some couth. When the picnic is going to be held tomorrow or even today, there's time to stir this quick condiment together because it starts with a jar of good prepared mustard, not mustard powder, and so doesn't need mellowing time.

Good with sausages, smoked turkey, cold meats and cheeses; excellent dabbed in a sandwich or added to mayonnaise for chicken salad.

Boil the orange zest with 2 cups water for 5 minutes. Drain; discard liquid. Add zest to the mustard.

Chop the marmalade and raisins medium-coarse, most easily done in a food processor. Add to the mustard with the horseradish and optional pepper sauce.

Taste for sweetness and hotness; add sugar, more horseradish, and/or more pepper sauce if needed. Scrape into a jar; cover.

The mustard keeps indefinitely in the cupboard or refrigerator; it only gets better with time.

OTHER SHORTCUT MUSTARDS: You can concoct many kinds from an 8-ounce jar of Dijon mustard. Here are sketches of three. Add other seasonings to your taste.

Horseradish Mustard: Stir in 2 tablespoons drained horseradish, your own (page 102) or purchased; add, if you like, a minced garlic clove and a pinch of allspice.

"Honey" Mustard: Stir in ⅓ cup (packed) light-brown sugar.

Herbed Mustard: Add 1 teaspoon dried tarragon, a pinch of dried thyme, a little mashed garlic, a little honey, a pinch of allspice, and a pinch of freshly ground pepper.

Makes about 1½ cups

Zest (colored rind only, no pith) of a large orange (or substitute zest of 2 lemons), shredded

8-ounce jar smooth Dijon-style mustard

⅓ cup bitter-orange marmalade (Scotch-style)

⅓ cup golden raisins

1 tablespoon drained horseradish, or more for hotter mustard

Dash of Tabasco or other hot pepper sauce, optional

Granulated sugar, if needed

EGGY POTATO & BACON SALAD

Serves 6

2 pounds boiling or all-
    purpose potatoes (5 or 6
    medium), scrubbed but
    not peeled
Salt
6 ounces (6 to 8 slices)
    lean thick-cut bacon,
    diced fine
1 small onion, diced
    (about ½ cup), or ½ cup
    sliced scallions (white
    part only)
1 large clove garlic, minced
1 tablespoon granulated
    sugar
2 tablespoons all-purpose
    flour
½ cup, or as needed, beef
    or chicken broth, or milk
    or water
¼ cup, or to taste, cider
    vinegar
1 teaspoon celery seed
½ cup diced tender celery,
    optional
3 large eggs, simmered 10
    minutes, shelled, diced
Pepper, to taste
Herbs, optional:
    ¼ to ⅓ cup minced
    parsley leaves; 2
    tablespoons, or to taste,
    snipped chives

irtually a one-dish meal when served warm in hot-supper season, this hearty salad is also splendid at room temperature as part of a picnic, cookout, or summer lunch.

Cover the potatoes with cold water, add 1 teaspoon salt, and boil gently until barely tender when tested, about 20 minutes; avoid overcooking. Drain; when cool enough to touch, peel and slice ¼ inch thick; cover and keep warm.

Cook the bacon slowly in a skillet until crisp; pour the bacon and its fat into a strainer set over a bowl. Return 3 tablespoons fat to the skillet; reserve the bacon.

Cook the onions and garlic slowly in the fat until tender, stirring often, 5 to 7 minutes. Sprinkle with the sugar, raise the heat, and cook another minute, stirring. Add the flour and stir briefly over the heat; gradually add the broth, then the vinegar and celery seed; cook 5 minutes, stirring. The sauce should be pourable; if not, add more liquid. Add the optional celery.

Pour the hot dressing over the warm potatoes; add the eggs and reserved bacon; toss lightly to mix. Taste and season with salt and pepper and, if needed, a little more vinegar. If the salad seems too dense, add a little more broth (or milk or water) to achieve a creamy, spoonable texture. Sprinkle with herbs, if they are used.

Serve warm or cool, or refrigerate overnight to mellow, then let return to room temperature before serving.

If the salad has become stodgy in texture during its rest, add liquid (water, milk, mayonnaise, or sour cream) and toss it again.

COOK'S CHOICE: The quantity of bacon and/or eggs may be greater or less; the eggs can be omitted entirely. Celery can supplement the celery seed, if you'd like a little crunch. Make sure the salad is well seasoned and sufficiently tart, but don't omit the sugar, which is a balancing element, not a sweetening.

"Whipped cream is good on shortcake. Plain cream is better. Shortcake made with cake mixture may be cake, but it's not shortcake."

—ANN BATCHELDER.

SUMMER FRUIT SHORTCAKE

In a real shortcake, let the balance of power lie with the fruit. Have your shortcake layers more crusty than doughy.

—ANN BATCHELDER

he true American shortcake is a disk of fresh-baked baking-powder biscuit (*never* cake), split into layers and, if you do it right, spread with butter before it's honored with the presence of bursting-ripe strawberries, raspberries, or peaches.

This is a crumbly, messy, lovely dessert, the juicier the better—perhaps the best dish ever devised this side of the Atlantic. Diet the rest of the year, if you must, but have shortcake at least once a summer, with its proper complement of cream.

Serves 6 generously

FRUIT:
4 to 6 cups fresh raspberries or strawberries, or about 2 pounds ripe peaches
¾ to 1 cup superfine sugar

SHORTCAKE:
Unsalted butter for coating the pan
2 cups all-purpose flour
3 tablespoons granulated sugar
2½ teaspoons baking powder
½ teaspoon salt
4 tablespoons (½ stick) cold unsalted butter, in ½-inch slices

Fruit—berries: Sort the berries, then rinse and drain them (but only if a rinse is necessary). If the strawberries are large, halve or slice them. Stir the berries with the sugar; crush a few of them to encourage syrup to form. Reserve the berries.

Peaches: Skin and slice the fruit; stir the slices with the sugar, then crush a few pieces to create a syrup. Reserve the fruit. (Berries may be prepared a few hours ahead of time and this is feasible for peaches, too, if they are sprinkled with ascorbic acid powder—see Ascorbic Acid Powder, right).

Preheat the oven to 400°. Generously butter a round 8-inch cake pan.

Cake: Sift together the flour, sugar, baking powder, and salt; cut in the butter with a pastry blender or two knives until the mixture is in medium-coarse flakes. Stir in the cream, using a fork or the tip of a knife, just until moistened. Scrape the dough onto a lightly floured work surface and knead it lightly, only two or three strokes. Pat the dough into the prepared pan; the top needn't be patted smooth.

⅔ cup light cream
Additional butter for
  baked layers, optional

TOPPING:
1 cup chilled heavy cream

NOT FOR SUMMER ONLY:
An out-of-season shortcake
topped with poached fruit (or
premium fruit out of a jar) is
a welcome dessert in
seriously wintry weather.
One version: Simmer fresh or
dried apples or pears and a
few cranberries (or use dried
peaches or apricots, without
the cranberries) in syrup
enlivened with strips of
lemon zest and a scrap of
cinnamon stick. Top the
warm shortcake with warm
fruit and some of the juice to
make a sort of upside-down
cobbler, to serve with cream.

Bake until golden-brown and firm, about 15 minutes.

Set the pan on a cake rack and leave until the shortcake has firmed up but is still warm, 20 to 25 minutes.

Shortly before serving, remove the cake from the pan and split it into two layers (a long serrated knife works best). Optionally, spread the cut sides of the layers with softened butter. Set the bottom half, cut side up, on the serving plate. Cover with half of the sugared fruit and a share of its syrup.

Set the top half in place, again with the cut side up. Cover with the remaining fruit and juice.

Cut the shortcake into wedges at the table; if you have a pie server, use it to lift the wedges with minimal crumbling.

Pass the heavy cream, or if whipped cream is your pleasure, whip it until it's softly thickened, sweetening it a little if you wish. Some of the whipped cream can be dolloped on top of the cake in the fashion that will best show off the fruit.

———

ASCORBIC ACID POWDER (a.k.a. VITAMIN C) & CITRIC ACID: Often used to prevent darkening of cut fruit that's destined to be frozen, ascorbic acid is sold as crystals or as vitamin C tablets (in drugstores) or in combination with sugar in small cans (in groceries). If you're using the grocer's version, see the label for the quantity to use. If you have crystalline ascorbic acid, about ½ teaspoon will be enough for the 2 pounds of peaches in this recipe.

Citric acid crystals (that's what's in the little jars labeled "sour salt" at the grocer's) will also prevent the darkening of cut fruit, but it possesses more sourness than ascorbic acid and thus it affects the flavor of the fruit more.

Both acids are found naturally in fruits (lemons contain both); as they are not an additive that has been invented in a laboratory, using them shouldn't worry the nutritionally pure-minded.

AFTER WE'VE BEEN FOR A SWIM

Buttered Crabmeat & Lobster, or Buttered Lobster Alone (below), in individual casseroles

Heated Angel Rolls (page 266)

Cucumber Shreds with Sesame & Soy (below)

Summer Potato Salad (below)

Cherry, Blueberry, or Plum Picnic Cake (page 57), with softened vanilla ice cream as sauce; or a bowl of fresh ripe fruit to choose from

To drink: *White wine spritzers or chilled dry white wine*

This one o'clock lunch requires you to do nothing at the last minute besides heating seafood in a bath of hot butter and popping the rolls into the oven to warm in a paper bag, so it's quite good when you expect guests whose company you prefer to pots and pans.

The menu is ideal for crabmeat and/or lobster lovers who aren't in a position (or of a mind) to tackle hot, steamed crustaceans in their shells; and, further, the main dish is pure seafood, with no saucy diversions. The accompaniments are a little relish of cucumbers seasoned with sesame seeds and soy sauce and a potato salad made along the lines of French *pommes à la huile,* but more interesting, I think. A fruited Picnic Cake or fresh fruit is suggested for dessert; a fruit sherbet would also be appropriate.

The menu can easily be converted to hearty-snack size by serving the hot seafood in rolls—see the note following the recipe— and accompanying the rolls with sliced bursting-ripe tomatoes or a scoop of coleslaw.

CRABBY COMMENTS:
Please don't jeopardize the excellence of this simple dish by substituting Alaskan king crab—a good enough creature no doubt, but not what's wanted here—and don't even think of using a crab analog. This fake crabmeat is marketed in look-alike chunks made almost entirely from processed white-meated fish imbued with flavors extracted from genuine crab; it's identifiable at the fish market by the uncanny symmetry of the pieces and the (also uncanny) red coloring painted on each chunk.

GRADES OF CRABMEAT:
Lump or backfin crabmeat is most expensive because the pieces are largest. Flake meat (bits and pieces) and claw meat (also in bits, and brownish) are less choice grades, but so long as it has been properly handled and sold while still perfectly fresh, all meat from blue crabs is equally tasty. For this recipe, lump crabmeat will make the best appearance.

BUTTERED CRABMEAT & LOBSTER, OR BUTTERED LOBSTER ALONE

or this luscious lunch, start on the day before by steaming and picking some live lobsters as outlined in Basic Lobster (page 60); cook six 1¼ pound lobsters if you're serving lobster alone, or two or three lobsters if the dish will also contain Chesapeake Bay crabmeat, which you'll find pasteurized (it has been cooked) and sealed into tins in the cold case of any first-rate fish market. You'll need from 1 to 1½ pounds, depending on the opulence of the appetites you expect.

This seafood combination came my way first in Baltimore, which is of course deep in the home country of wonderful crabmeat and not a place we usually think of in connection with lobster. It's a delectable pairing for which you want the best crabmeat you can buy, unless you can catch, steam, and pick the meat from your own "beautiful swimmers." Once in a while we can net a few blue crabs here on Long Island, but they're never as large as a middling-size blue from the Chesapeake.

The object here is to imbue the seafood with butter and vice-versa, meanwhile getting it piping hot without overcooking it. If you're planning to have this dish when you steam and pick out the lobsters, it's not a bad idea to undercook them slightly; remove them from the steamer 3 to 5 minutes (depending on their size) before they're done.

Melt the butter in a wide nonreactive skillet over medium heat. When it is foamy and barely melted, add the

Serves 6

*About 6 cups (combined)
pasteurized best-quality
crabmeat and cooked
lobster meat, half and
half, or cooked lobster
meat alone (see Basic
Lobster, page 60)
½ pound (2 sticks) best-
quality unsalted butter,
more if desired
Fat and coral from the
lobsters, if available
Salt and pepper, to taste
A little ground hot red
pepper, optional*
Accompaniment: *Lemon
wedges*

**SEASONING WITH
SESAME:** Hulled white
sesame seeds are used here,
although there's a dark kind
too, much used in the Orient.
Store sesame seeds in the
freezer to keep their rich
cargo of oil from becoming
rancid. The sesame oil to use,
if you include it, is the dark,
flavorful oil pressed from
roasted seeds. After it's
opened, refrigerate it.

lobster fat and coral, if you have them, and stir for 1 or 2 minutes. If there is no fat and/or coral, add the crabmeat and lobster as soon as the butter foams. Heat the panful carefully, turning the pieces without breaking or mashing them, until they are very hot through, 5 minutes or a bit more. Don't allow any browning at all.

Add salt, if it's needed, and pepper(s) to taste. Serve in individual casseroles with plenty of lemon wedges.

HOT SEAFOOD IN A ROLL: More casually, serve this dish in lobster-roll style: Split best-quality frankfurter rolls down the top, warm them well, and fill them with the buttered seafood and its juices. Alternatively, serve the crabmeat and lobster (or just lobster) in casseroles with the rolls alongside, to be dealt with by each eater as he/she pleases.

CUCUMBER SHREDS WITH SESAME & SOY

Here's a refreshing side-salad inspired by the Japanese sliced cucumbers and *daikon* I learned from Sono Rosenberg, friend, fine cook, and editorial colleague in jobs past. The recipe for "Sono's Sesame Cucumbers" was published in a magazine food column I was writing a few years back; it was paid a pirate's compliment by being lifted, title and all, for a diet cookbook. The borrower's name has faded into the mists, but this delicious relish continues to be a summertime asset at our house.

We like the cucumbers shredded, rather than sliced as in Sono's original, and served in side dishes with simply cooked chicken or fish or other seafood.

If a firm specimen of *daikon,* or white radish,

turns up, a piece about the size of one cucumber can be shredded and added to two shredded cucumbers and the seasonings listed; it's a delicious pairing.

Peel the cucumbers and either shred them the long way on a coarse-toothed grater or a mandoline, or use the julienne disk of a food processor to make the longest possible shreds. Drain the shreds in a colander for an hour or so, then squeeze out surplus moisture by twisting the cucumbers in a cloth.

Stir the sesame seeds in a skillet over low heat until golden, then grind them coarsely in a mortar, blender, or spice mill.

Mix the vinegar, soy sauce, sugar, and optional sesame oil; add the sesame seeds. Toss with the cucumbers; taste and adjust seasonings, adding salt if it's needed. The cucumbers can be served at once, but they're better after an hour or two at room temperature.

---

6 to 8 side-dish servings

3 cucumbers
2 tablespoons hulled white
   sesame seeds
3 tablespoons Oriental rice
   vinegar
2 tablespoons soy sauce
½ teaspoon granulated
   sugar
Few drops of Oriental dark
   sesame oil, optional (see
   Seasoning with Sesame,
   page 73)
Salt, optional

SUMMER POTATO SALAD

nce I had become addicted to this more or less French way of making a fresh-tasting, full-flavored potato salad, all the old ways—especially the customary use of cold potatoes—went by the board.

The seasonings follow my likings, but they can of course be changed; the method is what counts (but taste carefully as you compound the salad). When my herb patch is in good production, I often toss in minced tarragon, a few tiny leaves of fresh thyme, chervil, and even a sneaky leaf or two (chopped) of fresh mint. Shallots can replace the scallions and, in fact, they would be a French cook's preference.

The secrets of the salad aren't so secret. *One:* Start with thin-skinned, firm, rather waxy-fleshed potatoes, not "bakers," which crumble too much. (Lately I've been delighted by the availability of a potato variety called Yukon Gold, which is perfect for the purpose; red-skinned potatoes are fine, too.) *Second secret:* Peel the cooked potatoes as soon as you can touch them without flinching and marinate them while they're still warm. *Finally,* don't chill this salad. It can be made two or three hours ahead of time, as the recipe outlines, and allowed to rest peaceably at room temperature until it's wanted.

Leftover salad should of course be stored in the fridge. It will stiffen up, so when the second appearance comes around, add a little water, broth, mayonnaise, sour cream, or even yogurt to restore some of the original texture.

Serves 6 to 8

2½ pounds small "boiling" potatoes, such as Yukon Gold, scrubbed but not peeled
½ cup, or more if needed, hot chicken or beef broth (broth made with a good-quality bouillon cube is okay)
½ cup dry vermouth or dry white wine
½ cup, or more if needed, extra-virgin olive oil
¼ cup, or as needed, white wine vinegar
Salt and pepper, to taste
Herbs: Minced Italian-style parsley, a good handful; a small amount (depending on the eaters' love for onions) chopped tender scallions, white part only, or a good handful of snipped fresh chives

Boil the potatoes in water to cover (or steam them) just until tender, not overcooked; small spuds will take about 20 minutes.

Drain and cool the potatoes until they can be handled; peel them and slice them chunkily, ⅜ to ½ inch thick, into a mixing bowl.

Pour the hot broth and the vermouth over the potatoes, turn them a few times with a rubber spatula, and leave them to imbibe the liquid for a few minutes; they will be a little soupy at this point.

Add the oil and vinegar and some salt and pepper; turn the potatoes gently, taste the mixture, and adjust the seasoning. Leave the salad, covered, at room temperature for up to 3 hours.

Near serving time, taste the salad again quite critically and add more oil, vinegar, salt, and pepper if your palate decides they are indicated. Sprinkle the chopped herbs and your choice of scallions or chives over the salad and fold them in. The salad is now ready to serve, but it can wait for another half-hour or so.

TAKE IT, OR LEAVE IT, PICNIC OR LUNCH

Savory Chicken & Veal Loaf with Herbed Mayonnaise (below)

Dark-brown bread & butter sandwiches, or buttered pumpernickel, or crisp flatbread or breadsticks

Pre-Pasta Macaroni Salad (below) or Summer Potato Salad (page 74)

Crunchables: Cherry tomatoes, cucumber sticks, celery, pickles, hot peppers, green olives, thick-cut potato chips, and so forth

Pineapple Cake for the Fern Dell (below)

To drink: Either a rosé (on the dry side) or a white wine, and/or soft drinks

T he exceedingly nummy pineapple upside-down cake that rounds off this packable repast always recalls for me (and for my siblings) many youthful outings to one particular place, the Fern Dell in Los Angeles, whose attractions were a shady ravine in a dry country and, sometimes, a chance to go up the mountain to the Griffith Observatory on top.

We often went picnicking, too, on the palm-dotted lawns of the Palisades above the ocean in Santa Monica, where there were tables and benches and stone fireplaces, but we had another excuse, a fishy one, for a more exciting picnic. In grunion season we went to the wide beach below the Palisades, across the Pacific highway, for a bonfire, a feast, and a sing-song whose pretext was the moonlight pastime called grunion-hunting.

Grunion are small fish of the smelt tribe; they swim inshore at the peak of the high tide on certain full-moon nights in order to lay their eggs at the fringe of the waves that reach highest up the beach. (The hatchlings are carried to sea on the next full-moon tide.)

The sport was to catch the grunion bare-handed—nets and such were forbidden. Though grunion-hunters were pleased to take home enough of the tasty little creatures for a fish fry (I don't remember ever catching very many), the grunion were mostly an excuse for being on the beach at night, around a driftwood fire.

Sans a grunion excuse, the picnic that follows can be served anywhere. The chicken and veal loaf and macaroni salad are especially commended to those who may have forgotten about such simple dishes.

INSTEAD OF VEAL SHANKS: Shanks are excellent for this loaf because they're more flavorful than most parts of the veal calf. But you might check the butcher's cold case for neck, breast, or stew meat from the shoulder, all sensibly priced cuts. After all, when he's finished packaging his cutlets at a million dollars a pound, the butcher must dispose of the rest of his veal critter(s) somehow, so the remnants, so to speak, are often bargains.

Makes 8 servings

1 pound veal shanks
1 pound chicken thighs
1 medium onion, sliced
1 rib celery, cut up
1 or 2 bay leaves
2 carrots, scraped and cut into sticks
1 clove garlic, flattened
2 or 3 sprigs parsley
Pinch of crumbled dried thyme
½ teaspoon, or to taste, salt
Pinch of white pepper
Chicken broth, diluted beef broth, or water
¼ cup roasted, skinned, and diced sweet red peppers, fresh or bottled
2 tablespoons minced parsley
½ teaspoon minced fresh tarragon or ¼ teaspoon dried tarragon, soaked briefly and drained
Fresh lemon juice, to taste

SAVORY CHICKEN & VEAL LOAF WITH HERBED MAYONNAISE

andsome and colorful, a little sparkly, this cold loaf is a hybrid—a cross between pressed chicken and jellied veal, with zippier seasonings than either antecedent can boast. Savory for a lunch on a warm day, it's also worth a thought for supper in any season.

Cover the veal and chicken with cold water, bring to a boil, and boil 5 minutes. Discard the liquid. Rinse the meats in cold water; reserve the chicken.

Return the rinsed veal to the pot and add the onion, celery, bay leaves, carrots, garlic, parsley sprigs, thyme, ½ teaspoon salt, and pepper; add broth or water to cover, bring to a boil, lower the heat, and simmer 20 minutes. Add the chicken; bring to a boil again, then cook at a simmer until the meats are very tender, 40 minutes to 1 hour.

Remove the meats and vegetables and reserve them. Strain the broth, then boil it until it has reduced to 2 cups, skimming it once or twice as it reduces.

Meanwhile, remove the skin, bones, and gristle from the chicken and veal. Cut the meat into ½-inch-thick chunks; pry out and add to the meats any marrow to be found in the veal bone. Dice the carrots and add them to the meat with the diced red peppers, minced parsley, and tarragon. (Discard the remaining flavoring vegetables.)

Taste the reduced broth and add enough salt, lemon juice, and mustard for well-balanced and emphatic flavor, remembering that chilling will mute the impact of the seasonings somewhat.

Soak the gelatin in the cold water until soft, about 5 minutes, then stir it into the hot stock to dissolve. Stir in the meats and vegetables.

*Dijon-style mustard, to
  taste
1½ envelopes unflavored
  gelatin
¼ cup water
Garnish: Fresh greens
Sauce: Lemony
  mayonnaise with added
  parsley, chives, and
  tarragon
Optional accompaniment:
  Crisp toast or flatbread*

Pack the mixture firmly into a 6-cup loaf pan. Cover the top with plastic or foil and, optionally, add a light weight (a second loaf pan with a can of food set inside will do the job). Chill the loaf until firmly set, 6 hours or more. The loaf can be held for 2 or 3 days before it is unmolded for serving.

Slice and serve the loaf from its pan for a picnic. At home, unmold the loaf and serve it whole on greens with a garnish, or slice it and arrange the slices on shredded greens. (For unmolding pointers, see page 218). Pass the mayonnaise separately.

PRE-PASTA MACARONI SALAD

MACARONI SHAPES: If another shape of macaroni is substituted for elbows, choose a small size of such types as bow ties or butterflies, ditali, spirals, or sea shells. Large tubular shapes such as ziti— sometimes used in ultra-fashionable renderings of this simple salad—are too big for a comfortable bite, and they also tend to collapse unless they are half-raw.

Talking of calling a spade a shovel, I'm dropping "pasta" in favor of "macaroni" for this grandparent of the pasta salads purveyed by stylish take-outs. We've appreciated it around our house as far back as the memory of the cook runneth, and so have some highly sophisticated guests who have been treated to its homely charms. Although it doesn't pretend to the drop-dead chic of its "pasta" relatives, the real thing—a salad along the lines below—is also much better to eat than most versions, especially those deli-department salads whose long shelf life is their chief merit.

Don't chill the salad after it's assembled if you can help it, but if time permits do allow it to rest for an hour or more to develop flavor. If it must be refrigerated the texture will tighten, so at serving time you'll need to add more dressing or a little liquid (milk, sour cream, or yogurt, with perhaps a little pickle juice or other acid) to restore the creaminess of the dressing. Taste the salad again at that point and adjust the seasonings, which have a way

---

Serves 8

*½ pound (2 cups) small
elbow macaroni (see
Macaroni Shapes, below)
2½ tablespoons corn or
peanut oil (not olive oil)
¼ cup, or to taste, fresh
lemon juice, or white-
wine or tarragon vinegar
3 cups, combined total, of
your choice of diced or
sliced radishes,
cucumbers, celery,
Jerusalem artichokes, or
jicama
1 cup, total, in preferred
proportions, sliced
scallions, chopped
shallots or red onion,
diced red or green sweet
peppers
½ cup minced parsley
¼ cup, or to taste, of
good-quality India relish,
or diced bread-and-
butter or sweet or sour
pickles
2 to 3 tablespoons diced
bottled pimientos or
pimiento-stuffed olives
Optional, for piquancy:
2 tablespoons diced
pickled jalapeño peppers*

DRESSING:
*¾ cup, or needed,
mayonnaise, plus milk or
yogurt to thin it slightly
Salt and pepper, to taste
Garnish: Additional
minced parsley; or
cherry tomatoes; or
radish roses*

of changing their balance in the refrigerator. Let the reseasoned dish return to room temperature again, if you can.

Cook the macaroni in well-salted boiling water according to package directions until it's tender but not soft. Drain at once and stir in the oil and ¼ cup lemon juice or vinegar. Let marinate at room temperature for 1 hour if feasible. If not feasible, proceed with the recipe as soon as the macaroni has cooled.

About an hour before serving time, add all other ingredients except the dressing and toss with two spoons. Pour on the dressing and mix again.

Taste and season carefully with salt, pepper, and more lemon juice or vinegar (or more pickles or India relish), and so on, whatever your palate thinks it needs. The salad should be highly flavored and its texture should be creamy but not soupy; add more dressing if it's needed.

Let the salad rest, covered but not refrigerated, until serving time. Serve garnished or not, as preferred. Refrigerate leftovers.

SUIT YOURSELF—OTHER VERSIONS OF THE SALAD: A tender bowlful of macaroni salad is nostalgic as is for picnics, summertime lunches, and cookouts as a go-along for anything from hot dogs to grilled steak.

With Poultry, Eggs, or Meat: The salad makes an all-in-one lunch or supper if substance is added by tossing in diced chicken, roast beef, corned beef, smoked tongue, ham, or hard-cooked eggs, or any combination thereof, in any amounts you like. If the additions are substantial, you can put more plates on the table.

With Fish or Seafood: Drain, flake, and add a tall can (1 pound) of salmon to the basic macaroni (or use tuna, or flaked leftover fish of any kind) and round out the textures and flavors with plenty of diced celery, some minced fresh dill, parsley, and chives, and a dressing of mayonnaise mixed with sour cream. (Enlarged this way, the salad will serve two or three more hungry mouths.)

Seasoning Switches: Onion lovers will add more of their favorite Allium—perhaps chives or sliced scallion greens—to the seasonings of any version. Herb fanciers are likely to add to the basic salad some snipped chives, minced tarragon, thyme, and chervil, and extra parsley.

PINEAPPLE CAKE FOR THE FERN DELL

 n the arid Los Angeles basin of Southern California, green things grow only where they're watered a *lot*, so one of the miraculous places of my childhood was Griffith Park. In that mostly wild reservation of brushy foothills, the highest hill was crowned by the Observatory, to which school children were taken to see the electrically replicated wonders of the night sky in the Planetarium.

The Fern Dell was (is?) a deep ravine with a brook and paths wandering between shady banks covered with ferns; the green lushness was enchanting to visitors coming in from the dry hills all about. There were tables for eating and fireplaces for cooking, so it was a grand place for family picnics.

By the time we were young teen-agers, my older sister and I took turns making the picnic dessert, which was almost always pineapple upside-down cake baked in an iron skillet. Very proud we were when it was turned out onto a platter in all its brown-gold glory, then carefully placed in a carrying carton (Tupperware was yet to come).

I'm still fond of this very American cake, perhaps not least because I first dared to depart from a recipe when making it. We used, for the batter, my mother's reliable recipe for one-two-three-four cake, and once I substituted syrup from the pineapple can for the milk; it wasn't a disaster, in fact it was delicious, and that's the way I've made the cake ever since when there has been an excuse for a sticky, fruity, delightful, and altogether excessive dessert. The recipe below has changed very little since then.

Today, made with the same amount of batter,

OTHER PICNIC DESSERTS THAT TRAVEL: When composing your own picnic menu, see the Index for the whereabouts of recipes for cookies and for Cherry, Blueberry, or Plum Picnic Cake; Upside-Down Fruited Ginger Cake; Blueberry & Pound Cake Pudding; Honey Pecan Pie; and Hazelnut Cheese Tart. Any or all will travel well in a picnic "tote."

*Makes a 10-inch cake
serving 8 or more*

FRUIT LAYER:
5 tablespoons unsalted
  butter
⅔ cup (packed) light-
  brown sugar
1 20-ounce can sliced
  pineapple, drained, the
  juice or syrup reserved
Optional addition:
  A handful of walnut
  halves, or fresh
  cranberries, or candied
  cherries

CAKE BATTER:
2 cups sifted cake flour
2 teaspoons baking
  powder
1 teaspoon salt
8 tablespoons (1 stick)
  plus 2 tablespoons
  unsalted butter
1¼ cups granulated sugar,
  if pineapple is packed in
  juice; 1 cup if it is
  packed in syrup
3 large eggs, separated
¾ teaspoon lemon extract
½ teaspoon vanilla extract
⅔ cup reserved pineapple
  juice or syrup
Optional accompaniment:
  Whipped cream

the cake is less bulky than the original because canned pineapple comes in smaller and thinner slices; there used to be eight wide slices to a large can, now there are ten in a slimmer can. That's no problem, but the old slices filled a ten-inch skillet more neatly and completely.

Sliced pineapple is now often packed in pineapple juice instead of syrup, but I think the sweetened fruit is preferable for this dessert.

Preheat the oven to 350°.

Fruit layer: Melt the butter in a 10-inch cast-iron skillet or other heavy flameproof pan of similar size. Add the brown sugar and stir over the heat until the mixture is lump-free and bubbly. Reserve.

Pat the pineapple slices fairly dry with paper towels, then arrange them in the skillet, cutting some, if you wish, to make a pleasing pattern. Optionally, place a nut half, a few cranberries, or a cherry in the center of each slice and here and there in other spaces. Set aside.

Cake: Sift together the flour, baking powder, and salt.

Cream the butter well; cream in the sugar, then beat in the egg yolks one at a time; beat until very fluffy. Add the lemon extract and vanilla.

At low speed, beat in one-third of the dry ingredients, then half of the juice or syrup, continuing to alternate additions and ending with dry ingredients. Beat briefly until smooth.

Whisk or beat the egg whites until they form medium-stiff peaks when the beater is lifted. Stir about a fourth of the whites into the batter, then fold in the rest with a rubber spatula.

Scape the batter over the fruit and smooth the top. Bake in the center of the oven for about 45 minutes, or until a cake tester emerges dry when the center is pierced and the sides of the cake have shrunk from the pan.

Cool in the pan for a minute or two, then carefully turn the cake out onto a rack (or a platter, if you prefer). If any fruit adheres to the pan, lift it with a metal spatula and put it back where it belongs.

This cake tastes best after it has cooled almost to room temperature, but it's still excellent the next day. It

OWL SALAD AND OTHER GOOFY EATS: The home cook's desire to thrill her eatership used to be expressed in such fripperies as the owl salad described in the text. Nowadays, though, it seems often to appear as a yearning to reproduce fast food, or the dishes sold by takeouts, or the "convenience" foods that take up the lion's share of shelf space in markets. A fully unscientific survey made in idle moments not long ago turned up recipe requests for such delights as deli-counter coleslaw; Cheez-Whiz, or a "cheese like Velveeta," or "a cheese sauce that tastes like [deleted] brand"; a pizza sauce like that of the [deleted] chain; New England-style chow mein, whatever that may be; fried chicken like Kentucky Fried; and brownies and cakes "like Sara Lee's." Those recipe-requesters who didn't want to copycat fast foods wanted to make some dishes that just may be equally vile. How about chicken presoaked in salad-dressing mix, or frozen cooked chicken sauced with marmalade, or pickles flavored with cinnamon candies?

John Thorne, in his good book *Simple Cooking,* says of such "truly awful recipes" that they "conjure instant elegance from dross.... Like any truly brilliant swindle, they thrill us most when we know we're being taken."

really needs no sauce, but some people like whipped cream with it.

———

WHOO-OOSE SALAD? Those bygone thick slices of pineapple were involved in another delicacy at our house, a children's birthday-party number we knew as "owl salad." (Some people called a related concoction "candlelight salad," according to the food writers Jane and Michael Stern, who have written delightfully about such American exotica; besides pineapple and banana, it included coconut, mayonnaise, and pimiento.)

For owl salad, a slice of pineapple went onto a plate adorned with lettuce; half a banana was anchored upright in the center of the slice, a split maraschino cherry (carcinogenic red dye and all) was perched on the banana as "eyes," and whipped cream was plopped around the base. (A nest? Feathers?) This was a dish only the very young could admire—and we did—but the Sterns swear that their candlelight salad was also served to grownups.

As Ann Batchelder wrote in her *Cookbook,* "Salads made into candles, pinwheels, butterflies, and rag dolls are not salads. Let's think up another name."

A DINNER TO *ASK* A PERSON TO

We should look for someone to eat and drink with before looking for something to eat and drink.

—EPICURUS, *APHORISMS*

Dr. Samuel Johnson's sniffish remark, which I've taken the liberty of adapting in the title of this section, was, in full, "This was a good dinner enough, to be sure, but it was not a dinner to *ask* a man to."

Nowadays we need to rethink the Johnsonian view of the kind of dinner he felt he was entitled to at someone else's table, although the good doctor was neither the first nor the last to believe that a "company" dinner should be quite a production. In modern terms Dr. Johnson was wrong about what's due to a guest, unless he was speaking as a greedy fellow (which, one gathers, he was).

Today, we almost always do better as hosts when we don't worry about whether the food—which must be very good, don't misunderstand me—will be sufficiently up-to-the-minute and decidedly showy, like one of the spreads demonstrated by pretty ladies on television. We do best when we think like Epicurus, or when we take

Balthazar's position in *The Comedy of Errors*—"Small cheer and great welcome makes a merry feast."

The cheer (read "eats") in the dinners Mrs. Witty offers in the following pages won't be judged to be all *that* small, she hopes, just because the menus are designed for family-alone or for family-plus-friends; in either case, the "great welcome" is up to you.

These meals are meant to be "good dinners enough" to invite friends to (or at least *my* friends). They are meant to be simple (meaning without pretentiousness), to taste very good, and to be achievable without exhausting either the cook or the food budget. As Angelo Pellegrini, that wise, earthy professor with one foot in the Old World and one in the New, once wrote, what we all need is to "see the dinner hour in perspective, as an element in the good life." And the good life goes on every day, not just when there are guests.

A menu postscript: Not a word of the foregoing essay on everyday eating that's good enough for company (or vice versa) should be read to mean that you shouldn't do your best to wow the dinner audience (eatience?) with a dandy dessert from time to time. I have included in this chapter some of my own and my family's favorites, which no one in his/her right mind should be able to ignore.

Is There Anything Else for Dinner?

Yes there is, in other chapters. Look in the lunch-picnic-cookout section and in the supper chapter for dishes and combinations that may well suit your notions of dinner. Check those pages (and see the Index and the Seasonal Recipe Lists) for dishes involving lobster (for which, you will begin to suspect, Mrs. Witty has a weakness), other seafood, chicken, and ham; and look for such "made" dishes as hearty salads and soups.

You can always redesignate as "dinner" one of the baked-bean or chowder suppers, or (especially in warm weather) one or two of the more substantial lunches. It all comes down to semantics—a meal, after all, is only what you choose to call it—lunch, dinner, midday dinner, evening dinner, or supper. Or breakfast.

ASSIMILATED ITALIAN

Antipasto of Marinated Jerusalem Artichokes (below) and slices of fine salami; oil-cured black olives; roasted red sweet peppers garnished with anchovy fillets; wedges of ripe tomato

Purchased Italian breadsticks or Buttery Breadsticks (page 225)

Linguine with Clams & Pancetta (below)

Raspberry & White Wine Ice (below), plus Twice-Baked Orange & Nut Cookies (below) or purchased sugar wafers

To drink: A white wine, preferably Italian—perhaps an Orvieto

Playing fast and loose with culinary roots by adopting ethnic specialties is nothing new in American cuisine, and here we go again with an only somewhat Italian dinner. The meal, however, *does* have Italian influences, and that's my excuse, Your Honor...

Antipasto has long been taken to our hearts on this side of the Atlantic, and here I've built an antipasto course around an Italian treatment of the Jerusalem artichoke. (That native of the New World traveled to Italy long ago and received a warm welcome.)

Pasta sauced with clams, with or without tomatoes, made it

into the ranks of "American" food quite a while back; my version below has a white clam sauce.

The twice-baked cookies are recognizably *biscotti* in spirit if not in substance, and like fully authentic biscotti they are good companions for the deep-flavored fruit ice that completes the menu.

If switching dishes for the beginning and/or the finale of this menu appeals to you, possibilities for a first course include crudités, either pristine or with a Dipping Vinaigrette; or Orange & Lemon Salad with Mint; or the Tapenade of a Different Color. For dessert, pleasant alternatives to those listed are Raspberry & Rhubarb Parfait, Berry Bavarian, or simply an opulent bowl of fresh fruits of the season. (See the Index for the recipes.)

MARINATED JERUSALEM ARTICHOKES (SUNROOTS)

orking out this recipe, I discovered for myself why the "Jerusalem artichoke" (which as everyone knows is neither from the Holy Land nor an artichoke) acquired that name. These knobby tubers of a native American sunflower (*Helianthus tuberosus*) do indeed taste much like the fleshy bottoms of globe artichokes when they are fixed in certain ways, including this one. Marinated with herbs, garlic, olive oil, and wine vinegar, they are an appetizing item for an antipasto platter, or a dandy relish with a sandwich or cold meats.

Sunroots (an old name that sounds better to me than the craw-sticking "sunchokes," a market name thought up by wholesalers) can be used raw in salads for their special nutty crispness; they can be transformed into pungent pickles and relishes, or cooked plain-buttered, or mashed, or in gratins, purées, and soups. Existing recipes scarcely scratch the surface; the vegetable repays experimentation, especially during the winter and spring months when the roots seem to be at their best.

The sunroot traveled to Europe from the New World long ago; called *topinambour* in France and *girasole* in Italy, the North American novelty became quite fashionable; in fact, I've found one chef's recipe that tried to reproduce its flavor by combining sweet potatoes with real artichoke hearts, which would be quite a reversal now, considering the price commanded by artichoke hearts in any form whatsoever.

GETTING "ARTICHOKES" INTO A PICKLE: In the U.S., Jerusalem artichokes didn't cut much of a figure on the *haute* culinary scene until their recent rediscovery by marketers, but the vegetable has always been highly valued by home gardeners and by the cottage-industry entrepreneurs who make "artichoke" pickles for fancy-food shops. For a very good pickle recipe, look in *Better Than Store-Bought,* which I co-authored a few years back.

Makes about 3 cups

1 pound Jerusalem
    artichokes
Salt, to taste
⅓ cup white wine vinegar
    or Oriental rice vinegar
⅓ cup water
2 large cloves garlic, sliced
Herbs:
1 teaspoon mixed dried
    Italian herbs, or ¼
    teaspoon each thyme,
    basil, and oregano, plus
    a pinch each of rosemary
    and sweet marjoram
Big pinch of dried red
    pepper flakes, or small
    pinch of ground hot red
    pepper
Big pinch of granulated
    sugar
2 or 3 thin slices lemon,
    halved and seeded
¾ cup, or as needed, mild
    olive oil

**BLANCHING SMOKED
BACON:** If thick-cut bacon
replaces the pancetta,
simmer the slices in a quart
of water for 10 minutes.
Drain, rinse, and pat dry with
paper toweling; dice and
proceed with the recipe.

MARINATED JERUSALEM ARTICHOKES (CONTINUED)

For easy peeling, rinse the roots, drop them into boiling water, and blanch them for 3 or 4 minutes; cool in cold water and pare off the skins. (Alternatively, scrape them while raw.)

Cut the roots into more or less uniform ½-inch chunks. Drop the chunks into boiling salted water and cook them until tender but not soft, 5 to 10 minutes. Drain the roots and place them in a quart jar.

In the same pan simmer together the vinegar, ⅓ cup water, garlic, salt to taste (I'd use about 1½ teaspoons), herbs, pepper, sugar, and lemon. Pour the mixture over the roots, then add oil to cover. Cap the jar, shake it to distribute the seasonings, and refrigerate the roots at least overnight before serving them.

The marinated roots improve with further mellowing. They'll keep for at least 2 weeks; shake the jar occasionally during storage to redistribute the seasonings.

LINGUINE WITH CLAMS & PANCETTA

Pasta with white clam sauce—"white" meaning the sauce has no tomatoes—was an Italian dish that quickly won my Californian heart when I explored now-forgotten New York City restaurants during my student days at Columbia University. As soon as I had a kitchen (so-called) of my own, no time was lost in recreating the dish, although canned clams were mostly what I could get in the neighborhood. Once in a while they were razor clams from Oregon, vastly better than common kinds and now a real rarity. Later, during my first summers on eastern Long Island, I often went clam digging in local bays and used the Eastern quahogs I was able to capture in still more versions of this quick and delectable dish.

Serves 4 to 6

1 pound linguine or
  regular spaghetti,
  preferably imported

SAUCE:
¼ pound pancetta, diced,
  or ¼ pound (about 6
  slices) thick-cut bacon,
  blanched and diced (see
  Blanching Smoked
  Bacon, left)
2 tablespoons mild olive or
  vegetable oil
6 tender scallions, sliced,
  with a little of the green
  tops
3 large cloves garlic,
  minced
½ cup dry white wine
1 cup chopped freshly
  steamed hard clams
  (about 18 good-sized
  Cherrystones or small
  chowders), juice reserved
  (see cleaning and
  cooking directions on
  page 39); or two 10-
  ounce cans (or three 6-to
  7-ounce cans) chopped
  clams, liquid reserved
1 to 1½ cups, as needed,
  clam broth
Freshly ground pepper, to
  taste
3 tablespoons unsalted
  butter
¼ cup minced parsley

In its most basic version,. it requires only olive oil, garlic, clams, fresh pepper, parsley, and pasta.

The recipe here is gussied up a little with additions of pancetta—unsmoked Italian bacon—a little white wine, and scallions. (If you'd like to try the basic recipe, sauté the garlic—I'd use more than the recipe lists if the scallions are omitted—add clam juice, simmer briefly, add clams, butter, and parsley, simmer again, and there you are.)

Cook linguine according to package directions until just tender, about 10 minutes.

While the pasta cooks, make the sauce: Cook the pancetta or bacon pieces in 1 tablespoon of the oil in a heavy skillet over medium or low heat, stirring, until golden, 5 to 8 minutes; do not brown. Lift the pieces from the fat and reserve them.

Discard all but 1 tablespoon of the fat in the pan; add the remaining oil, scallions, and garlic and cook, stirring, over medium heat until wilted but not browned, about 3 minutes. Add the wine; simmer a moment; add the clams and their liquid and the additional broth and simmer briskly for 2 or 3 minutes to reduce the sauce slightly. Return the pancetta or bacon.

Spoon about one-third of the sauce into the beaker of a blender or food processor and whirl it to a purée; return the purée to the sauce. Stir in the pepper, butter, and parsley; reheat the sauce without boiling it and keep it warm if it's not used at once.

Drain the linguine thoroughly. Ladle some of the sauce into a warmed serving bowl. Add the linguine; toss briefly, add the remaining sauce, and toss thoroughly with two forks. Serve at once, or cover and let meditate for a minute or two, especially if the sauce is quite liquid.

———

A TRICK WORTH REMEMBERING: Other pasta dishes as well as this one are all the better for it if you purée part of the sauce, which helps the chunky elements to cling to the pasta strands instead of slipping off. Further, it does nothing but good to let the sauced hot pasta rest for two or three minutes, covered, before it's served; the strands can then imbibe some of the sauce and gain character in the interval between the pot and the plate.

RASPBERRY & WHITE-WINE ICE

nlike many ices and sorbets, this rosy beauty stays silky-smooth for weeks in the freezer, so it's a good thing to have on hand at any season. It's a refreshing dessert as is, and it's even more intriguing when a little crème de cassis—black-currant liqueur—is drizzled on to enhance the fragrance of the raspberries.

The ice, without the cassis, is also suitable for service as a palate-refresher midway through a dinner of several courses, if such a fancy occasion should arise.

Makes a little over 1½ pints

3 cups fresh raspberries or a 12-ounce bag of frozen unsweetened raspberries
1 cup granulated sugar
⅔ cup water
1½ cups dry white wine
¼ cup crème de cassis, optional

OPTIONAL TOPPING:
Additional crème de cassis

Purée the raspberries in a food processor or blender. Press the purée through a fine sieve once or twice to remove the seeds; discard the seeds. Chill the purée.

Heat the sugar and water together and boil the syrup, uncovered, 3 minutes. Remove from the heat; stir in the wine and the cassis, if it's being used. Cool, then chill thoroughly.

Stir in the raspberry purée and freeze in an ice-cream maker according to manufacturer's instructions. Store the finished ice in a covered container in the freezer.

Making the dessert without an ice-cream maker: Pour the mixture into a shallow metal baking pan and place uncovered in the deep-freeze until mushy, about 3 hours. Scrape into the food processor or bowl of an electric mixer; beat until fluffy, working quickly to minimize melting. Return to the pan, cover tightly with foil, and freeze until firm, 2 to 3 hours. If the ice hasn't been served within a few hours of freezing, scrape it into a freezer container, cover it tightly, and return it to the freezer for storage.

To serve, scoop into chilled dessert glasses and, if you like, top each portion with a tablespoonful of crème de cassis.

TWICE-BAKED ORANGE & NUT COOKIES

hockful of almonds and candied orange peel and most delicately spiced, these cookies add a festive dimension to coffee- or tea-time, or to a barebones dessert. They keep well, if they are hidden with reasonable cunning. (Make that a *lot* of cunning.)

Makes 3 to 3½ dozen

8 tablespoons (1 stick)
  unsalted butter
⅔ cup granulated sugar
2 large eggs
¼ teaspoon almond
  extract
1 tablespoon finely minced
  or grated lemon zest
  (colored rind only, no
  pith)
2½ cups all-purpose flour
1 tablespoon baking
  powder
¾ teaspoon salt
¼ teaspoon ground
  cinnamon
¼ teaspoon freshly grated
  nutmeg
¼ teaspoon ground mace
⅓ cup minced candied
  orange peel, preferably
  homemade
⅓ cup coarsely chopped
  toasted natural almonds
  (see page 276)
Milk for brushing

Preheat the oven to 350°.

Cream together the butter and sugar; beat in the eggs. Add the almond extract and lemon zest.

Sift together the flour, baking powder, salt, and spices. Stir into the creamed mixture; mix in the candied peel and almonds, working the dough well with a spoon (or kneading it by hand in the bowl) until it is thoroughly mixed and compact.

Divide the dough in half. Cover a baking sheet with foil. Shape the dough firmly into two compact flat loaves, placed well apart on the pan; make each about 12 inches long and 2½ inches wide and slightly higher in the center than the sides. Brush the loaves with milk, smoothing all surfaces with the bristles of the brush as you do so.

Bake the loaves about 20 minutes, until they are firm to touch and slightly browned. Remove from the oven; slip the foil from the pan onto a wire rack and let the loaves cool for 15 minutes.

Meanwhile, reset the oven to 300°.

Slice the loaves slightly on the bias into bars ½ inch wide. Lay the slices flat on the cooled baking sheet and bake 10 minutes, or until the top side has taken on slightly more color; turn the slices and bake up to 10 minutes longer, looking at them frequently to prevent the cookies from overbrowning.

Cool on racks, then store airtight. The cookies will keep for several weeks.

SUMMERTIME SAMPLER

Herb-Broiled Chickens (below)

Old New England Corn Pudding (below)

Pot-Steamed Baby Zucchini (below)

*Ice-cold watermelon or other melon in season, or Berry
Bavarian (below)*

*To drink: A light red wine, such as an Italian Barolo, or a
Gamay or premium jug wine from California; or beer*

---

ummer is almost the only season when you can revel in broiled chicken seasoned with a buttery mixture of herbs stuffed under the skin, unless you can lay hands on fresh herbs at the greengrocer's at other times of year (or are able to grow your own supply indoors). Therefore the rest of this menu is also summery, with offerings of fresh corn, infant squash, and, for dessert, either watermelon or a Bavarian cream of fresh berries.

The New England corn pudding, however, can be an off-season dish if you like, thanks to the general availability of excellent canned or frozen whole-kernel corn. Made with such stand-ins for summer ears, the pudding will still have more flavor and sweetness than the dish eaten by the Nantucketers, who had only field corn for cooking. Even young and tender, field corn would be unlikely to appeal to us today.

Serves 4 to 6

8 tablespoons (1 stick)
 unsalted butter
¾ teaspoon salt
Several grinds of pepper
1 or 2 cloves garlic, minced
Herbs: Small handful each
 of minced parsley and
 snipped chives; about 3
 tablespoons (any
 combination) of minced
 fresh thyme leaves,
 tarragon, chervil, or
 sweet marjoram; a little
 minced fresh rosemary,
 optional
1 tablespoon fresh lemon
 juice
2 broiler-fryer chickens,
 split, backbones and
 wing tips removed,
 rinsed and patted dry

HERB-BROILED CHICKENS

he basic how-to's of plain-broiling chicken are in every general cookbook, but it can be quite challenging to season a bird so it will take wing, so to speak. An excellent way to meet the challenge is one I came across soon after our vacationtime herb patch was established.

Stuffing fresh herbs and quite a lot of butter under the skin of a chicken is surprisingly easy to do—the skin is barely attached to the meat below, and the herbs can impart their flavor without falling off or, even worse, burning.

The birds can be broiled a few hours ahead and cooled, then served at room temperature, not cold.

Preheat the broiler at its highest setting, with a shelf placed so the surface of the chicken will be about 6 inches from the element (broiling should be slow).

Cream the butter with the salt, pepper, garlic, herbs, and lemon juice. Divide it into 4 portions.

Using your fingers, push two-thirds of each butter portion under the skin of a chicken half, poking it in from all sides. Spread the butter evenly by smoothing the skin. Arrange the chicken halves skin down on the broiler-pan rack; place the remaining butter in the cavities.

Broil the chicken slowly, using a basting brush to distribute the butter in the cavities as soon as it melts; brush the flesh side again with the buttery juices from time to time. When lightly browned—about 15 minutes—turn the pieces with tongs and broil the skin side, brushing the pieces occasionally with pan juices, until they are done; the skin should be crisp and lightly browned, with a dappling of green showing through, about 20 minutes.

With a knife or poultry shears, separate the halves into serving pieces and arrange them on a warm platter.

For a sauce: Heat the pan juices with a little wine or stock, lemon juice, more herbs, and salt and pepper; pour it over the platter of chicken.

IN PLACE OF FRESH CORN: With modern hybrid corn, none of the sugar called for in the ancestor recipe is needed if the ears are young and fresh, as they should be. If the available fresh corn doesn't measure up, high-quality canned or frozen whole-kernel corn is a better bet. Not all brands are equal, and neither are types; white "shoe-peg" corn is especially tender and sweet, though pale. Of gold-kerneled corn, brands packed with very little liquid tend to be the best.

Serves 6 generously

Unsalted butter for coating the baking dish
About 12 large ears fresh sweet corn, enough to yield 3 cups pulp; or 3 cups of puréed canned or frozen corn
2 large eggs
1½ cups whole milk, light cream, or half-and-half
1 teaspoon salt
⅛ teaspoon white pepper
Pinch of freshly grated nutmeg
⅓ cup finely crushed pilot crackers or other lightly salted crackers
3 tablespoons melted unsalted butter

TOPPING:
¼ cup cracker crumbs
2 tablespoons additional melted unsalted butter

OLD NEW ENGLAND CORN PUDDING

antucket was the home of the summer corn pudding that inspired this year-around update. The old "receipt" called for a great deal of sugar to make more palatable the unripe field corn used before the development of modern sweet corn.

The crumbs the Nantucketers would have used were fine-rolled cracker-barrel or common crackers, which are still available, tooth-bending as ever, from one or two New England mail-order suppliers.

Preheat oven to 325°. Butter a 2-quart baking or soufflé dish.

Fresh corn: To remove pulp, hold each ear upright; slit the rows of kernels lengthwise with a sharp knife; with the back of the knife, press and scrape out all pulp. Measure.

Canned or frozen corn: Whirl the corn in a food processor or blender until puréed medium-fine, not smooth. Measure.

Beat the eggs with cream, seasonings, and 3 cups corn pulp or puréed corn. Stir in the cracker crumbs and melted butter. Pour into the baking dish.

Topping: Stir the crumbs with the butter to mix well. Sprinkle over the pudding.

Bake in center of oven until slightly puffed and golden with firm edges, about 1 hour; center should be slightly soft.

Serve hot, with additional melted butter if it seems a good idea; or cool and refrigerate the pudding to reheat later.

Reheating: Cover the baking dish with foil. Set dish in a larger pan, pour in simmering water to come partway up the dish, and bake in 375° oven until pudding is hot, about 30 minutes.

POT-STEAMED BABY ZUCCHINI

o be cooked this way, zucchini should be tiny and fresh off the vine, shiny and taut-skinned, not the least bit withered or rubbery. The smallest are most delectable, but squash up to 6 inches long will do if they're halved in each direction.

Scrub the zucchini and trim their ends; leave tiny ones whole; halve or quarter them if larger.

Melt the butter in a heavy pot. Add the zucchini, salt them lightly, roll them in the butter, add 2 or 3 tablespoons of water, and cover the pot absolutely tight.

Steam the zucchini gently over low heat, shaking the pot occasionally, just until they begin to be tender, perhaps 10 minutes in all. Check quickly on the pan juices when shaking the squash and add a few drops of water if necessary to maintain gentle steaming.

When the zucchini are done, uncover the pot, correct the seasoning, and add a few drops of lemon juice if the idea appeals; they should be served promptly, while in their first buttery bloom.

INFANTICIDE IN THE SQUASH PATCH: For gardeners, it's a yearly question: What to do with a surfeit of squash, especially after they've become enormous?

First, be ruthless; pick summer squashes (any kind) when they're still bearing their blossoms. Pick daily! (If you must throw them away, it's easier then.)

Then consider things to do with baby squashes: Slice thin coins into green salads...Stuff and bake squash blossoms...Put squash chunks into ratatouille (big specimens will do)...Shred coarsely, steam with a branch of basil, sauce with butter or sour cream...Make an Italian zucchini frittata...Add ginger and lemon to golden squash and make marmalade...Cut zucchini into sticks, dust with flour, and deep-fry (in olive oil, preferably) for "French-fries"...Make zucchini pickles...Make a French-style cream soup.

Serves 6

2½ pounds tiny zucchini
4 tablespoons (½ stick) unsalted butter
Salt and white pepper, to taste
Drops of fresh lemon juice, optional

SQUASH WISDOM: Having grown up on summer squashes that were picked before their blossoms had had a chance to wither, I was baffled, when I first moved "back East," to see huge, hard-skinned pattypans and yellow squashes and zucchini that had far outgrown their youth. (West Coast pattypans were silver-dollar size.) Happily, there's more market wisdom about vegetables now, and baby squashes are sold almost everywhere. If you can't buy 'em, grow 'em.

BERRY BAVARIAN

osy and opulent-looking but not especially rich, here's a fruit cream that is much simpler to make than the ancestral Bavarian cream based on an egg custard. For the berry purée, raspberries are everyone's first choice, but it's smart to use the best berries of the moment—straw-, logan-, boysen-, and so on according to season.

A plain or fluted ring mold or a bundt cake pan will show this pretty dessert to best advantage without undue fanciness.

Serves 6

2 pints fresh raspberries or other berries, rinsed (if dusty) and very well drained
1 cup superfine sugar
2 tablespoons strained fresh lemon juice
1½ envelopes (4 generous teaspoons) unflavored gelatin
⅓ cup cold water
1½ cups chilled heavy cream
Oil for coating the mold
Garnish: *1 cup additional berries chilled with ¼ cup superfine sugar, or Raspberry Sauce (page 143), or Two-Berry Sauce (page 206).*

Purée the berries in a blender or food processor, then strain the purée through a fine sieve to remove seeds. You should have 1 cup purée; if there is a tablespoonful more or less, it isn't crucial. If the surplus is much more than that, reserve it to add to the sauce. Stir the sugar and lemon juice into the purée until the sugar has dissolved.

Sprinkle the gelatin over the cold water in a small saucepan and let it soften for 5 minutes. Set the pan over very low heat and stir constantly until the gelatin has dissolved; don't allow the mixture to come anywhere near boiling. Cool to lukewarm.

Stir the purée into the gelatin base; chill until the mixture has thickened to the consistency of egg white.

Beat the cream in a chilled bowl with chilled beaters just until it forms soft peaks. Whisk a spoonful of the cream into the fruit mixture, then fold the fruit portion into the remaining whipped cream. Spoon into a lightly oiled 6-cup mold. Refrigerate, covered, until set, about 3 hours. (The dessert may be made up to a day ahead.)

If the garnish is to be additional berries, toss them with the additional sugar and refrigerate.

Shortly before serving, unmold the cream: Dip the mold briefly into very warm water, invert a chilled serving plate over the mold, hold the two together, and turn out the cream.

Garnish the dessert with the sugared berries and their syrup, or spoon a little of the chosen sauce over the top and pass the rest at the table.

DINNER AT NANNY'S

*Platter of green-ripe California olives,
radishes, baby turnips, and strips of red pepper and kohlrabi
or jicama, with Dipping Vinaigrette (below)*

Nanny's Braised Wineburgers (below)

*The Real Mashed Potatoes (below)
Remolded Broccoli with Butter & Lemon Sauce (below) or
Hollandaise (page 195)*

*Green Tomato Fool (below) and
Old-Fashioned Sugar Cookies (page 232)*

To drink: *A hearty red wine, not a subtle one; consider a
Pinot Noir, a Merlot, or a Zinfandel*

Nanny is one of my several sisters, all of them blessed with one or more talents, cookery not the least among them. (Lest I be accused of female chauvinism, let me add that our one brother, George Stroop, is no slouch in the food department, either.) Nancy Stroop, I've always thought, is possessed of an uncanny sense for seasoning—I've known her to sniff the aroma of a soup and decide whether or not it was sufficiently salted. The central dish of this dinner is one I've learned from her.

Mashed potatoes—*good* mashed potatoes, which seem to be the object of an enthusiastic revival on all sides, lately—are an excellent reason for rejoicing that good things from tables gone by are being readopted. (Have you noticed that children seem to love mashed potatoes from their first baby taste, unlike, say, green peas or squash? Is it the creamy yet faintly grainy texture, the slippy-slidiness that requires the jaws to do no chomping? However it may begin, a liking for mashed potatoes, with or without gravy on top, seems to stay with most of us for a lifetime.)

The dinner also includes a handsome presentation of broccoli and a dessert developed as a new use for green tomatoes when I found myself in possession of a big basketful from a North Shore farm a few autumns ago. The dessert can be chilled and served as a "fool," as here, or it can be soft-frozen to become a creamy semi-freddo.

DIPPING VINAIGRETTE

 vinaigrette, these days, is whatever the maker *says* it is—it can be thick or thin, classically simple, or intricate. This one is designed to complement the crudités suggested for this particular menu. As with all other vinaigrettes—some are outlined on page 274—it's eater's choice as to precise seasonings.

Makes about 1¼ cups

¼ cup red wine vinegar
2 tablespoons water
⅔ cup good olive oil, mild- or rich-flavored according to preference
Seasonings to taste:
   Garlic, anchovy paste, Dijon-style mustard, salt and pepper, very finely minced parsley as an option
1 large egg yolk, optional

Whisk together the vinegar and water, then slowly whisk in the oil. Season with a squeeze of garlic, a dab of anchovy paste, a little Dijon-style mustard, and ample salt and pepper; parsley, minced to a pulp, is optional.

Taste carefully; correct the seasonings. To stabilize the sauce for a stay on a buffet table, beat in an egg yolk if you don't mind violating the classic rules for vinaigrettes.

NANNY'S BRAISED WINEBURGERS

ne of the few truly original notions I've come across in a few decades of sampling, these wine-braised beef patties with an unexpected condiment tucked into their centers are the invention of my sister Nancy.

The flavor of the secret horseradish is surprisingly subtle, zesty but almost too elusive to identify; there is just enough of the "short" wine sauce to gloss the patties. Real mashed potatoes are perfect with this; but noodles aren't bad either.

Serves 6

*2 pounds high-quality
    chopped beef
Salt and pepper, to taste
Horseradish, fresh grated
    (see Prepared Horse-
    radish, below) or bottled
A little unsalted butter,
    preferably Clarified
    Butter (page 268)
1 to 1½ cups, or as
    needed, sturdy red wine
1 bay leaf, torn up
Pinch of crumbled dried
    thyme*

CHOOSING A ROOT: If you
find a source of fresh
horseradish, choose a smooth
root with skin that hasn't
begun to "green" again. If all
available roots are greenish,
pare deeply to remove the
thick layer just under the
skin—you can see it outlined
in cross-section—to avoid
bitterness. With a normal
root, just pare or scrape the
thin skin off a chunk before
grating the flesh. The rest of
the root will keep a few
weeks in the fridge, or you
may want to make your own
jarful of Prepared
Horseradish as described in
the accompanying recipe.

NANNY'S BRAISED WINEBURGERS (CONTINUED)

Season the meat with salt and pepper and form it
into 12 thin patties. On each of 6 patties spread 1 tablespoon freshly grated (or well-drained bottled) horseradish.
Cover with a second patty; seal the edges; flatten to ½-
inch thickness.

Brown both sides of the hamburgers in the butter
over medium heat in an enameled or other nonreactive
skillet; this will take about 5 minutes. If there is much
more fat than you started with, pour off most of it.

Add ¼ inch of red wine to the pan; strew the bay leaf
and thyme over the meat. Cook over medium heat, turning
and basting the hamburgers often, until they are done to
taste and the sauce has reduced to a dark syrupy glaze,
about 8 minutes.

Serve with a little of the sauce over each patty.

HORSERADISH & BEEF: These two have a celebrated
affinity—think of the shavings of pungent fresh horseradish served with the real roast beef still sometimes met
with in England. Fresh horseradish is worth looking for
because it has flavor, not just hotness; unfortunately, it's
not a common item in supermarkets. Anyone who has a
garden and prefers fresh to bottled can grow it easily; once
planted, it will yield a supply of roots almost forever.

In big cities fresh horseradish is often in the market
just before the season of Passover and Easter. It is the
"bitter herb" placed on the Passover table, and it has
come to be used with several foods of the Easter season in
certain European cuisines.

PREPARED HORSERADISH

Grate the pared root in a food processor fitted with a
grating disk; or cube it, then chop it with the steel blade in
the machine (or in a blender) with enough white or cider
vinegar to assist the process. However you do the job, keep
your face away from the pungent fumes or you'll cry many
tears.

Mix the pulp with enough additional vinegar to cover
it well; add a good big pinch of salt and another of
granulated sugar for each half-cup. Refrigerated, horseradish keeps for weeks, but the fresher it is the better it
tastes.

THE REAL MASHED POTATOES

*L*et's stop waltzing... and talk the real
mashed potatoes.
—GEORGE C. WRIGHT

A lump in a dish of mashed potato is like a
button in the contribution plate. Not negotiable.
—ANN BATCHELDER

 light, piping-hot mass, creamy and buttery and irresistible and *smooth*, is what we're discussing when we talk about the real mashed potatoes... no other versions need apply, although I have heard of people who say they want lumps in theirs.

Talking or even thinking calories in this connection seems pointless; dieters who have a mashed-potato craving should settle for a French-style purée—quite another kettle of spuds—which can be kept low in calories.

Well, there *is* a middle ground for the dish. Milk can replace cream, and butter can be kept to a prudent measure; but once in a while, perhaps if mashed potatoes are to be an indulgence—maybe as a one-dish supper, after a weary day—lashings of cream and butter don't seem so wicked.

The method of this recipe isn't traditional, but it's the best way to go unless you have an heirloom potato masher (like our heavy wooden one) and feel prodigiously ready to use it. Using a food mill (or a potato ricer, if you have one) makes it possible to cook and "mill" the potatoes an hour or more ahead, then finish them at the last minute; this can't be done with truly mashed potatoes.

"The success of a dish is not
following the book. It's having
done the dish often enough to
get it right."

—NICOLAS FREELING, *The*
Kitchen.

Serves 6

*8 medium-large baking
 potatoes, or 4 "bakers"
 and 4 all-purpose or
 "boiling" potatoes (see
 All Eyes on the Potato—
 Kinds to Use, below)
Salt, to taste
1 cup, at least, cream,
 half-and-half, or milk
White pepper, to taste
Unsalted butter, as desired*

**ALL EYES ON THE POTA-
TO—KINDS TO USE:**
Precise recipes for mashed
potatoes should be taken
with grains of salt, because
it's impossible to know how
much liquid will be required
by a potato you haven't met
personally. Example: Baking
potatoes are mealy and dry
and, to me, the most flavorful
kind; they absorb perhaps
twice as much liquid as
boiling types and much more
than all-purpose potatoes,
which fall somewhere
between bakers and boilers.
You can split the difference
by using part of each kind, or
settle for all-purpose spuds.

THE REAL MASHED POTATOES (CONTINUED)

Peel and halve the potatoes and drop them into
lightly salted boiling water just to cover. Boil gently, partly
covered, until the potatoes are tender to a fork but not
soggy, 20 to 30 minutes.

Fork the potatoes immediately into a food mill fitted
with a medium disk. Discard the cooking water, set the
mill over the cooking pot, and mill the potatoes into it.

At this point the light heap of potato pulp—which
should not be stirred until the final steps—can wait,
covered with a cloth, for up to an hour.

Set the pot over low heat, pour about ½ cup of the
cream or milk around the sides of the potatoes, and heat,
beating the pulp with a whisk or slotted spoon; add more
liquid until the consistency suits you; make sure the
potatoes are very hot. Beat in salt, white pepper, and
butter. Heap the potatoes lightly in a warmed dish and
serve them immediately.

———

THE GARLIC VERSION: Mashed potatoes enriched
with mellow-cooked garlic are perfect with pork roast,
succulent with sausages, and a change with fried chicken.
The flavor is full and rounded but subtle, without the
sharpness of raw or undercooked garlic. You need quite a
lot of garlic, at least half a dozen good-sized cloves.

Peel and halve a handful of garlic cloves (if there are
green sprouts inside, remove them). Simmer the garlic,
covered, in 1 cup of milk with 2 tablespoons butter (or just
use 1 cup of cream, or half-and-half), until the cloves are
soft. Mash or sieve together the garlic and liquid, or whirl
them in a blender. Beat the garlic cream, with more liquid
if needed, plus butter, salt, and pepper, into potatoes that
have been pressed through a food mill or ricer as described.

WALTZING WITH LEFTOVERS: Spud-lovers who have
their wits about them wouldn't be caught dead cooking
and mashing just enough potatoes for one meal; they
know that a bowlful of leftovers is money in the bank, to
be squandered on improvisations. At our house it's
salmon or tuna cakes, but no noses are turned up at re-
mashed mashed potatoes browned in a skillet for breakfast, or stirred into a vegetable soup to lend body.

Nostalgic fishcakes: Smash up the solidified potatoes
with about two-thirds as much tuna, salmon, or leftover
cooked cod or haddock; this is easily done in an electric
mixer. While you're about it mix in an egg (or two, if the
batch is large), a tiny bit of grated onion or onion juice,
and some chopped parsley. Pat into flat cakes, dust with
flour, and brown the cakes slowly in mixed vegetable oil
and butter in a skillet. Pass the tartar sauce.

REMOLDED BROCCOLI WITH BUTTER & LEMON SAUCE

Serves 6

*About 3 pounds fresh
    broccoli
Pot of boiling salted water
Butter & Lemon Sauce,
    below, or Hollandaise
    (page 195)*

hen a handsome hot vegetable course is in order, molding broccoli into an emerald dome is an attractive way to convert a potful of florets into a more pulled-together shape for serving. (See Remolded Purple & White Cauliflower below, for another possibility.)

For a salad, the florets can be quickly chilled in ice water, drained, molded, and turned out to be served with a highly seasoned vinaigrette (see the Index) instead of the Butter & Lemon Sauce.

Remove the broccoli tops from the main stems; trim the florets, splitting any large ones so they'll all be about the same size. Drop the broccoli into the boiling salted water and cook briskly just until tender but still firm, testing often to prevent overcooking; cooking time will depend on the size of the florets. Pour a little cold water into the pot to stop the boiling. Drain.

Select a relatively deep 6-cup bowl. Arrange broccoli florets in the bowl, heads down and close together, to line the bottom and sides; fill the center with the rest of the broccoli pieces, including the stems, if you've cooked them (see Main Stems on the following page). Press down lightly with a small plate. (At this point the bowl of warm broccoli may be held for a few minutes in a warm oven.)

Cover the bowl of broccoli with a warmed serving dish and turn out the mold, holding the bowl and dish firmly together. Spoon a little of the butter sauce over the broccoli and serve at once with the remaining sauce.

REMOLDED PURPLE & WHITE CAULIFLOWER: The notion of reconstructing broccoli into a superdome came

MAIN STEMS: Pare the skin from the heavy stalks, quarter them lengthwise, and cut into 1-inch pieces. Add to the boiling water first; let the pot boil again before adding the florets. They'll be done when the florets are.

from a recipe for cauliflower written in the 1920s by Mme St. Ange, whose *Livre de Cuisine* was surely the *Mastering the Art of French Cooking* of her day in France. Having borrowed her idea for broccoli, I've borrowed it further for the purple cauliflower of autumn (it's green after cooking), which I sometimes combine with regular cauliflower to make a handsomely patterned mold.

Serve the two-cauliflower mold hot, with the butter sauce below (or Hollandaise—see the Index). If regular white cauliflower is all you can get, you're still okay, right back where Mme St Ange left off.

BUTTER & LEMON SAUCE

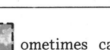

Sometimes called "mock Hollandaise," this butter sauce (which is "bastard sauce" to the candid French) is less intensely rich than the real thing and it's also conveniently pourable.

Makes about 2 cups

8 tablespoons (1 stick) unsalted butter
2 tablespoons all-purpose flour
1½ cups boiling water or fat-free chicken broth
2 large egg yolks, beaten
1 tablespoon, or more to taste, fresh lemon juice
Salt and white pepper, to taste

Melt 2 tablespoons of the butter in a small heavy saucepan over medium heat; whisk in the flour and cook until foaming. Whisk in the hot water or broth; cook until the sauce simmers; lower the heat to very low.

Whisk a spoonful of sauce into the egg yolks, then whisk the egg mixture gradually into the pan of sauce. Add 1 tablespoon lemon juice, then whisk in the remaining butter a tablespoon-size slice at a time. Taste carefully and season with salt and pepper and more lemon juice, if you think it's needed.

———

SAME SAUCE, DIFFERENT DISHES: Just as the recipe describes it, butter sauce is often served over poached fish as well as vegetables. For fish, it can be made with a portion of the poaching liquid instead of chicken broth, and it might be embellished with minced herbs—minced parsley, finely snipped chives, a little tarragon or chervil. If the fish happened to be cod, I'd include a few capers instead of the herbs.

GREEN TOMATO FOOL

ade-green unripe tomatoes are the mystery base of this tart-sweet-creamy dessert, which is something of a palate-fooler. It's reminiscent in color and flavor of a gooseberry fool; it can be chilled and served in classic fool fashion, or it can be soft-frozen and offered as a semifreddo, as you please.

Rhubarb makes an excellent fool or semifreddo, too, as outlined after the main recipe.

Serve 6

1½ pounds completely green tomatoes, untinged with yellow or white
3 long strips (½ inch wide) lemon zest (colored rind only, no pith)
½ teaspoon, or to taste, ground coriander
Big pinch or more, of ground mace or freshly grated nutmeg
1 cup granulated sugar
1 to 2 tablespoons fresh lemon juice
1 cup chilled heavy cream
3 drops each vanilla and almond extract

Pare the skin from the green tomatoes (a swivel peeler works best); chop to make 3 cups. Combine in a saucepan with the lemon zest, ¼ teaspoon of the coriander, pinch of mace or nutmeg, and the sugar; stir, then simmer over low heat until thick and jammy, about 40 minutes. Remove the lemon zest.

Purée the mixture in a processor or blender, then press through a fine sieve to remove any seeds. Add 1 tablespoon lemon juice and another ¼ teaspoon coriander; chill.

At least an hour before serving time, taste and add more lemon juice if needed to balance sweetness; correct for spiciness, adding more coriander and ground mace (or nutmeg) if you judge they're needed. (Freezing, if you choose the semifreddo version below, will mute the flavor of the mixture.)

Whip the cream to the soft-peak stage, whip in the vanilla and almond, and fold together the cream and the purée. Chill for at least an hour in a serving bowl. For a semifreddo, read on.

SOFT-FROZEN GREEN TOMATO FOOL

For a frozen fool along the lines of an Italian semifreddo, turn the mixture into a shallow cake pan, cover with foil, and place in the freezer about 1 hour, or until soft-frozen throughout, stirring the frozen edges into the center after about half an hour. If it's too hard at serving time, let the mixture soften in the refrigerator for 20 minutes. (Leftovers can be held, frozen, for several days.)

———

THE RHUBARB VERSION: Omit the coriander, mace, lemon juice, and almond extract. If you like, use orange zest in place of lemon zest. Substitute 1½ pounds of diced red rhubarb (frozen is fine) for the green tomatoes; cooking time will be shorter. When puréed, the rhubarb should be thick as medium applesauce; if not, drain off and reduce the syrup by simmering, then return it to the purée. Correct the sweetening; chill.

Beat the chilled heavy cream with a few drops of vanilla until it forms soft peaks; fold into the rhubarb, leaving swirls and streaks of color. Chill in a serving bowl, or freeze as a semifreddo.

FINE FOR A BIRTHDAY

Ann Seranne's Great Hunk of Beef (below) served with pan gravy

Garlic Variation of The Real Mashed Potatoes (page 103) or Creamy Potato Gratin (the ham & potato scallop on page 157, without the ham)

California Succotash (below) or Sautéed Red & Green Tomato Slices (below)

Salad of Mixed Greens & Oranges (below)

Springtime Fruit Tart with a Meringue Lattice (below) or Crustless Hazelnut "Cheesecake" (below)

To drink: Such a roast deserves a good Burgundy, but any full-bodied red wine is an appropriate choice

As long ago as the late sixties, the renowned food expert Ann Seranne described in an interview her magical method for roasting beef to crusty perfection outside and juicy pinkness inside, without the need to watch the oven or baste the meat. I've been using it ever since (signed testimonials from happy eaters on request); and I've also seen it reprinted in a cookbook without credit for the bright idea, which seems a shame. Her way is so well worth knowing about that I'm repeating it here, with much appreciation, for another generational go-around.

With this great hunk of beef I'm suggesting either garlicky mashed potatoes or a creamy potato gratin, plus a version of succotash I still like best after spending many years in the native region of lima-bean succotash. Then there's a vegetable alternative, a platter of sliced and sautéed red and green tomatoes, which I'd advise you to keep in mind for a delectable summer breakfast.

What we have for dessert is a strawberry-rhubarb pie with a difference—it's a tart topped with a lattice of the tenderest meringue I've ever come across. Or you can choose the crustless "cheesecake" studded with hazelnuts, a quickly assembled and quickly baked variant of my hazelnut cheesecake/tart.

ANN SERANNE'S GREAT HUNK OF BEEF

nn's way with beef is to put a room-temperature rib roast into an extra-hot oven and roast it for a very short time; it's then left in the turned-off oven for at least 2 hours. The meat is then ready to carve, but if your schedule requires it, the roast can stay put for up to 4 hours and still emerge at serving temperature.

This works like a charm for a trimmed roast (with the short ribs cut off) of 2 to 4 ribs, in a weight range from a little over 4 to about 12 pounds. The usual allowance is 2 servings to each rib, except perhaps in macho steak houses.

TO PREPARE ANN SERANNE'S RIB ROAST

Meat preparation: Take the roast from the refrigerator and let it reach room temperature; allow about an hour per rib. Rub salt and pepper generously into all surfaces; dust flour over the upper (fat) side and rub it in well. Stand the roast on its rib ends in a shallow roasting pan.

Roasting: Preheat the oven to 500°. Roast the beef uncovered for the precise time called for below; set a timer. When the timer rings, turn off the oven and leave the meat in peace for at least 2 hours. Don't open the oven at all until serving time.

Timing: Roast a 2-rib cut weighing from 4 to 5 pounds 25 to 30 minutes;
for 3 ribs (8 to 9 pounds), 40 to 45 minutes;
for 4 ribs (11 to 12 pounds, the maximum size for this method), 55 to 60 minutes.

Gravy made with the pan juices: When the roast has been removed, what's left in the pan is too good to ignore.

> *"...I am a great eater of beef, and I believe that does harm to my wit."*
>
> —SHAKESPEARE, *Twelfth Night.*

THE WELL-COOKED VEGETABLE MAKES A COMEBACK: Besides the vegetables in succotash—a dish that's abominable if half-cooked—some others really need to be better-cooked than they were as one of the worst clichés of almost-bygone *nouvelle* cuisine.

A rude shock to the diner's tooth, and so underdone as to be tasteless, "nouvelle"-cooked broccoli, onions, winter squash, turnips, carrots, celery, leeks, beets, sweet potatoes, and baby limas are a mistake. Better to save the brief, brief cooking for such tender things as snow peas, baby green beans or peas, slant-cut asparagus, and Chinese cabbage.

Don't insult broccoli and carrots and such with a mere quick pass through heat. If they're cooked until just right, neither hard, rubbery, nor mushy, they'll have more going for them than pretty looks alone.

Spoon off all possible fat, set the pan on a stove burner over medium heat, and stir in 1 to 2 cups (depending on how abundant the drippings are) of beef broth (canned will do). I'd add a bay leaf, a slice of onion, and a little thyme, but that's optional. Boil the liquid for a few minutes, scraping the brown bits free of the pan bottom, until the consistency suits; season with salt and plenty of pepper and strain into a warmed gravy boat.

For gravy with more body, mix a tablespoon of cornstarch with 2 tablespoons of cold water and begin stirring the mixture slowly into the boiling gravy; stop adding cornstarch just before it has thickened enough; cook a moment longer, until the gravy is clear and bright.

CALIFORNIA SUCCOTASH

ack there and back then, our family succotash was based on corn (of course), but the beans weren't the limas or shell beans used on the East Coast—they were "string" beans, now more aptly called snap beans or green beans since stringiness has been deleted from their genes.

The mostly Midwestern cooks who took their recipes West with them knew that long-simmered beans and corn develop flavors that scarcely cooked veggies can't match, and they were right. Don't be tempted to make this succotash in a tearing hurry —the cooking time has already been cut way back from the old-fashioned two hours-plus. Succotash reheats well, so it can be made ahead.

Beans that aren't in their first youth—well, beans that are frankly mature—are better for this dish than very young ones because they've had time on the vine to develop beany character. (Old-fashioned Kentucky Wonders, bulgy with developing seeds, would be ideal.) The bacon and onion round off the flavor of this all-American combination, but either or both can be omitted.

Serves 6

2 or 3 slices bacon, cut
   into squares or slivers
2 generous slices onion,
   diced
About 3 cups water
1 pound green beans, cut
   short or diced
2 cups corn cut from the
   cob (See Cutting Kernels,
   page 25), or high-
   quality canned or frozen
   whole-kernel corn
Salt and pepper, to taste
A little unsalted butter or
   sweet cream, optional

Combine the bacon and/or onion with the water in a saucepan, bring them to a boil, then simmer, covered, for 10 minutes or so. (If both are omitted, bring the water to a boil before adding the beans and proceeding with the cooking.) Add the beans, bring to a boil, cover partially, and simmer for half an hour or more, depending on the maturity of the beans; they should be tender before the corn is added.

Spread the corn over the beans; season with salt and pepper; partly cover the pan and simmer the succotash up to 30 minutes longer, until the corn is well done and most of the liquid has been absorbed. (Don't worry about overcooking this dish; it's supposed to be mellow, not half-raw in the fashion of nouvelle-cuisine vegetables.)

Toss the vegetables together, season with more salt and pepper if needed, add butter or cream if you like, and serve the succotash piping hot.

SAUTÉED RED & GREEN TOMATO SLICES

platter of fried ripe and green tomatoes is not just colorful to the eye—it also pleases the palate with its contrasting flavors and textures. The red slices are juicy and somewhat sweet; the green ones are firm and tart inside their crisp coats. The creamy pan sauce, optional here, is traditional with fried tomatoes, but the touch of basil isn't traditional (it's good, though).

Fried tomatoes can be the making of a fine breakfast, alongside ham or sausage or bacon with eggs, or on their own, accompanied by whole-grain toast. They're good with grits, too, if your fancy lies that way, or scrapple. For other meals, either red or green tomatoes (or both) go harmoniously with fried chicken, or a slice of clam pie, a steak, a hamburger, or broiled fish.

Serves 6

*3 medium-large ripe
 tomatoes
3 medium-large completely
 green tomatoes, untinged
 with yellow or white
Salt and pepper, to taste
Cornmeal or flour for
 coating slices
For frying: Half oil and
 half butter, or oil alone,
 or clear bacon fat*

OPTIONAL SAUCE:
*1 cup, or more, cream or
 half-and-half
A little fresh or dried basil,
 chopped or crumbled,
 optional
Salt and pepper, to taste*

GREEN WITH ENVY?
Unripe tomatoes are an
unsung asset of the summer
garden, where we tend to
leave them to ripen until the
end of the season; when
killing frost is about to strike,
they may or may not make it
to the kitchen.

To lobby for a change, I've
included this recipe showing
how the red and green fruits
complement one another.
Only habitual thinking keeps
this fruit/vegetable from
being used for its own sake.

Elsewhere in these pages
you'll find an intriguing
dessert made from green
tomatoes; other recipes—for
green-tomato pickles,
mincemeat, relishes, and
pie—can be found in
cookbooks of the down-to-
earth persuasion.

SAUTÉED RED & GREEN TOMATO SLICES (CONTINUED)

Cut a thin slice from each end of each tomato; core
and slice thick, 2 or 3 slices each. Season the slices with
salt and pepper; coat with cornmeal, pressing it in well, or
with flour, dusting off excess.

Heat ¼ inch of fat in a large skillet (better yet, use
two pans) until medium-hot. Fry the green tomatoes
rather slowly over medium heat until the undersides are
golden and crisp (don't let them get too brown, to preserve
their looks).

When the green slices are turned to cook the second
side, start frying the red tomatoes, which cook faster and
should be browned more; try for crisp coats on slices that
still hold their shape.

Add fat to the pan(s) as needed. As slices are finished, keep them warm on a platter.

For the optional sauce: Pour the cream into the
pan(s) after the tomatoes have been removed, add the
basil if it's used, and simmer the sauce for 2 or 3 minutes,
stirring, to reduce it a little; add salt and pepper. Pour the
sauce around, not over, the slices, or serve it separately.

SALAD OF MIXED GREENS & ORANGES

 hole cookbooks have been written on the
art of making green salads. All very fine,
but all we *really* need is a talent for
washing greens free of grit, then drying them in a
rolled towel or a salad spinner.

Assemble a bowlful of crisp dark-green salad
makings—I like stemmed sprigs of watercress and/or
arugula (roquette)—and add a head or two of Belgian
endive, cut into thin slivers, and a generous portion of
halved seedless orange sections, free of membrane.

Toss with good olive oil, coarse salt, fresh-ground
pepper, lemon juice, and a pinch, if you have it, of chopped
fresh or crumbled dried sweet marjoram.

SPRINGTIME FRUIT TART WITH A MERINGUE LATTICE

A LATE-BREAKING BULLETIN ON THE STATE OF MERINGUE: There's a dim clue to the meringue mystery (*right*) in a piece by a long-ago chef that I read while this book was in the proof stage. Possibly the meringue method I've used here grew from a practice he cites; it seems that pastry cooks have been known to make (and perhaps they still make?) meringues that include a little cornstarch, added with the sugar. I haven't tried the dry-cornstarch caper yet, but I will.

Never mind motherhood and apple pie—to me, a glorious American symbol, especially in springtime, is rhubarb and strawberry pie, a rosy confection that's lapped up even by people who think they don't like rhubarb. It's pure heaven for me and other *rhubarbniks*.

Here the fruits (well, one fruit, one vegetable) are combined for presentation in a tart shell, mostly because a tart is prettier than a pie for a special occasion. The topping is made with an unusual meringue that remains tender and weep-proof even after long refrigeration. When and how it came into being is a small kitchen mystery.

I came across one version in a letter to a newspaper's food page a few years ago and tried it; the meringue was excellent and I made notes in my kitchen book. Soon afterward, while browsing through a haul of second-hand cookbooks, I found another version in a collection (modern) of what were supposed to be very old American regional recipes. Well, that booklet (and others I have since seen from the same author) has many anachronisms—some are real howlers—so the writer's claim that the recipes are log-cabin antiques must be doubted a lot. Which leaves the meringue mystery where it was.

Back to the pie: Frozen rhubarb works, and so do frozen berries (let them thaw before making the filling) if it isn't the season for fresh. The filling can go into a shell baked in a pie pan if you don't want a tart, and the meringue can be spooned on rather than piped; see the note on mile-high meringue.

Serves 6 to 8

Baked 9- or 10-inch tart
shell (page 280)

FILLING:
4 cups sliced rhubarb
⅓ cup water
1½ cups granulated sugar
blended with 1
tablespoon cornstarch
2 large egg yolks, beaten
3 cups fresh, ripe
strawberries, halved if
large

MERINGUE:
2 teaspoons cornstarch
5 tablespoons granulated
sugar
⅓ cup water
2 large egg whites
Pinch of salt
¼ teaspoon almond
extract

**FOR A MILE-HIGH
MERINGUE:** For a tall,
piled-on topping for any pie
or tart, the ingredients are ½
cup water, 1 tablespoon
cornstarch, 6 to 7
tablespoons sugar, a pinch of
salt, 3 egg whites, another
drop or two of flavoring. Bake
a deep meringue about 30
minutes.

SPRINGTIME FRUIT TART WITH A MERINGUE LATTICE (CONTINUED)

Tart shell: Make, bake, and cool the tart shell.

Filling: Combine the rhubarb and water and simmer until the rhubarb has softened, about 5 minutes. Stir in the sugar-starch mixture and cool until lightly thickened; stir in the egg yolks. Off the heat, fold in the strawberries. Pour at once into the tart shell.

Preheat the oven to 325°.

Meringue: Blend the cornstarch with 1 tablespoon of the sugar in a small saucepan; blend in the water. Stir over medium heat until the mixture clears and thickens, about 2 minutes. Let cool until tepid.

Beat the egg whites and salt until foamy, then gradually beat in the cornstarch mixture; continue to beat while gradually adding the remaining 4 tablespoons sugar. Add the almond extract and beat until very fluffy.

Scoop the meringue into a pastry bag fitted with a star tip and pipe a lattice and border onto the filling.

Bake at 325° about 20 minutes, or until the meringue has become golden-brown here and there. Cool the tart before serving it. Refrigerate leftovers.

CRUSTLESS HAZELNUT "CHEESECAKE"

tart with the recipe for Hazelnut Cheese Tart on page 151. Omit the crust; bake the filling in a buttered 1-quart soufflé dish set on a baking sheet. Bake at 350° for 30 minutes. Serve at room temperature, spooning the "cheesecake" from the dish. Pass Two-Berry Sauce (page 206) or Chunky Orange Sauce (page 16).

TURKEY, CUT DOWN TO SIZE

Orange & Lemon Salad with Mint (below), plus crispbread, breadsticks, or other crunchy accompaniment

Turkey Sausages in Garlic Cream (below)
Orzo "Risotto" (below), or hot buttered brown or long-grain white rice

Panned Spinach (below),
or any seasonable green vegetable,
steamed and buttered

Bundled Blueberry Pastries (below) or Pecan or Black-Walnut Graham Torte (page 240)

To drink: Gewürztraminer, a white Zinfandel, or Sauvignon Blanc

Well, all right, just for once we'll start dinner with the salad—it works well enough when the "salad" position in the meal (which is after the main course, according to me) will be occupied by something else that's green and succulent, such as the Panned Spinach suggested for this dinner.

Remember when "veal" tonnato was first being made with turkey breast, then newly available as a separate chunk of the Big Bird? Cutting up large turkeys into meal-size units was a step in the right direction, as was marketing ground turkey, which is used in the main dish here to replace veal one more time—this time, pricey veal cutlets.

Moving right along to the dessert—Armagnac-scented blueberries baked in crisp bundles of phyllo pastry. This is entertaining to make and educational, too, if you've never played with phyllo, but above all it's a delicious innovation. As an alternative, therc's a graham torte rich with ground nuts; use black walnuts if you can lay hands on them, but pecans are fine, too.

ORANGE & LEMON SALAD WITH MINT

ich Mediterranean citrus groves must have been the birthplace of the first salad like this one. The version I first tasted was made with unpeeled fruit, a strong mouthful for one who doesn't like the impact of a *lot* of citrus oil. Accordingly, for this sunny salad I peel at least half of the fruit, if it's thin skinned and very ripe, or peel all of it if it's thick skinned. If all the peel is removed, some of the outer layer—the zest—can be grated into the dressing; you can suit yourself.

Oranges and lemons are at their best in winter, making this salad especially good then. Heavy navel oranges with bright, thin skins and fully ripe lemons—Meyer lemons, if they can be had—are the ones to choose. Light or immature fruit is sure to disappoint, so it's worth taking the trouble to heft and inspect each specimen when you buy.

Serves 6

3 large thin-skinned
  seedless oranges
3 well-ripened lemons,
  Meyer variety for choice
3 tablespoons crumbled
  dried mint or a larger
  measure of chopped
  fresh mint
¼ to ⅓ cup extra-virgin
  olive oil
Salt and pepper, to taste
Large head tender lettuce
  or equivalent in
  watercress or other
  greens

Decide how much peel you want to include. At a minimum, scrub 1 orange and grate off all the outer rind (zest) and reserve it; pare the white pulp from that orange and the skin and pulp from the remaining fruit. Cut the fruit into sections or thin slices; remove any seeds.

For a salad rich in citrus peel, scrub, trim ends, and slice one, two, or all of the fruits with the peels on; halve the slices and remove any seeds.

Put the fruit into a bowl; add the reserved zest, if any, and the mint; add oil, salt, and pepper. Toss, then let marinate for an hour or two.

At mealtime, taste and add more salt, pepper, or mint if needed. Tear the washed and crisped greens into a salad bowl, tip in the fruit and dressing, toss, and serve.

CHIVE BLOSSOMS AND THE SHAKERS: Food history tells of no better American cooks than the Shakers, whose simple but highly intelligent food reached standards in the last century that are worth noticing.

Shakers were great herbalists, helping support their communities by growing, drying, and selling a great variety of herbs in addition to other foodstuffs, and they used herbs imaginatively in their kitchens. One Shaker recipe, for a blue-flower omelet, taught me suddenly what should have been obvious—chive blossoms, as well as chive leaves, are good to eat. Although I'd grown chives and admired their blue flowers through many seasons, it took that recipe—a whack alongside the head, so to speak—to make me aware of the tastiness of the blooms. Now I clip chive blossoms for June salads as well as omelets, and sometimes I drop a long-stemmed chive flower into a bottle of homemade herb vinegar, where its form remains attractive even after its color fades.

ORANGE & ONION SALAD, WITH OR WITHOUT CHIVE BLOSSOMS: Use 2 or 3 sweet onions—red onions look smashing, but Vidalia or Maui or Walla Walla onions, though pale, are considerably sweeter—and 3 of the best seedless oranges available.

First make the dressing: Beat together ½ cup vegetable oil or mild olive oil, 3 tablespoons white-wine vinegar or lemon juice, 1 to 2 tablespoons crumbled dried mint leaves, and salt and white pepper to taste; optionally, add a few snipped chives or, in season, 2 or 3 blue chive blossoms, pulled apart. Let the dressing mellow for ½ hour to 2 hours.

At mealtime, put salad greens on individual plates; arrange sliced oranges, with or without their peel, and thin rings of peeled onion over the greens; spoon on the dressing.

TURKEY SAUSAGES IN GARLIC CREAM

escended from a pleasing mid-European dish of cubed veal in sour cream, this recipe has been reorganized to use new-fangled ground turkey instead of old-fangled (and monstrously expensive) veal. The turkey, shaped into freeform "sausages," cooks faster than the original veal chunks, which helps when time is a consideration.

The soul of the dish is the well-tamed garlic in the sauce—at least three big cloves, better five. The garlic flavor is marvelously mellowed and savory; it complements instead of competing. This may be hard to believe unless you have cooked the classic French dish of chicken with 40 cloves of garlic, or unless you've tried Alice Waters's way of baking whole heads of garlic to buttery softness and spreading the pulp on grainy country bread. If you fall among the skeptics in spite of these citations, I can only ask you to trust me until you've tasted.

Serves 6

TURKEY SAUSAGES:
1¼ pounds ground turkey
⅓ cup fresh bread crumbs,
  not too fine
½ small clove garlic,
  minced or pressed
½ teaspoon crumbled
  dried thyme, or
  combined thyme and
  sweet marjoram
1 teaspoon salt
Pepper, to taste
1 large egg
2 to 3 tablespoons milk,
  broth, or water

FOR COOKING:
All-purpose flour for
  dredging
2 tablespoons vegetable oil
3 tablespoons unsalted
  butter

GARLIC CREAM:
3 to 5 large cloves garlic,
  peeled and flattened (see
  Flattening and Peeling
  Garlic, below)
1½ cups, more if needed,
  chicken broth
1 bay leaf
1 cup dairy sour cream
  mixed with 1 tablespoon
  cornstarch
Fresh lemon juice, as
  needed
Garnish: Minced parsley
Optional accompaniment:
  Hot buttered egg noodles
  sprinkled with poppy
  seeds or toasted sesame
  seeds

Mix the turkey, crumbs, minced garlic, herbs, salt, pepper, egg, and 2 tablespoons milk, broth, or water, beating well with a big spoon. The mixture should be light, so add more liquid if it's needed.

Shape heaping tablespoonfuls into short, thick sausage shapes with blunt ends, making about 18. Roll each sausage in flour to coat.

Heat half of the oil and butter in a heavy skillet over medium heat and brown half of the sausages gently on all sides; remove and keep warm. Cook the second batch, using more of the fat as needed, and remove from the pan.

Toss the garlic into the fat remaining in skillet and cook the cloves a few seconds until pale gold; don't brown them. Return the sausages, add the broth and bay leaf, and cook, covered, over medium-low heat, turning the sausages several times, for 20 to 30 minutes, until they're tender. During cooking add more broth or water if needed to prevent sticking.

Remove the sausages and keep them warm. Discard the bay leaf. Mash the butter-soft garlic into the pan juices. Stir in the sour cream and cornstarch mixture; cook over low heat until the sauce has thickened smoothly. Taste and adjust the seasoning with salt, pepper, and lemon juice. Return the sausages to the sauce and reheat gently, shaking the pan.

Pour into a deep platter and sprinkle with parsley. Add, optionally, an attractive border of hot buttered egg noodles sprinkled with poppy seeds or toasted sesame seeds.

GARLIC LORE

Choosing: The garlic to choose is young, firm and juicy—squeeze the head before you lay your money down. As garlic gets older the flavor gets stronger (you can confirm this when peeling or chopping). Garlic that's actually sending up sprouts shouldn't be used, but if the green sprout is still inside the clove, just dig it out and proceed, if sprouting garlic is all you have.

In earliest spring, when old-crop garlic begins to get the growing urge, the fresh crop, often pink garlic from Mexico, begins coming in; it's worth looking for.

Flattening & peeling garlic: Put the clove on a work surface, lay the flat of a big knife over it, and hit it with a fist. (Or swat the clove with the bottom of a saucepan.) The papery skin will come away easily and the green sprout, if there is one, will be visible and can be removed.

Press propaganda: Much nonsense has been written about

the evils of the garlic press. I often chop garlic, especially if I need a lot of it, but I own and use two or three presses and try as I might, I've found no difference in the actual flavor of pressed and minced garlic. The press divides garlic so finely that more of the volatile elements do reach the nose in a hurry, while the larger bits of minced garlic are more reticent, so the impact is stronger, yes; but is the flavor different? I don't think so. But what *can* change the flavor of garlic is using a press that isn't kept perfectly clean.

Storing Garlic: Don't refrigerate your garlic supply, even in a cute little earthenware jar, or it will sprout before its time. A cool and airy spot outside the refrigerator is better. Our working supply is kept in a small wire basket within reach; the reserve hangs from a hook in a home-made "braid" made by stringing fine, fat bulbs together through their papery necks, using cotton string and a darning needle.

ORZO "RISOTTO"

rzo is an unusual pasta because it seems to have originated in Greece or there-abouts, which is perhaps why it was ignored so long in specialized cookbooks that focus on Italian pasta shapes. Orzo grains look like cream-colored rice, but they cook faster and are softer than rice when done.

This pasta takes well to cooking by the risotto method used here, which yields tender-firm grains bathed in a little creamy "sauce," but it's also perfectly fine—especially if it's to be served as a sauce-blotting side dish—when cooked plain, as the box label directs.

For a fast hot lunch or light supper, an orzo "risotto," with the grated cheese added at the end and more cheese passed at the table, is most satisfying, and it's ready in half the cooking time required by rice.

ORDERING UP ORZO: This neat pasta shape is turned out in several sizes by various manufacturers; if you like its versatility, you may want to look for orzo in more than one size or brand. The smallest grains are handsome in clear soup; any size can be used in heartier soups and for recipes such as this one.

Serves 6

*2 tablespoons unsalted
    butter*
*3 to 4 tablespoons minced
    mild onion or scallions,
    white part only*
1 clove garlic, minced
2 cups orzo
1 bay leaf
*4 cups heated chicken
    broth*
Salt and pepper, to taste
*Additional unsalted butter
    and grated Parmesan
    cheese, optional*

Melt the 2 tablespoons butter in a heavy saucepan; stir in the onion or scallions and garlic and cook slowly until soft, about 5 minutes, without browning.

Stir in the orzo and cook briefly, stirring, until the grains turn golden-brown here and there. Add the bay leaf and 2 cups of the broth and simmer uncovered until most of the liquid has been absorbed, about 3 minutes. Add the remaining broth; cover and simmer about 7 minutes longer, or until most of the broth has disappeared and a grain or two meet your personal tooth-test of doneness. (It's best not to overcook this pasta.)

Season with salt and pepper; optionally, add a lump of butter and a little grated Parmesan, if you like.

PANNED SPINACH

f the Chinese hadn't invented stir-frying as the perfect way to preserve the color and character of vegetables, the Italians would have done so, judging from this Italian way of dealing with fresh spinach.

This is one of the many non-Oriental dishes for which a big wok is the handiest cooking vessel. Lacking a wok, use a very large skillet or sauté pan.

Serves 6

2½ pounds fresh spinach
¼ cup excellent olive oil
*2 cloves garlic, flattened
    and peeled*
Salt, to taste
Fresh lemon juice, to taste
Garnish: *Lemon wedges*

If the spinach is prewashed and packaged, pick it over, tear off the coarse stems, and rinse it; drain well.

If it's fresh-pulled, cut off the roots and wash the leaves through at least two or three sinkfuls of cold water, lifting them out each time to leave the grit behind. Pull off the coarse stems; drain well.

Heat the oil not quite to smoking in a wok or other big pan over high heat; add the garlic and cook for a moment without letting it brown. Add the spinach, cook for half a minute, then toss-cook vigorously until the leaves are wilted, glossy, and fragrant, a matter of minutes.

Sprinkle with salt and a few drops of lemon, toss again, and serve in a hot dish, with extra wedges of lemon.

BUNDLED BLUEBERRY PASTRIES

iny wild blueberries, with their firm texture and unique earthy tartness, are the fruit of choice for filling these crisp, buttery pastries with perky bundled tops. The dessert if scented with Armagnac, a powerful and princely brandy that's just right with the wild fruit.

Look for wild blueberries in bags in the grocer's freezer, where you'll also find phyllo leaves. Cultivated blueberries and Cognac can be used but the recommended combination is celestial. Using tame blueberries requires reducing the brandy by half, because they're much juicier than wild fruit.

Serves 6

3 cups wild blueberries, thawed if frozen

⅓ cup granulated sugar

½ cup Armagnac, Cognac, or other brandy

¾ cup Clarified Butter (see page 268), cooled but pourable

1 cup coarse, slightly dried fresh bread crumbs (no crusts)

24 large sheets room-temperature phyllo pastry (12 × 16 inches), thawed in the package if frozen

Superfine sugar for sprinkling

Optional accompaniment: Armagnac-flavored whipped cream

Combine the blueberries, granulated sugar, and Armagnac and leave for 15 minutes.

Sprinkle 2 tablespoons clarified butter over the crumbs and toss well; leave for 10 to 15 minutes.

Heat the oven to 350°. Cover a large baking sheet with foil; brush the foil lightly with clarified butter.

Add the crumbs to the blueberries; toss.

On your work surface, set out the remaining clarified butter, a pastry brush, the package of phyllo, a slightly dampened cloth (or sheets of plastic), a ruler, a sharp knife, a ½-cup measure, and the bowl of filling.

Count out the 24 sheets of phyllo and cover the stack with the damp cloth. Rewrap and refrigerate the rest of the package for another use. (Keep the waiting phyllo covered as you work, because dried-out sheets will shatter.)

Trim 4 inches from one end of the stack of phyllo to make 12-inch squares, using the ruler and knife. (Save the trimmings for another use, if you feel creative.) Re-cover the stack with the cloth.

Assembling the bundles: Lay out 1 sheet of phyllo;

WORKING WITH PHYLLO:
The paper-thin dough sheets called phyllo (or filo) must not be allowed to dry out while they are being rolled, folded, or otherwise manipulated, or they'll end up as a heap of scraps. Keep phyllo in its package until work begins, and keep sheets removed from the package covered with a damp cloth or sheet of plastic until they're needed on the job.

brush lightly with clarified butter, cover with a second sheet, and butter it. Lay a third sheet diagonally, with its points midway between the points of the first two, and butter it; add a fourth sheet in the same position; butter it. Place ½ cup of filling in the center, gather the points of the phyllo to make a bundle, and twist the "neck" of the bundle loosely, spreading the points. Set the bundle on the baking sheet and brush butter over the bulge. Repeat until you have 6 pastries, placing them well apart on the baking sheet. Sprinkle the tops lightly with superfine sugar.

Bake the pastries in the center of the oven for 35 minutes, or until they are golden and crisp. Remove from the oven and sprinkle lightly with additional sugar. Slip the foil and the pastries onto a wire rack; cool.

Serve at room temperature with, if you like, lightly sweetened whipped cream flavored with a few drops of Armagnac.

SLUNKING TOWARD DINNER

Slunk—an Oven-Baked Chowder (below)

California Succotash (page 112)

Winter salad: *Quick Citrus Coleslaw (below), or another
seasonal salad*

Summer salad: *Platter of sliced, salted, & peppered ripe
tomatoes*

Something crisp—*flatbread, Buttery Breadsticks (page 225),
or sea toast—with the salad*

Summer dessert:
*Fresh berries with Uncooked Lime or Lemon Curd (below)
and Cookies*

Winter dessert:
*Rummy & Raisiny, Topless & Bottomless Sweet-Potato ''Pie''
(below)*

To Drink: *A glass of French Muscadet, or Long Island
Chardonnay, or your favorite crisp California white*

Fishermen on Long Island's Great South Bay, an enormous coastal inlet east of New York City and west of where we live now, gave the name "slunk" to a non-soupy hot potful concocted with clams, potatoes, and onions. If they threw in such other shellfish as oysters, mussels, or periwinkles, slunk became Fire Island Hurrah.

Another notable dry chowder was Nantucket stifle, made with the same ingredients as slunk, plus salt pork and butter. (Recall, in *Moby Dick*, the clam and cod chowders, apparently much along the lines of slunk and stifle, eaten on Nantucket by Ishmael and Queequeg.)

On the Chesapeake, fishing families used to serve an oven chowder similar to both stifle and slunk but containing clams, salt pork, potatoes, onions, milk, fresh corn kernels, *and* a thickening of crushed soda crackers. So, if you'd like to rejigger the recipe in this menu, you'll have both precedents and guidance.

Not much more is needed for a meal built around this dish; I've included salad suggestions, a quick and delicious lemon or lime curd to serve with berries when berries are in season, and, for a winter dessert there's a particular delight, a crustless "pie" based on grated raw sweet potatoes enriched with raisins and aromatized with a little dark rum.

THE RIGHT POTATOES for slunk are all-purpose spuds. Baking potatoes are next best; "boiling" varieties are too dense and damp.

SLUNK—AN OVEN-BAKED CHOWDER

Serves 6

2 pints shucked medium clams, drained, juice strained and reserved (about 1½ to 2 cups juice)
½ cup finely diced salt pork
6 tablespoons (¾ stick) unsalted butter
1½ cups chopped onion
4 or 5 medium potatoes (about 1½ pounds), peeled and sliced thin (see The Right Potatoes, above)
Pepper to taste
⅔ to 1 cup crushed pilot crackers, sea toast, or saltines with unsalted tops
2 cups, or as needed, light cream, half-and-half, or mixed light cream and milk

ven if it's called "clam hash"—yet another name I've come across for this many-monickered potful—slunk is a soul-satisfying dish that deserves to be preserved, along with our endangered clam beds.

Preheat the oven to 325°.

Chop the clams coarsely, adding their juice to the reserved juice.

Sauté the salt pork in a heavy skillet over medium heat, stirring constantly, until crisp and golden. Remove and reserve the pork.

Discard the fat in the pan and wipe it clean. Melt 3 tablespoons of the butter in it, add the onion, and cook, stirring, over medium heat until the pieces are soft but not browned, 3 to 5 minutes. Add the sliced potatoes and cook, stirring once or twice, until steaming hot, about 5 minutes; if necessary to prevent sticking, add more of the butter. Remove from the heat; add the pork bits.

Spoon half of the mixture into a casserole or beanpot. Season with a little pepper (no salt—the clams, clam juice, and pork are all salty). Add half of the chopped clams, then a sprinkling of pepper, then half of the cracker crumbs. Repeat the layers, ending with crumbs. Dot the remaining butter over the top.

Heat the clam juice and 1 cup of the light cream together; pour it over the casserole, moistening the top evenly. If the liquid doesn't reach to the base of the crumb topping, add the rest of the cream (it's not necessary to heat it) plus, if needed, a little more cream (or milk or water).

Cover the slunk and bake it for 1 to 1¼ hours, or until the ingredients are very tender. If it seems too dry before it's done, add a little milk. Remove the cover and let the top brown lightly at the end.

Serve directly from the baking dish.

QUICK CITRUS COLESLAW

oleslaw made from your everyday winter cabbage can be a mouthful reminiscent of Naugahyde unless it's made far enough ahead of time to let the dressing tenderize the shreds. If you'd like winter slaw that's tender from the start, look for Savoy cabbage, distinguished by its handsome crinkly leaves and good green color.

This slaw has a citrusy glow and nip because of two pantry items we like to keep on hand. Wedges of Preserved Lemons, a long-keeping Moroccan speciality (see page 168), will give it unique character; however, fresh lemon zest will do very well if preserved lemons aren't an inhabitant of the refrigerator. For the other special flavoring, any orange marmalade will do, but marmalade made from bitter oranges, tangerines, or Temple oranges would be best.

Shred the cabbage fine or chop it to confetti-size bits.

Rinse the preserved lemon sections, if used, and mince. Heat the preserved lemon or lemon zest to boiling with the vinegar, water, marmalade, and sugar. Pour over the cabbage, toss to mix, and leave a few minutes.

Add just enough mayonnaise to make a creamy dressing and toss again; taste and add salt or other seasonings if needed.

OLD-STYLE SAVOY SLAW: This is dressed with a sweet-tart mixture made with our foremothers' standby, evaporated milk. Shred a medium head of Savoy. Stir together ⅓ cup evaporated milk and 3 to 4 tablespoons sugar, granulated or light brown, and ½ teaspoon salt. Stir in 3 tablespoons excellent cider vinegar. Let this thicken, then taste and adjust for acidity, salt, and sweetness. Toss with the cabbage, and it's ready to serve.

Serves 6 to 8

1 medium head Savoy cabbage, about 1½ pounds
2 sections Preserved Lemons (page 168), or 1 to 2 teaspoons grated lemon zest (colored rind only, no pith)
¼ cup cider vinegar
¼ cup water
2 to 3 tablespoons bitter orange or other orange marmalade
1 tablespoon granulated sugar
Mayonnaise, as needed
Salt, as needed

Uncooked Lime or Lemon Curd

ere is a quick twist on conventional recipes for lime (or lemon) curd—also called "cheese" or "butter"—which must be cooked, and in a double boiler at that. Cooked curd keeps for months, but this one should be stored for a short time only. It's a versatile component or sauce for desserts, and it's a fine spread for breakfast toast.

The curd is no less than splendid when made with the scarce Key limes for which the pie was named, but it's still good if based on the juice of regular limes or lemons. A better choice, though, is extra-zesty bottled Florida lime juice, which doesn't seem to be from *Key* limes; the label reads "*Key West* lime juice," a crucial difference if we're talking truth-in-labeling. It's usually stocked in fancy-food shops.

Makes 3 cups

8 tablespoons (1 stick)
  unsalted butter
5 large egg yolks
1 14-ounce can sweetened
  condensed milk (1⅓
  cups)
⅓ teaspoon salt
½ cup lime juice,
  preferably from Key
  limes, fresh or bottled, or
  strained fresh lemon
  juice
½ teaspoon grated lime or
  lemon zest (colored rind
  only, no pith); if lime zest
  is unavailable because
  bottled juice is used, zest
  may be omitted

Melt the butter; reserve.

Beat or whisk the egg yolks thoroughly with the condensed milk and salt (a blender or food processor is easiest), then beat in the hot butter. Continuing to beat (or with the machine running), add the juice (and the zest, if used) and mix.

Strain the curd through a fine sieve if you'd like a flawless texture, but it isn't essential, especially if the zest has been included.

Scrape into a storage jar, cover, and refrigerate; the curd will thicken further. It keeps for 10 days or more.

LITTLE LEMON OR LIME TARTLETS. Enough to make you hum "Polly, put the kettle on, we'll all have tea."

Make Lemon Cookie-Crust (page 151) or other pie or tart pastry (see the Index) and roll it out quite thin (⅛ inch, if possible; this is easier to do between two sheets of plastic wrap).

A KEY LIME LAMENT: In all my cooking years I've had my hands on only one batch of genuine Key limes, which are tiny and extremely juicy, green at first and later yellow, and worth killing for. They just aren't available in markets, although I wonder if Mexican limes, which are supposed to be the same species, couldn't be imported if a lime lobby demanded it.

Cut the dough into rounds and press the rounds into tiny muffin or tart tins (the size of the rounds will depend on the size of your pans). Bake the pastry cups in a preheated 375° oven until crisp and golden-brown, about 10 minutes. Remove the tartlet shells from the oven, cool them in their pans for 10 minutes, remove them carefully, and let them cool completely on a rack.

Store the tartlet shells in a covered container until near serving time, then fill them lightly with Uncooked Lime or Lemon Curd. A tiny tuft of whipped cream is an optional finish.

Extra shells will keep for 2 or 3 days.

RUMMY & RAISINY, TOPLESS & BOTTOMLESS SWEET-POTATO "PIE"

ooks like a pie, tastes like a pie, but it's totally crustless, which may or may not be of interest to calorie-watchers. This little number is made from shredded raw sweet potatoes—no boiling and mashing are involved— and it's rich with raisins and fragrant with dark rum. There's still a hint of crunchiness in its texture when the baking is finished.

Those with an eye for culinary genealogy will perceive that this non-pie is related, under its furbelows, to the very American dish called sweet-potato pone; unlike that rich pudding, however, it contains no butter. (It can be made with light cream, but that's optional.)

Because it needs fairly long baking, I like to make this when the oven is being used for another dish at the same time.

CHOOSING THE SWEETEST POTATO: A sweet potato that's not too dry is the one that's right for this dessert—in other words, what's popularly termed a "yam." There's a brief discussion of the confusion on page 134.

Serves 8

2 medium-size sweet
  potatoes (about ¾
  pound)
3 tablespoons dark rum
½ cup dark raisins
2 large eggs
½ cup (packed) dark-
  brown sugar
½ teaspoon salt
¼ teaspoon ground
  allspice
1 cup evaporated milk,
  light cream, or milk
Oil or cooking spray for
  coating the pan
Granulated sugar for
  sprinkling
Optional garnish or
  accompaniment:
  Whipped cream,
  Cultured Cream (Crème
  Fraîche) (page 269), or
  dairy sour cream

*RUMMY & RAISINY, TOPLESS & BOTTOMLESS SWEET-
POTATO "PIE" (CONTINUED)*

Preheat the oven to 350°.

Pare and shred the sweet potatoes medium-coarse to make 2 cups; toss the shreds with the rum and raisins and let them imbibe flavor for a few minutes.

Beat the eggs, brown sugar, salt, allspice, and milk or cream until smooth. Stir into the sweet potatoes and raisins.

Coat a 9-inch glass or metal pie pan with oil or cooking spray. Set it on a baking sheet on the center shelf of the oven and pour in the sweet-potato mixture; pat down any shreds that poke above the surface. (Otherwise, they may become tough.)

Bake for 30 minutes, then cover lightly with aluminum foil and continue to bake for another hour, or until a sample shred is only faintly crunchy.

Sprinkle a little granulated sugar over the pie and cool it on a rack. Plan to serve it at room temperature or while only faintly warm.

At serving time, garnish the top, if you like, with spoonfuls or rosettes of whipped cream, or pass a bowl of whipped cream, Cultured Cream, or sour cream.

MOVE OVER, PORK CHOPS

Slow-Baked Minimalist Pork Ribs (below)

Spicy Sweet-Potato Sticks (below)

Cauliflower Slaw (below)

Angel Biscuits or Rolls (page 226)

Raspberry & Rhubarb Parfait (below) and plain cookies, or
Cranberry, Raisin & Nut Pie (page 209)

To drink: *A Johannisberg Riesling or Pinot Blanc from*
California, or good beer

The meaty pork ribs called "country style" bake to melting tenderness in a slow oven, an impossible feat for present-day pork chops. (Pigs are now being bred for leanness, so their chops are likely to be dry unless a genius is at the stove.) Country ribs have streaks of fat throughout that make them literally self-basting and therefore succulent. Perhaps they aren't a meat to be served often, but they are indeed pleasing in flavor. Not fancy, just good.

For dessert, there's either a two-fruit parfait of raspberries and rhubarb or a pie of cranberries, raisins, and nuts.

SLOW-BAKED MINIMALIST PORK RIBS

llow 2 meaty country-style pork ribs per person, or about 5 pounds to serve 6. Bake the ribs as described in the first part of the recipe for Country-Style Pork Ribs Two Ways that starts on page 49.

No sauce is needed, just salt and pepper before cooking the ribs.

SPICY SWEET-POTATO STICKS

I YAM WHAT I YAM, OR AM I? THE SWEET-POTATO PUZZLEMENT: Oh what a tangled web "sweet potatoes" find themselves in. The ones with dark orange flesh are commonly called "yams" (which they aren't); among all the sweet potatoes they're first choice for these recipes, but paler kinds will do. Some sweet potatoes are drier in texture than "yams" and will need slightly longer cooking.

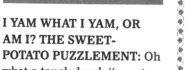elicately spiced, lightly sweetened with honey, and glazed, these sweet potatoes take only 15 minutes, from paring the tubers to dishing them up. Also swift to prepare are the citrus-flavored "sweets" following the recipe.

There's yet another fruitful possibility, sweet potatoes with apples, to enjoy when firm, tart apples have come to market. Just add 1 large apple (Granny Smith or a comparable variety), pared and cut into sticks the size of the sweet-potato pieces. Cook the dish that same way, but replace the ginger, cardamom, and cloves with ½ teaspoon cinnamon and a sprinkle of nutmeg.

All the versions are just right with a pork roast, smoked ham, or poultry as well as the ribs.

Serves 6

*3 large sweet potatoes,
1½ to 2 pounds total
(see I Yam What I Yam,
... left)*
2 tablespoons vegetable oil
*3 tablespoons unsalted
butter*
*Seasonings: Salt, white
pepper, ground ginger,
ground cardamom,
ground cloves*
*½ cup, or as needed,
water*
3 tablespoons honey

Pare the sweet potatoes and cut into short sticks ¼ inch thick. (I use the food-processor disk designed for French-fries.)

Heat the oil and butter in a wok or skillet over medium-high heat; don't let the fat brown. Add the potato sticks and toss to coat; season with salt, white pepper, about ¼ teaspoon each of ginger and cardamom, and a small pinch of cloves. Add ½ cup water, adjust the heat to medium-low, and cook, tossing often but gently, for 5 minutes, adding drops of water if needed to prevent sticking.

Add the honey and continue to toss-cook until the sticks are just tender and nicely glazed, perhaps 3 minutes. Check the seasonings and serve promptly.

SWEET-POTATO STICKS WITH ORANGE & HONEY: Omit the ginger, cardamom, and cloves; cook the potatoes with 1 tablespoon freshly grated orange zest (colored rind only, no pith) and, if you have it, a little ground coriander.

For the fresh orange zest I sometimes substitute about 2 tablespoons of chopped candied orange peel. I don't recommend this unless you have home-made candied peel—science has not yet detected any flavor in the kind sold in supermarkets.

CAULIFLOWER SLAW

 ere's a way to make a toothsome salad from fresh cauliflower, no formal recipe needed. You *do* need good raw material—unblemished cauliflower that's firm, creamy white, and tempting. To serve 6, a medium-size head is about right.

Pull the cauliflower into florets, discarding the tough core. Slice each section from stem end to head as thin as possible, using your sharpest knife (don't worry about some crumbling here and there). Stir about ¾ cup mayonnaise with enough buttermilk (or substitute well-stirred yogurt) to thin it to pouring consistency. Season the dressing highly with prepared mustard, lemon juice or white wine vinegar, white pepper, and salt to taste. Toss the cauliflower and dressing gently together, taste the salad, and add more seasonings with as free a hand as required.

This salad should be rather mustardy, I think, and a few drops of hot pepper sauce are a good addition. Let the salad rest and mellow for an hour, if the time is available.

RHUBARB RHAPSODY: For a while there, after American food began to aspire to the status of *haute cuisine*—something that began in the nouvelle-ish late seventies, when I was an editor for a food magazine—rhubarb was among those edibles considered pretty much beneath notice, a stalky country-cousin vegetable masquerading as a fruit. Rhubarb was something everyone knew about and maybe even *liked*, but no gastronome-who-was-anybody would have thought of dishing it up for company.

This has changed—rhubarb has been discovered by the previously haughty. It's therefore at risk of appearing in some strange recipes, but not to worry if it does; there will always be those who appreciate the ways God intended: rhubarb and strawberry pie, rhubarb crisp, rhubarb bread and cake and fool and chutney and other good and earthy things—like this dessert.

I'm glad that our own two clumps of rhubarb, growing peacefully in a flower border where they look very handsome, will go on supplying us for a good long time.

RASPBERRY & RHUBARB PARFAIT

*R*aspberries are best not washed. After all, one must have faith in something.

—ANN BATCHELDER

"In itself, rhubarb can be, in some circumstances, good. What is it, a fruit or a vegetable?"
"A weed, I think, but not necessarily a damned weed."

—IDWAL JONES, *HIGH BONNET*

verybody was looking forward to a taste of the July crop of raspberries but the pickings had been slim—what to do? This delicate dessert—first devised as a stretcher—turned out to have a misty charm all its own, so it has been repeated often and with pleasure. Its rich texture derives from perfectly sweetened and cooked rhubarb, a suave backdrop for the more assertive flavor of the raspberries.

Tender, pink-skinned rhubarb is the kind to use, but it's not always hanging around the garden or the greengrocer's in raspberry season; frozen rhubarb, if it was young and rosy to begin with, will work fine.

At times when fresh rhubarb is at hand but raspberries aren't, we use raspberries frozen the summer before, or, if they're all gone, commercially packed berries. If they have been sugared, count their syrup as part of the sweetening when adding sugar to the rhubarb.

Serves 6

3 cups diced tender
    rhubarb (½-inch pieces)
1 teaspoon finely grated
    orange zest (colored rind
    only, no pith)
¾ cup granulated sugar
2 cups raspberries, fresh
    or frozen (no need to
    thaw)
1 cup heavy cream, chilled
½ teaspoon vanilla
    extract, or ¼ teaspoon
    almond extract
Garnish: More rasp-
    berries, or candied mint
    leaves or candied orange
    peel

Cook the rhubarb, orange zest, and sugar gently in a heavy saucepan over low heat until the rhubarb is just tender, turning the pieces once or twice. Cool.

Fold the raspberries gently into the cooled rhubarb and chill from 1 to 6 hours.

Near serving time, whip the cream to soft peaks; beat in the flavoring. Layer the chilled fruit and cream in parfait glasses or wine goblets, beginning with fruit and ending with cream.

The parfaits can be held in the refrigerator for up to an hour. Garnish with a few raspberries, a candied mint leaf, or slivers of candied orange peel, whatever appeals to the eye.

ROAMING THE RHUBARB PATCH: Any reader with half an eye will have perceived that Mrs. W and her family like rhubarb a lot. We like it in several ways in this book—besides the recipe above, there's a rhubarb variation of green tomato fool on page 108, and a meringue-topped springtime tart involving rhubarb is to be seen on page 115.

BEANFEAST WITH A COMPANY DESSERT

Peppers, Plus (below)

Red-Wine Beans with a Ham Bone (below)

Blueberry Corn Bread or Muffins (below) or Fresh Corn Popovers (page 43)

Salad of tender leaf lettuce tossed with olive oil, tarragon vinegar, and a pinch of salt

Dark Chocolate Mousse with Raspberry Sauce (below) or Very Chocolate Ice Cream (page 204), also with the Raspberry Sauce

To drink: *Premium red jug wine; or iced tea*

To my way of thinking no apologies are necessary when a splendid dish of beans—any beans—has been lovingly prepared for either family alone or family-plus-a-guest-or-two. Add corn bread or muffins blossoming with blueberries (or popovers studded with kernels of corn) and a few leaves of green salad, and—even before the dessert—you will have *dined,* and never mind what Dr. Johnson had to say about the kind of dinner he preferred to be asked to.

With either of the desserts in this menu, White Chocolate Marshmallow Sauce (page 205) would be an alternative topping.

PEPPERS, PLUS

s a small, quick extra at the beginning of this meal, roasted peppers with anchovies will whet the appetite and harmonize nicely with what's to come. This is a "starter" that can be made most respectably with peppers from a jar, if you prefer them to fresh.

Drain the peppers, cut them into strips, and arrange them on endive or other greens on small plates. Drain the anchovies and drape several over each serving, according to anchovy appetites. Drizzle a little oil over the portions; garnish them with lemon and olives.

ROASTING YOUR OWN: Roast red peppers on a grill (or a cake rack) set over a gas burner set on high, turning them often, until they are blackened all over. (Or do this under the broiler.) Enclose them in a plastic bag until cool enough to touch, then rub and scrape off the charred skins; remove the seeds. Sprinkle with a little salt and a little oil and refrigerate, covered, for up to a week.

RED-WINE BEANS WITH A HAM BONE

tart with deep-red beans, cook them with a ham bone (country ham, if possible), add aromatic sweet red peppers, onions, and herbs, dye the potful deeper crimson with tomato and a good slosh of red wine, tuck in any leftover chunks of ham trimmed from the bone, and you have a really rib-warming dish.

Serves 6

1 large jar (24 ounces) roasted sweet red peppers
Endive or other greens
2 or 3 cans (2-ounce size) anchovy fillets in oil
Additional olive oil
Garnish: Lemon wedges; oil-cured black olives

CAN DO: Two cans (19-ounce size or thereabouts) of dark red kidney beans can replace home-cooked. Drain off their sticky juice, rinse them, and drain again. Replace the bean liquid with beef broth or water. Instead of using the ham bone, which needs time to release its flavor, combine the beans with the sautéed vegetables, garlic, tomato paste, wine, herbs, and a double quantity of ham chunks. Cook in a covered casserole in a 325° oven; allow an hour. Check and adjust seasonings toward the end of cooking.

The beans taste even better the second time around so, if it's at all possible, prepare the dish a day before you need it so the ingredients can swap flavors and mellow. Any leftovers will freeze well.

The bone from a country ham is first choice for flavoring, but a bone from any other type will do so long as the ham is a smoky and flavorful one.

Serves 10 or more

1 pound dried dark-red kidney beans or other red beans
A meaty bone from a smoked ham or half-ham
Optional for the beans: Bay leaf, dried thyme, parsley, a cut-up onion
3 tablespoons bacon drippings, vegetable oil, or unsalted butter
1½ cups coarsely chopped yellow onions
1½ cups coarsely chopped red or green sweet peppers, or a mixture
3 large cloves garlic, chopped
6-ounce can Italian tomato paste
1 to 1½ cups full-flavored red wine
2 large bay leaves
Dried thyme, or mixed dried Italian herbs
1 to 2 cups diced leftover ham, optional
Salt and pepper, to taste
1 tablespoon red wine vinegar
Tabasco or other hot pepper sauce, optional

Soak the beans overnight or by the fast method (soaking and cooking notes are below); cook them slowly with the ham bone, in water to cover, until they pass the split-skin test. (Optionally, a bay leaf, a little thyme, parsley, and a cut-up onion can go into the cooking water.)

Warm the bacon fat, oil, or butter in a skillet; sauté the onions and peppers, stirring, until soft and golden but not browned. Add the garlic, tomato paste, red wine, bay leaves and other herbs; bring the mixture to a boil, simmer a minute or two, and add it to the beans.

Simmer the beans slowly, partly covered, until tender. Add the optional ham chunks, salt and pepper, and wine vinegar. Simmer uncovered for a few minutes to reduce the liquid if the sauce is soupy; if it's stodgy, add hot water. Taste, adjust seasonings, and add, optionally, a little Tabasco or other hot pepper sauce.

Cool the beans uncovered, then remove the bone, cutting off and returning any meat to the pot, and refrigerate overnight to mellow if time permits.

Reheat the beans slowly, adding a little more liquid if needed.

SPEEDING UP THE BEANS: Dry beans are traditionally soaked overnight before they're cooked. Here is a shortcut, included for anyone who has missed it: Bring sorted, rinsed, and drained beans to a boil with water rising 2 inches over them. Boil 1 minute, turn off the heat, cover, and let stand 1 hour. Drain the beans and cook in plenty of fresh water.

BEAN COOKERY: Precook beans at a simmer, not a boil. If they're to be cooked further, as in this recipe, they are ready for the next step when a bean, blown upon in a spoon, splits its skin but is still firm. I like to add onion and seasoning herbs to the precooking water, but salt should never be added until the beans are almost done, or they'll toughen.

Cooking time for any kind of dried legumes can vary a lot; new-crop beans can take a surprisingly short time, while older beans can take hours.

BLUEBERRY CORN BREAD OR MUFFINS

hen it turns out to be a wild huckleberry year—a sometime thing here, not to be counted on—a few handfuls of berries gathered around the edges of the yard are tossed into the batter for this bread as a celebration of such wee wild bounties. At other times I use wild blueberries from the grocer's freezer case, which have more flavor than the big tame berries grown for market. (But those will do, too.)

This batter, without the berries, is fine for cornsticks (see page 209), if you possess an iron pan for baking them; it will make about 12.

Makes an 8-inch square panful, or 12 muffins

Unsalted butter for
  coating the pan
1⅓ cups yellow cornmeal,
  preferably stone-ground
1 cup all-purpose flour
2 tablespoons granulated
  sugar
1 tablespoon baking
  powder
¾ teaspoon salt
1½ cups fresh or frozen
  blueberries or
  huckleberries, rinsed and
  towel-dried
2 large eggs
1 cup milk
¼ cup melted unsalted
  butter

Preheat the oven to 400°. Butter an 8-inch square baking pan or a 12-cup muffin tin.

Sift the cornmeal, flour, sugar, baking powder, and salt into a large bowl. Add the blueberries and toss them gently to distribute and coat them.

Beat the eggs and milk together, then add the melted butter. Stir lightly into the dry ingredients, mixing just until the dry ingredients are lightly moistened; don't overmix the batter even a little or you'll risk ending up with tough muffins or corn bread.

Spoon the batter into the baking pan and smooth the surface, or divide it among the muffin cups. Bake in the center of the oven until golden brown and firm to the touch, 25 to 30 minutes for corn bread, 20 to 25 minutes for muffins. Leave in the pan for 5 minutes, then remove the muffins, or cut the bread into squares, and serve hot.

Leftover corn bread or muffins will keep at room temperature, wrapped in foil or plastic, for a day or two; or they may be frozen. Before serving again, rewarm either, wrapped in foil, in a 325° oven for about 15 minutes if unfrozen. Reheating will take about twice as long for still-frozen items.

DARK CHOCOLATE MOUSSE WITH RASPBERRY SAUCE

he sauce of raspberries touched with a little liqueur sets up a vivid resonance of flavors when paired with this dark, intensely chocolately mousse. Its flavor is bittersweet; for more sweetness, use 2 ounces of unsweetened and ¾ cup of semisweet chocolate.

Serves 8

Oil for coating the molds
2 teaspoons unflavored
  gelatin
2 tablespoons water
½ cup strong coffee,
  preferably espresso (see
  Express Espresso, right)
3 squares (3 ounces)
  unsweetened chocolate,
  chopped
½ cup (3 ounces)
  semisweet chocolate,
  either cut-up bulk
  chocolate or chocolate
  bits
6 large eggs, separated
6 tablespoons granulated
  sugar
¼ teaspoon salt
Raspberry Sauce (right)
Optional garnish: About
  ½ cup heavy cream

Lightly oil 8 soufflé dishes, coffee cups, or molds.

Sprinkle the gelatin over 2 tablespoons water; soak 5 minutes, or until softened.

Heat the coffee to simmering in a heavy pan; add the gelatin and stir over low heat until it dissolves. Add all the chocolate and stir until smooth. Remove from the heat.

Beat the egg yolks to mix; add the sugar and salt and beat until very light. Stir in a big spoonful of the chocolate mixture, then blend into the remaining chocolate mixture. Beat the egg whites until stiff but still glossy; whisk a large spoonful of egg whites into the mousse, then pour the mousse over the remaining egg whites and fold the mixtures together with a rubber spatula just until no streaks can be seen.

Spoon the mousse into the lightly oiled soufflé dishes, coffee cups, or molds. Cover and chill for several hours or overnight, until well set. (The mousse will keep, refrigerated, for several days.)

To serve, dip the containers one at a time into very warm water and hold for a moment, just until an edge of mousse can be loosened with a finger. Unmold the mousses onto chilled individual dessert plates. Pour a pool of Raspberry Sauce around each and, if you like, pour a thread of cream in a looping ring pattern in the pool.

DARK THOUGHTS: CHOCOLATE. Supermarket brands of cooking chocolate are perfectly fine for almost every kitchen purpose but, like major brands of anything, they aren't the ultimate choice for an occasional special creation such as this mousse, or perhaps a wicked fudge cake.

If you, too, enjoy browsing in the catalogs of fine-food and fine-cookware purveyors, take a look at their offerings of high-quality semisweet, bittersweet, and white chocolate, which can be bought in large blocks and kept on hand. A sampling of premium chocolate from, say, Maid of Scandinavia or Williams-Sonoma will prove, if there are doubts, that grocers' chocolate and the superior brands aren't created equal. Other sources of bulk chocolate of good quality are confectioners' shops where candy is actually made, not just sold.

Makes about 1½ cups

3 cups fresh raspberries, rinsed and drained, or 3 cups unsweetened frozen berries (no need to thaw)
⅓ cup superfine sugar
2 tablespoons liqueur or fruit brandy— Framboise, kirsch, cherry brandy, or orange-flavored liqueur such as Triple Sec, Cointreau, or Grand Marnier

EXPRESS ESPRESSO: To keep on hand for adding a touch of coffee flavoring whenever it's wanted in a sweet dish, a small jar of concentrated espresso is worth the space it takes in the refrigerator.

Use very fine-ground espresso (or French roast) coffee. Measure ¼ cup into a funnel lined with filter paper (or a cone-type coffee filter) and pour 1½ cups of boiling water slowly through it. The fraction of a cup of extract will be very strong; if you want it stronger, filter it through the grounds a second time. Capped and refrigerated, it keeps for months and months. Dilute it with water to use in recipes calling for strong coffee.

RASPBERRY SAUCE

ot just a soul-mate for Dark Chocolate Mousse, this quickly made sauce is also remarkably good over dark chocolate ice cream. It will keep in the fridge for several days.

If you should have a berry bonanza, you can multiply the batch and freeze some of it; it will keep its quality for a year or more. For fresher flavor, though, you might omit the liqueur from the portion to be frozen; add it after thawing the sauce.

Purée fresh or unthawed frozen raspberries in a blender or food processor until as smooth as possible. Press the purée through a fine-mesh sieve over a bowl to rid it of as many seeds as you can. You should have about 1⅓ cups of purée.

Stir in the sugar until completely dissolved; stir in the liqueur. Serve, or refrigerate in a covered jar for 3 or 4 days; can be frozen for up to 1 year.

CALL IT *CAL*-MEX: LOW-OCTANE HOT STUFF

Beforehand, *Margaritas; or cold beer all the way*

Carnitas (Little Pork Nuggets), below, with warmed corn tortillas or crisp tortilla chips

Pretty Good Chili con Carne (below)

Beans for Chili (below) or
Garlic Garbanzos to go with Chili (page 49)

The jalapeño version of Chinese-Cabbage Coleslaw (page 215)
or a platter of sweet red and green pepper rings and pickled
jalapeños or other hot peppers

Hazelnut Cheese Tart (below) or Raspberry & White Wine Ice
(page 92)

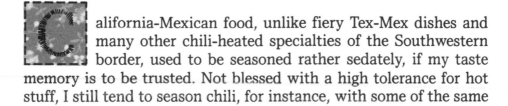

alifornia-Mexican food, unlike fiery Tex-Mex dishes and many other chili-heated specialties of the Southwestern border, used to be seasoned rather sedately, if my taste memory is to be trusted. Not blessed with a high tolerance for hot stuff, I still tend to season chili, for instance, with some of the same moderation I recall in the "Mexican" foods I first tasted.

Take the wares of the Tamale Man, who came around with his steaming containers in quiet Santa Monica when my siblings and I were quite small. My mother, unlike some of her California neighbors—nearly all were transplants from elsewhere—tended to be open to new foods (she was herself an unusually good cook), so thanks to her adventurousness we experienced Mexican food, or at least tamales, while young. (Just as we experienced avocados, and loquats, and guavas, and ranch-raised rabbit, and artichokes, and chayote, and barracuda.)

Properly steamed in corn-husk wrappings, the Tamale Man's wares smelled and tasted deliciously of corn; they had a bit of meat (not a lot) inside and were made with very little "hot" seasoning. All in all, they were something young gringo palates could take to. As later we all took to the mild local versions of chili.

The main items of this menu are authentic only in my own West Coast terms. I've included a personal notion or two, such as the preparation of the garbanzos, and desserts that are anything but traditional. As for the chili: My excellent food friends from New Mexico and Texas would make the chili *their* way, and it would be good, but not as "Californian" as mine.

Just to keep the cross-cultural franchise, a choice of desserts that are absolutely inauthentic in Southwestern terms rounds off this menu; choose Hazelnut Cheese Tart for a creamy windup, or palate-cleansing Raspberry & White Wine Ice.

CARNITAS (LITTLE PORK NUGGETS)

ooked with just salt and pepper and served warm, these meltingly tender bites of pork are a classic nibble from Old Mexico. For a not-so-classic version with a flavor rather like that of a French pâté, the meat is first marinated with a little garlic, thyme, and bay, the optional seasonings listed; the cooking is done in the same fashion. (In this hybrid version the pork nuggets are no longer carnitas, except for convenient reference.) In either guise, carnitas tend to disappear fast as an accompaniment for drinks. Plain carnitas are estimable in tacos sauced with guacamole, too—see the directions following the main recipe.

With little additional effort the batch can be doubled to make a big potful; carnitas freeze and reheat well.

Makes 2 to 3 cups

2 pounds pork shoulder
  meat, trimmed (reserve
  fat) and cubed (1 inch)
1 tablespoon coarse
  (kosher) salt
About ½ teaspoon freshly
  ground pepper
Fat or oil for coating the
  pot
Optional seasonings: 1 or
  2 cloves garlic, minced
2 bay leaves, broken, or ¼
  teaspoon Powdered Bay
  Leaves (page 274)
½ teaspoon crumbled
  dried thyme

If the pork is to be cooked immediately, rub salt and pepper into the meat cubes and bits of trimmed-off and reserved fat; cook as directed below.

To marinate the meat, either rub the meat and fat with salt and pepper, or use salt, pepper, and all the optional seasonings; refrigerate 6 to 12 hours in a plastic bag.

Preheat the oven to 250°.

Rub a little fat or oil around the inside of a heavy iron or enameled iron pot. Set over medium-high heat, add the pork, and stir and turn the pieces with a spatula just until all surfaces are gray. Put on a completely tight lid; transfer to the oven.

Bake 2 to 3 hours, stirring every half-hour, until the pieces are very tender, almost falling apart; uncover the pot for the last 10 minutes.

Lift the meat cubes from the cooking fat, leaving behind any fat scraps. If the carnitas are to be served at once, drain them on paper towels.

THE PART OF THE PIG FOR CARNITAS: Another cut of pork should not be substituted for shoulder in this recipe. That part of the animal has the right blend of fat and lean fibers for the purpose, whereas the loin doesn't; neither does the leg (ham).

Strain and keep the flavorful fat for storing leftovers (below) and for use in cooking.

Serve either plain or herbed carnitas warm, with wooden picks, as an appetizer; or make tacos (below) with plain carnitas.

Storing: Cover carnitas with strained fat and refrigerate for a few days; or freeze for up to 2 months.

Reheating: Warm cubes in a little of the fat in a 250° oven; drain well.

TACOS, MORE OR LESS

or a simple version of this Mexican-style sandwich, very good on a do-it-yourself buffet, fold plain carnitas (above) into warm corn tortillas and douse them with your favorite salsa or with this quickly made guacamole:

GUACAMOLE FOR TACOS

Mash dead-ripe avocado coarsely with minced onion, a little chopped pulp of very ripe tomato, chopped jalapeño peppers (fresh, canned, or pickled), a little lime juice, and salt; proportions are to the cook's taste, but the guacamole should be mostly avocado, and it shouldn't be mashed too much. Chopped fresh coriander is the finishing touch, if it's available and all hands have acquired a taste for it.

———

AVOCADO AD LIB: Just as with chili con carne, for which every chilihead has the "one and only" recipe (to quote Bill Bridges in his *Great American Chili Book*), there's no agreement as to what, besides avocado, belongs in guacamole. The suggestions above are personal; suit yourself as to the kind or quantity of hot pepper(s), or how much onion or lime juice or tomato to use.

WHAT'S *NOT* IN MY CHILI:
All these ingredients (scout's honor) can be found, printed in black and white, in chili recipes collected over time.

Tequila, curry powder, sake, rosemary, tarragon, ginger ale, bottled chili sauce, butter, rum, caraway, honey, Scotch whisky, soy sauce, filé powder, ripe olives, chocolate, nutmeg, orange liqueur, Romano cheese.

Dried woodruff, fresh coriander leaves, Coca-cola, coffee, turmeric, cloves, celery, cocoa powder, Worcestershire sauce, Jack Daniel's whiskey, dry mustard, white wine, annatto paste, orange peel.

Bay leaves, water chestnuts, brown sugar, carrots, mustard seed, potatoes, molé powder, smoke flavoring, Bourbon, raisins, Jack cheese, applesauce, canned salsa, celery seed, peanuts, parsley, roasted Italian peppers, lemon or lime juice, nuts, sliced limes.

Anise seed, mushrooms, fresh ginger, bottled taco sauce, ordinary green (unripe) tomatoes, Dijon mustard, cardamom, brandy, canned chicken gumbo, goat cheese, cinnamon, bottled barbecue sauce, avocado, allspice, Parmesan cheese, consommè, juniper berries, red wine, canned pimientos, pickling spice, ketchup, canned onion or chili-beef soup, horseradish.

Bloody Mary mix, basil, and sauerkraut.

PRETTY GOOD CHILI CON CARNE

*T*HE BEST OF THE WORST: *of all the fearful and wonderful chili recipes I've gathered as a dedicated collector, the absolutely unbeatable worst is "Chili à la Frigidaire," dating from the 1930s, from which there's no way to go but up:*

- *A pound and a half of hamburger*
- *One small onion*
- *One large bottle of catsup*
- *One can of red kidney beans*

xcept in Texas, beans are often included in chili (which then becomes *chile con carne con frijoles*, strictly speaking, and speaking in Spanish), but I seem to have bent in the direction of Texas since my growing-up days in California, where the chili was quite beany. The friendly little "chili joints"—there was one called the Chili Bowl (what else?) in our suburban neighborhood—used to ladle out a bowlful that generally had more beans than meat. (Saltines and a glass of milk rounded out the order.) Members of the beans-in-the-bowl school can add 2 to 4 cups of Beans for Chili (page 150) when the potful of meat is three-quarters done.

Chili the way I make it is only mildly peppery, pretty much in the California tradition except for its beanlessness. After tasting carefully, the cook may want to ratchet up the heat when the chili has cooked for an hour. If commercial chili powder is used instead of the dried and ground peppers ("pure chile"), start with 2 tablespoons for this quantity of meat; include the paprika, but omit the oregano, cumin, and coriander. You may want to read the Chili Notes following the recipe before starting to cook.

Makes 1½ quarts

About ½ cup scraps of beef fat, or substitute 4 to 6 tablespoons vegetable oil or bacon fat
2 pounds lean beef (shank or rump), in ½-inch dice (see Chili Notes, right)
1½ cups chopped onion
4 cloves garlic, minced
1½ tablespoons mild pure ground chile (see Chili Notes, right)
¼ teaspoon hot ground chile (or ground hot red pepper)
2 tablespoons sweet or medium paprika, preferably imported
1 teaspoon ground or finely crumbled dried oregano, preferably the Mexican variety
1 teaspoon ground cumin
½ teaspoon ground coriander
½ teaspoon, or to taste, salt
16-ounce can Italian plum tomatoes, chopped, with their juice
2 tablespoons tomato paste
About 3 cups beef broth, or combined beef broth and beer
1 tablespoon masa harina (tortilla flour) or cornmeal
1 to 2 teaspoons red wine vinegar, optional
Accompaniment: Beans for Chili (page 150); or Garlic Garbanzos to Go with Chili (page 49); or hot whole-grain hominy, rice, or plain spaghetti

Stir the beef fat over medium heat in a large heavy pot until all possible fat has been tried out; remove and discard the scraps. If you don't have 4 to 6 tablespoons rendered fat, add vegetable oil.

Add a layer of beef cubes and stir over medium-high heat until browned; remove. Repeat with remaining meat in single-layer batches; reserve.

Cook the onion and garlic slowly in the fat, stirring often, until golden and soft, 8 to 10 minutes.

Return the meat; add the chiles, paprika, oregano, cumin, coriander, ½ teaspoon salt, tomatoes, and tomato paste. Bring to a simmer, then add enough beef broth or other liquid to almost cover the meat.

Simmer uncovered until the meat is very tender, about 2 hours; if necessary, add liquid from time to time to keep the meat almost covered.

Taste and add more of any seasoning that is needed. Mix the masa harina or cornmeal with a little water, stir it into the chili, and simmer for another 15 minutes to thicken the chili slightly.

If you're including the vinegar (not needed if beer is used), stir in 1 teaspoon and taste before deciding to add more.

If possible, cool, then refrigerate the chili overnight or longer to let it mellow. At serving time, reheat it slowly.

Serve in bowls, if you'd like to be classical, either straight or ladled over the beans or other accompaniment.

CHILI NOTES AND GLOSSARY

Chili or chili con carne: The dish itself, Southwestern in origin, not Mexican. By extension, as in "chili powder," it also applies to seasoning mixtures.

Chili powder (or chili mix): Comes in a jar, can, or foil pouch. Besides chilies (or chiles), chili powder usually contains such herbs as oregano, cumin, and coriander, plus paprika (for color) and often dried garlic. Some packaged "chili mixes" are available in grades of hotness that depend on the kinds of chiles they contain.

Chile: The purist's preferred spelling for any of numerous native American peppers, mostly very hot, each possessing its own character. A given chile (or chili, if you like) may have several names, depending on who's talking

CHILI CURMUDGEONS:
The Hot Pod prize for authorial acerbity about this dish should go to Henry Beard and Roy McKie, two droll fellows who define chili con carne as "Incendiary dogfood widely eaten in Texas," and a chili parlor as "A fistfight at which cooked beef is served." More to be pitied than censured, they are the authors of *Cooking: A Dictionary.*

or cooking. Among the lovely chile names are poblano, ancho, jalapeño, serrano, pasilla, cascabel, mulato, chipotle, arbol, guajillo, pequin, Anaheim, and Fresno. And then there are the hybrids . . .

Chile powder or ground pure chile: Pure dried and ground chiles (or chilies), without added spices or herbs. Available in various degrees of heat, mostly by mail order unless you're out West. Dried whole peppers, from the same sources, are favored by dedicated chili cooks—they're simmered and puréed before they go into the pot.

Chili grind or chili meat: Very coarsely ground beef, put through a plate with holes up to ¾ inch across. It's not available everywhere. Don't use regular ground beef for chili—you'll end up with mush. Tough meat—muscle meat, such as shank or rump—is better for chili than tender cuts. Like some purists (which I'm not), I prefer meat cut by hand. Cut beef into slices ½ inch thick; cut slices into ½-inch strips; stack several strips and cut them into cubes, and that's it.

Masa harina: Corn flour used for tortillas, unique in flavor because of way the grain is processed—it tastes like tortillas, and vice versa. Cornmeal can be substituted as a chili thickener.

BEANS FOR CHILI

ried beans—pinto, red kidney, or pink—are soaked, then simmered with a few seasonings that complement the chili they're to accompany.

Serves 6 or more

1 pound dried beans
1 ham hock
1 large onion, chopped
Seasonings: *salt, pepper, whole or ground hot red pepper or pepper flakes, or hot pepper sauce*

To 1 pound of picked-over beans that have been soaked overnight and drained, add 1 ham hock and 1 onion, chopped up; cover with fresh water and simmer slowly, partly covered, until the beans are tender.

Toward the end add salt, a little black pepper, and a little something hot: 2 or 3 small fresh or dried hot red peppers, left whole; or dashes of ground hot red pepper, dried red pepper flakes, or bottled pepper sauce. How much depends on individual taste; if doubtful, add hot stuff with a light hand and put pepper sauce on the table.

When the beans are done, remove the ham hock, chop the meat, and return it to the pot. Reheat for serving.

HAZELNUT CHEESE TART

his nutty tart, slimmer and less rich than a classic tall, stout cheesecake, is remarkably satisfying all the same. Golden raisins can replace the hazelnuts, if you like.

8 to 10 servings

LEMON COOKIE-CRUST:
1 cup all-purpose flour
3 tablespoons granulated
* sugar*
¼ teaspoon salt
½ teaspoon grated lemon
* zest (colored rind only,*
* no pith)*
6 tablespoons cold
* unsalted butter*
2 large egg yolks, beaten
* just to mix*

CHEESE & HAZELNUT
  FILLING:
1 pound large-curd cottage
* cheese*
½ to ⅔ cup granulated
* sugar*
2 tablespoons cornstarch
3 large eggs
½ cup milk or light cream,
* or ¼ cup of either plus*
* ¼ cup sour cream*
1½ teaspoons vanilla
* extract*
¼ teaspoon lemon extract
* or orange-flower water*
⅓ cup toasted, skinned,
* and sliced hazelnuts*
* (page 276)*
Sugar for top

Preheat the oven to 375°.

Cookie crust: Place the flour, sugar, salt, and lemon zest in the bowl of a food processor. (If you're not using the machine, see Making the Tart by Hand, below.) Pulse the machine briefly on and off to mix, then add the butter and pulse until the mixture is crumbly; add the egg yolks, then run the machine just until the dough forms a ball on top of the blade.

Press the dough over the bottom and up the sides of a 10-inch loose-bottomed tart pan, using your knuckles and fingers; the surface needn't be smooth.

Bake the crust in the center of the oven 12 to 14 minutes, until it's firm and the edges are lightly browned. Cool in the pan on a rack.

Reset the oven to 325°.

Filling: Whirl the cottage cheese in the food processor until very smooth, scraping down the sides once or twice. Add sugar to taste, cornstarch, eggs, milk or cream, and flavorings; blend well.

Return the prebaked tart shell to the center shelf of the oven and pour in the filling; sprinkle the hazelnuts on top.

Bake until the filling is firm except for a slightly jiggly center, about 30 minutes.

Sprinkle the top lightly with sugar. Cool the tart 10 minutes on a rack, then remove the rim of the pan and cool completely.

MAKING THE TART BY HAND: *For the crust:* Whisk together the dry ingredients and lemon zest; cut in the butter with two knives or a pastry blender; stir in the egg yolks, turn the dough onto your work surface, and knead

ORANGE-FLOWER WATER: To most palates nowadays this flavoring is too intensely floral to use by itself, although it has a long history in confectionery and baking. A few drops used together with vanilla, as in this recipe, adds a delightfully mysterious undernote of flavor.

it by hand until smooth. (Don't worry about overmixing this dough; it's impossible.)

For the filling: Push the cheese through a fine-meshed strainer once or twice, to make it as smooth as possible. Whisk together the sugar and cornstarch; add to the cheese with the eggs, milk or cream, and flavorings. Beat thoroughly with a whisk or egg beater.

INSPIRED BY ITALY: Replace the nuts in the Hazelnut Cheese Tart with certain other goodies and you have a delectably different version that's reminiscent of an Italian ricotta pie.

For this knockoff, you omit the hazelnuts but use all the other ingredients, plus these: 2 tablespoons chopped toasted almonds (or you could use pine nuts), 1 tablespoon each of chopped candied orange peel and candied citron (or 1½ tablespoons of candied orange peel alone), 1 teaspoon grated lemon peel, 2 tablespoons coarsely chopped golden raisins, and 2 tablespoons chopped semisweet chocolate (or use miniature chocolate bits).

Mix all these good things into the filling before pouring it into the baked tart crust, then bake the tart as described.

GOING RETRO

Tomato Aspic with Avocado (below) bedded on watercress or arugula or curly endive, served with a dab of mayonnaise or the sauce accompanying the recipe

Ham Scalloped with Potatoes à la Jacques (below)

Panned Spinach (page 123), with lemon wedges

Upside-Down Fruited Ginger Cake (below), with Cultured Cream (or Crème Fraîche) (page 269), English Pouring Custard (page 218), or lightly whipped cream,
or
ripe pears and/or crisp apples, plus a creamy cheese (Brie, Bel Paese, Explorateur, etc.) and crashingly crusty bread or rolls

To drink: A premium white jug wine; or, for a splurge, a good Chardonnay or fumé blanc

Perhaps because thoughts of autumn brought nostalgia when this menu was being written, it turns out that two or three of the dishes for this dinner exactly fit the definition of what is called "retro food" by gastronomic journalist, cookbook writer, and good friend Marian Burros. Well, so be it. Full speed backward; retro dinner herewith.

Really good tomato aspic—tangy and dense, meaty with tomato pulp—is a zesty dish whose turn for revival has come, and never mind whatever cycle of snobbery is ruling the nation's restaurants at the moment. Here we have aspic.

The foundation of this rendition of ham scalloped with potatoes—a homey dish many of us grew up on—is an exalted *gratin dauphinois* from the hands of chef, teacher, and author Jacques Pépin. Jacques' potatoes have never even *heard* of the curdling and cantankerousness typical of most American versions of scalloped potatoes; they have been silky, creamy, foolproof, and irresistible each of the many times I've prepared them since I had the pleasure of hands-on classes with the master.

Two traditions—upside-down cake and hot-water gingerbread—meet and mingle in the dessert. The last course could perfectly well be the alternative fruit and cheese, but I'll take the ginger cake.

TOMATO ASPIC

 n my California youth, tomato "jelly" often enfolded suave chunks of avocado, a fruit that grew in most backyards. I liked it then, with or without avocado. I still like it, especially when it's one of the aspics here.

The Horseradish Cream Sauce is optional and so is mayonnaise, the alternative suggestion.

ASPIC WITH OR WITHOUT AVOCADO

Serves 6 to 8

3 cans (1-pound size) Italian-style canned tomatoes, with their juice, or about 4 pounds fully ripe fresh tomatoes
Handful of fresh celery tops, roughly chopped
2 big slices onion
¼ red or green sweet pepper, roughly chopped
2 slices lemon, with peel
½ bay leaf
2 whole cloves
Seasonings: *Lemon juice, sugar, salt, white pepper, hot pepper sauce, Worcestershire sauce*
2 envelopes unflavored gelatin
1 avocado, fully ripe, optional
Horseradish Cream Sauce *(page 156; optional), or highly seasoned mayonnaise (optional), with added fresh herbs— parsley and chives, plus either chervil or tarragon*
Garnish: *Watercress, parsley, or other greens*

Chop the canned or fresh tomatoes and simmer them covered over medium heat with the celery tops, onion, sweet pepper, lemon, bay leaf, and cloves until the celery and onion are soft, about 15 minutes.

Press the tomatoes through a fine food mill or strainer; discard the debris. If any seeds have come through the mesh, strain again. Taste and season highly with lemon juice, a little sugar if needed to smooth the flavor, salt and white pepper, drops of hot pepper sauce, and 1 to 1½ teaspoons Worcestershire. The flavor should be assertive, like that of a very good tomato cocktail; don't underseason, as chilling will mute the flavors.

Measure 1 cup of the seasoned tomato juice into a small pan, sprinkle the gelatin over it, and let stand 5 minutes. Dissolve over low heat, stirring. Add the mixture to 3 cups of the remaining juice.

Chill until the mixture is thicker than syrup but not yet able to hold its shape. Pour into a 4-cup mold or 6 individual molds, rinsed out with cold water.

If the avocado is included, peel and cube it and fold the chunks gently into the thickening aspic; you'll need a 6-cup mold or 8 individual molds for this version.

Cover and refrigerate until set. The aspic can be made up to 24 hours ahead.

Unmold the aspic (for tips, see page 218); garnish with watercress, parsley, or other greens. Serve with Horseradish Cream Sauce or with well-seasoned and herb-enlivened mayonnaise.

SIMPLIFYING ESCOFFIER:
Whether taken as homage to
the master or otherwise,
Creamy Tomato Aspic (to the
right) exemplifies the
simplification of a dish that's
too elaborate for anyone but a
chef. It's based on Escoffier's
tomato mousse, which was a
major production involving,
besides tomatoes, velouté
sauce, calf's-foot jelly, and
much rubbing of ingredients
through a cloth. Here, it's
much less fancy and more
feasible.

RAW MATERIALS: Good
aspic can't be made from
tomato juice, which yields a
wan and weakling dish.
Brilliantly ripe fresh
tomatoes are first choice as
raw material, but high-
quality canned tomatoes do
very well. I usually look for
tomatoes canned in Italy, but
good labels also come from
California.

CREAMY TOMATO ASPIC

Make the aspic, reducing the measurement of tomato
purée by ¼ cup; taste and add a little more lemon juice,
salt, and hot pepper sauce as needed. Omit the avocado.
Chill the mixture until it's a thick syrup. Whip ¾ cup cold
heavy cream until it barely holds its shape—don't beat it
until stiff. Fold the cream into the aspic. Chill in a 6-cup
mold, first rinsed out with cold water. Serve with the
Horseradish Cream Sauce or with mayonnaise with added
fresh herbs.

HORSERADISH CREAM SAUCE

Combine 1 cup sour cream and 2 teaspoons drained
horseradish with salt, pepper, and fresh lemon juice to
taste, adding minced parsley, chives, or other herbs if you
wish. Taste carefully; the seasoning should be emphatic.

COPING CAPABLY WITH GELATIN

Gelatin: Recipes usually call for unflavored gelatin in
units of "envelopes," which used to contain 1 tablespoon,
the amount formerly needed to jell 2 cups of liquid. The
strength of gelatin has been increased over the years, so
the quantity in a packet has decreased accordingly. Just
use 1 envelope if you should come across and want to use a
recipe calling for 1 tablespoon of gelatin.

Gelatin troubleshooting: Sometimes a gelatin mixture
won't set no matter how you beg and implore. Certain
ingredients, such as uncooked pineapple, make jelling
impossible (gelatin packages warn of this), but sometimes
the problem is caused by imprecise measuring or by the
technique used—the gelatin may have been weakened by
heating in an overly acid mixture, for example.

Solution: Usually adding a little more gelatin will
solve the glitch. Soak a little additional gelatin—say half a
packet, for 2 cups of a problem mixture that hasn't set
after several hours—in ¼ cup of the mixture for 5 minutes, then dissolve it over hot water or very low heat. Mix
it into the stubborn dishful, if it's still liquid; if it has
thickened, set its container in a bowl of hot water; stir
until it melts before mixing in the additional gelatin.

HAM SCALLOPED WITH POTATOES À LA JACQUES

or this substantial main dish I've used Jacques Pépin's method of handling the spuds for his perfectly wonderful *gratin dauphinois*; but because of the addition of ham I've added a touch of nutmeg and omitted the Swiss cheese topping that gilds the original dish. To make Jacques' original dish, see the note following the recipe.

Preheat the oven to 400°.

Peel, rinse and dry the potatoes; slice them crosswise no more than ¼ inch thick, to make about 6 cups slices.

Combine the potatoes in a sauté pan or large saucepan with the milk and cream, garlic, salt, pepper, and nutmeg. Bring to a boil over medium heat, stirring with a wooden spatula to separate the slices and to prevent sticking. Let boil for a moment or two, just until the liquid has been thickened slightly by starch released by the potatoes.

Pour the potatoes into a buttered shallow baking and serving dish—an oval dish measuring 9 × 13 × 2 inches is perfect. Arrange the ham on top in an overlapping pattern, pushing part of each slice into the potatoes but leaving part on the surface.

Set the dish on a baking sheet. Bake the potatoes in the center of the oven for about 1 hour, until potatoes are tender when probed and the top has browned lightly. Remove and let rest for 10 minutes or more before serving.

JACQUES' ORIGINAL WAY: To make enough of the original gratin to serve 8 as a superb accompaniment for a roast of beef or lamb (or a baked ham), omit the ham and nutmeg; sprinkle the top with ½ cup shredded Swiss cheese, bake as described, and there you are.

Serves 6 as a main dish

2 pounds boiling potatoes
3½ cups half-and-half, or
  2 cups milk plus 1½
  cups cream
1 large clove garlic, minced
  very fine
¾ teaspoon salt
Generous amount of white
  pepper
2 pinches of freshly grated
  nutmeg
Unsalted butter for
  coating
1 pound cooked smoked
  ham, in pieces about 3
  inches square and ¼
  inch thick

UPSIDE-DOWN FRUITED GINGER CAKE

 t fully deserves to be called a cake, but this spicy, fruity confection will be seen by gingerbread fans for what it is—a variation on the theme of "hot-water gingerbread," as it used to be described.

For the fruit layer, fresh apples, oranges, pears, or peaches are excellent, and so are canned peaches, pears, or apricots. Perhaps best are dried fruits (peaches, pears, or apricots), with their glorious intensity of flavor.

Preheat oven to 350°.

Butter and sugar layer: Melt the butter, brown sugar, and corn syrup over very low heat in a flameproof 8-inch square or 9-inch round baking pan (the pan should be 2 inches deep), stirring until the butter has melted and blended smoothly with the sugar and syrup. Remove the pan from the heat and set aside while the fruit is prepared.

Apples, peaches, or pears: Remove the skins and cores or stones; cut the fruit into ¼-inch wedges; overlap the wedges closely in the pan over the butter mixture.

Oranges: Remove the skin and all white pith; halve the oranges lengthwise; slice the halves into half-moons ¼ inch thick. Arrange the pieces close together or overlapping in the pan.

Canned fruit: Drain well; overlap slices, or lay halves hollow sides down in the pan.

Dried fruit: Soak and simmer according to package directions; cool. Drain the fruit; arrange halves in the pan with hollow sides down, or cut into wedges and make an overlapping pattern.

The cake: Measure the butter and water into a saucepan; heat, stirring, just until the butter melts. Add the molasses and orange zest; cool to lukewarm.

Sift together into a mixing bowl the flour, sugar,

Makes an 8-inch square or 9-inch round cake

FRUIT LAYER:
3 tablespoons unsalted
  butter
¼ cup (packed) light-
  brown sugar
2 tablespoons light corn
  syrup
2 or 3 firm cooking apples
  or pears or ripe peaches;
  or 2 large seedless
  oranges; or equivalent
  amounts of canned
  pears, peaches, or
  apricots; or any of the
  latter three in dried
  form, soaked and
  simmered to reconstitute

CAKE:
6 tablespoons unsalted
  butter (or margarine is
  okay here)
1 cup water

⅔ cup unsulphured
  molasses
1 tablespoon grated
  orange zest (colored rind
  only, no pith), optional
2 cups all-purpose flour
½ cup granulated sugar
2 teaspoons baking
  powder
½ teaspoon salt
¼ teaspoon baking soda
1½ teaspoons ground
  ginger
1 teaspoon ground
  cinnamon
¼ teaspoon ground
  allspice
Big pinch of ground cloves
2 large eggs, beaten
Accompaniment: Cultured
  Cream (Crème Fraîche)
  (page 269) or English
  Pouring Custard (page
  218), or lightly whipped
  sweet cream

baking powder, salt, baking soda, ginger, cinnamon, all-spice, and cloves. Add the liquids and stir just until moistened. Add the eggs and whisk until smooth. Pour the batter over the fruit. Lift the pan a few inches and drop it onto the counter a time or two to settle everything snugly.

Bake the cake 45 to 50 minutes, or until it has shrunken slightly from the sides of the pan and a cake tester emerges dry after probing the center.

Cool 5 minutes in the pan, then turn the cake out onto a serving plate. If bits of fruit stay behind in the pan, lift them with a thin spatula and fit them into place.

Serve the cake warm or at room temperature, accompanied by Cultured Cream, English Pouring Custard, or whipped cream.

To rewarm any leftover cake, wrap it loosely in foil and heat it in a 350° oven for 10 to 15 minutes.

———

JUST GINGERBREAD: Make and bake the cake as described, omitting the fruit layer; simply grease the pan. Baking time will be a few minutes shorter. Delectable when served warm with vanilla ice cream or whipped cream.

REALLY GINGERING IT UP: If there's a hand (or a mere thumb) of fresh ginger in the house, a little of it will add liveliness to the flavor of either the upside-down cake or the plain gingerbread. Grate enough of the ginger (peel it only if the skin is tough) to make between ½ and 1 teaspoon of fine pulp. The best gadget for doing this is one of the most ancient, a small Oriental plaque of white porcelain studded with tiny hooked teeth. Reduce the ground ginger by ½ teaspoon.

DINNER FOR "DOC"

Fricasseed Rabbit with Creamy Gravy (below)

*Swiss-Style Skillet Potato Cake (page 193) or
Corn Oysters (page 25)*

*Bowl of green salad dressed with oil, wine vinegar, and fresh
herbs (tarragon, chervil, or dill, plus chives and garlic),
salt and pepper*

*Springtime Fruit Tart with Meringue Lattice (page 115) or the
bread & butter variation of Blueberry & Pound Cake Summer
Pudding (page 45)*

*To drink: A light red wine, perhaps a Gamay Beaujolais or
Barbera; if you'd prefer a white, try Chenin Blanc*

Pass this by (you needn't ask permission of the author) if rabbit is not a viand that appeals to you; a strong "anti" feeling toward any foodstuff can be overcome only by experience, not by words on a page, and all I can do is encourage.

Among Americans there are many who have never tasted this meat; the main exceptions seem to be West Coasters, hunters, and those wise folk who cherish dishes from their distant homelands. So—yes, I am taking up the cudgels for this underprized delicacy. Any adventurers out there?

FRICASSEED RABBIT WITH CREAMY GRAVY

s this dish shows, rabbit meat is fine-grained, delicate, and white—actually like veal—and it also has much less fat than poultry, which is cooked in many of the same ways. Further, rabbit figures in hundreds of recipes that are worth exploring. (French bistros, for instance, could scarcely survive without it.)

Any converts in the audience, as well as those who already esteem the meat, may want to try substituting rabbit for fowl in the recipe for Bean-pot Chicken on page 185. Conversely, chicken can be substituted in this recipe, pound for pound.

Preheat the oven to 325°.

Salt and pepper the pieces of rabbit generously, then coat them with flour; shake off excess flour.

Heat a large sauté pan, chicken fryer, iron or enameled iron skillet, or a flameproof casserole over medium heat until a few drops of water dance fast when flicked in. Put in 3 tablespoons of the oil and 3 tablespoons of the butter.

As soon as the fat is hot, lay the rabbit pieces in the pan, not quite touching. Brown the pieces evenly on all sides over medium to medium-high heat, turning them as necessary and adding more oil or butter if needed. This should take 10 minutes or so; don't rush it.

When the pieces have browned, pour in the water or broth, cover the pan tightly, and set it on the center shelf of the oven.

Steam-bake the rabbit gently until the pieces are tender and the liquid is almost all gone, about 1 hour; test the meat occasionally after 45 minutes, and be sure the liquid isn't boiling the meat—turn down the heat if that threatens.

Serves 6 to 8

2 young frying rabbits, about 2½ pounds each, disjointed (see Buying Rabbit, page 162)

Salt and pepper, to taste

All-purpose flour for dredging and for the gravy (or use 2 tablespoons cornstarch for the gravy)

¼ cup corn or peanut oil

4 tablespoons (½ stick) unsalted butter

2 cups water or chicken broth

3 cups milk, regular or low-fat, or more if needed

Garnish: Parsley, coarsely chopped or in small sprigs

BUYING RABBIT: Unless a local rancher raises meat rabbits, the supermarket freezer is the best bet for ready-to-cook meat.

Young rabbits, good for this recipe or for frying or sautéing, are about 2 months old and weigh 2½ to 3 pounds.

Slightly older animals, up to 14 weeks, are considered "roasters"; mature rabbits, up to a year old, are for stewing and such other long-cooked dishes as *hasenpfeffer*.

Wild rabbit, with its gamier flavor, is favored by connoisseurs for such dishes as civet of rabbit, highly seasoned with red wine, bacon, and onions, and for *hasenpfeffer*, too.

FRICASSEED RABBIT WITH CREAMY GRAVY (CONTINUED)

Transfer the rabbit pieces to a warmed platter, cover them with foil to keep them warm, and set the cooking pan over a stove burner.

If the pan contains too much fat to suit you, spoon off the excess. Add 3 cups milk and heat over low heat to simmering, scraping up and stirring in all the browned bits.

Stir 3½ tablespoons of flour (or 2 tablespoons cornstarch) with enough water or milk to make a thin paste. Stir it into the simmering liquid and cook, stirring, until the gravy has thickened, then let it boil, stirring, for a minute or two.

If the gravy is too thick or too thin, adjust its consistency with a little more milk or a very little additional thickening (be careful not to make library paste).

Taste the gravy and add salt and pepper to season it well. At this point, it may be sieved (or whirled in a blender) to make the brown speckles less noticeable, or it may be left appealingly natural; it's up to the cook. If the gravy is lumpy despite your best efforts, press it through a strainer or blender-whizz it, then reheat it if necessary.

Garnish the platter with parsley and pass the gravy at the table in a bowl or a boat.

———

STEPPING UP THE SEASONINGS: The fricassee above has minimal seasonings, really just salt and pepper; but a pinch or two of thyme leaves, a torn bay leaf, even a tablespoonful of diced onion, may be sprinkled over the pieces before they are baked. Further gussying-up—with sliced mushrooms, or browned, diced lean bacon, or both mushrooms and bacon—will reward, and white wine may be substituted for all or part of the cooking liquid.

DISJOINTING A WHOLE RABBIT: This is easier than cutting up a chicken. With a large sharp knife, disjoint the front legs at the shoulder; detach the hind legs at the joint; divide the saddle crosswise into two or more sections, depending on the size of the rabbit, and the job is done.

AND NOW FOR A CHICKEN COMPLETELY DIFFERENT...

Tapenade of a Different Color (below) served with cream cheese and toasted thin-sliced French bread

Lemon Chicken My Way (below)

Orzo "Risotto" (page 122), or hot curly noodles, or buttered brown rice or domestic Basmati rice

Chilled arugula (roquette) sprigs tossed with balsamic vinegar, or a bowl of chilled watercress sprigs accompanied by a shaker of coarse salt

Richard's Recaptured Angel Cake (below), with sugared berries and lightly whipped cream

To drink: *A full-bodied white wine—perhaps a choice Chardonnay*

One or two uncommon things are found in this menu, which is perhaps more suited to cool weather than warm. The tapenade starts the proceedings partly because Sally Kovalchick, highly appreciated editor of this book and longtime friend, liked its ancestral version so much, and partly because I find it altogether excellent as a kickoff for a dinner menu featuring Lemon Chicken.

My lemon chicken is not a bit like the Chinese-American (or American-Chinese?) dish of the same name, for which Pearl's Restaurant, in Manhattan, was especially famous; that chicken is flavored with a great slug of bottled lemon extract, and very good it is. The chicken in creamy-tart sauce here is especially splendid when made with Preserved Lemons—you can fix your own in the way described in this section—but the dish is not to be sneezed at when prepared with fresh citrus.

The dessert for this dinner is the best angel cake I've ever met, with its perfect accompaniments, fresh berries and cream.

A TAPENADE OF A DIFFERENT COLOR

 n my last book, *Fancy Pantry*, I included my favorite version of the dark, gleaming, and zesty Provençal mixture of oil-cured olives, anchovies, and capers called "tapenade," an appetizing compound that can be a spread for canapés, a stuffing for hard-cooked eggs, an inspiriter of drab salad dressings, and even a sauce for pasta. As I was traveling around the country shamelessly promoting that book, the food-wise host of a Boston radio program told me of tasting a tapenade of green olives. It sounded as good as he assured me it was.

Once home, I worked out the recipe below for a tapenade of half green Spanish olives and half black California olives—a good use for the Californians, which are bland and boring when served "straight." (It can also be made with green olives alone.) Either way the tapenade is drab looking (olive drab?), but its flavor makes up for any deficiencies in glamour. Serve it with thin-sliced and toasted French bread or something simple and not too salty in the cracker line—water biscuits, for instance, or lightly toasted American-style matzos.

As it keeps indefinitely in the fridge, this tapenade, like any version of the Provençal original, is useful to have on hand, especially if cocktail-hour food is frequently in demand. It's much appreciated by palates attuned to complicated and zesty flavors, so you may want to step up the seasonings after you've tasted this, possibly adding more capers, more anchovies, more garlic, and/or more lemon juice or herbs—a pinch of well-crumbled rosemary or oregano can be a pleasant addition. The tapenade is best served at room temperature.

THE BUSINESS OF TAPENADE: Antonin Carème, considered one of the immortals of French chefdom, said *"My business is to provoke your appetite; it is not for me to regulate it."*

That could also be said for tapenade; it will get you started, all right, but the rest is up to you.

Makes about 1⅓ cups

10-ounce jar large
  unstuffed green Spanish
  olives, drained, or half
  the green olives in the jar
  plus about ¾ to 1 cup
  pitted California black
  olives
2-ounce can anchovy
  fillets in olive oil,
  drained; or more to taste
1½ tablespoons, or more
  to taste, drained capers
1 large clove garlic,
  chopped
½ teaspoon finely
  crumbled dried thyme
¼ cup full-flavored olive
  oil, the fruitier the better
Freshly ground pepper,
  optional
A few drops of lemon
  juice, optional

A TAPENADE OF A DIFFERENT COLOR (CONTINUED)

Pit the green olives, unless you have succeeded in finding a pitted jarful (I haven't).

Chuck the olives into a blender or food processor with all the other ingredients except the pepper and lemon juice; start out with the minimum measurement of an ingredient where a range is indicated.

Run the machine, scraping down the sides of the container occasionally, until the texture of the tapenade suits you; green olives are firm-textured, not to say hard, so it takes a while to produce the smoothly puréed texture that's preferable for this mixture.

Taste and add, if you wish, a little freshly ground pepper and a very little lemon juice. If you judge it's a good idea, more anchovies, capers, thyme, or oil may be added to taste and the puréeing repeated.

The tapenade is now ready to serve if it's needed the same day but, like most savory mixtures, it improves if it's given time for mellowing; forward-looking hosts will note that it can—even should—be made ahead and refrigerated, well covered (it's pungent) for indefinite storage. If your plans permit, try to remove it from the refrigerator well ahead of serving time.

LEMON CHICKEN MY WAY

nce upon a time I made up a dish of chicken baked with lemon slices, a little tarragon, and cream—one of those "Why not?" notions—knowing that the cream would inevitably curdle and prevent the dish from looking as pretty as a kitchen calendar. The chicken was exceptionally tender, lemony, and lightly redolent of tarragon, and the creamy curds, it turned out, were easily smoothed for a handsomer sauce. With scarcely a change (other than sometimes using Preserved Lemons, as discussed on page 168), there have been many return engagements.

Serves 6

A 3½ pound chicken, or 3 pounds leg quarters, if preferred
3 tablespoons unsalted butter
1 tablespoon vegetable oil
Salt and pepper, to taste
1 teaspoon dried tarragon leaves, or 2 to 3 teaspoons fresh tarragon
1 fully ripe medium lemon, scrubbed, or wedges of Preserved Lemons (page 168)
2 cups heavy cream or undiluted evaporated milk
2 tablespoons all-purpose flour
1 teaspoon finely minced onion (see Onion Juice or Pulp, below)
Chicken broth, if needed

ONION JUICE OR PULP:
When only onion juice or a little finely minced onion is needed, as for Lemon Chicken, it's a fiddly job to haul out board and knife or a miniature chopper. Instead, press chunks of onion through a garlic press, or grate an onion on a ginger grater, which reduces food to a fine pulp with little effort.

Preheat the oven to 375°.

Disjoint the chicken into serving pieces, or separate the leg quarters into thighs and drumsticks. Rinse; wipe dry.

Melt the butter with the oil in a skillet over medium heat and cook the chicken pieces briefly on all sides, just until the flesh has firmed and the skin has become golden.

Arrange the pieces, skin side up, in a single layer in a large shallow baking dish. Season the pieces moderately with salt and pepper, then sprinkle them evenly with the dried or fresh tarragon leaves.

Remove and discard the ends of the lemon, cutting into them where the flesh begins. Halve them lengthwise, then slice the halves paper-thin; remove the seeds. Lay the slices over the chicken pieces. (If you are using Preserved Lemons, see Chicken with Moroccan Lemons, below.)

Whisk together the cream, flour, and onion. Spoon the mixture over the chicken, covering the lemon well. Cover the chicken with foil, crimping it lightly to the sides of the baking dish.

Bake the lemon chicken in the center of the oven until very tender, about 40 minutes. After 20 minutes, baste it occasionally with pan juices, re-covering the pan loosely with the foil. If necessary, add a little chicken broth or water to the dish to keep the sauce liquid enough for basting the chicken.

To serve, lift the chicken pieces with any lemon bits clinging to them and keep them warm in a deep platter (or return them to the baking dish after pouring out the liquid for the next step). Strain the sauce (or lift out the remaining lemon scraps) and whisk it or buzz it in a blender or food processor until smooth. Reheat the sauce; taste it carefully and season it with salt and pepper as needed, then pour it over the chicken.

CHICKEN WITH MOROCCAN LEMONS: I first made this chicken dish with fresh lemons—which should be fully ripe (heavy and fragrant and soft, not light and hard). Lately I've found it's also remarkably good when made with lemons preserved in salt, a staple of North African cuisine that has many uses—I put the peel into salads and sauces in place of fresh lemon juice and/or peel.

To use Preserved Lemons in Lemon Chicken: Allow a wedge to each section of chicken. Rinse the lemon wedges, and either keep or discard the soft pulp, as you prefer; if you retain the pulp, use less salt when seasoning the chicken. In other respects, follow the recipe.

PRESERVED LEMONS

 raditionally, preserved lemons are salted almost whole, with a couple of long, deep slashes in each; done that way, the preserving takes several weeks. Expert cooks of Moroccan food have devised shortcut methods like the one below, which is based on Paula Wolfert's.

Experimentally, I've shortened the preserving time even more by slicing the lemons into sixteen wedges instead of Paula's eight; so divided, the lemons are ready to use in three or four days instead of a week, if you're in a hurry to taste their delights.

The Lemon Chicken in this menu doesn't exhaust the ways to use this condiment/seasoning/preserve. Because either the peel alone or the peel and the pulp together are rich and mellow in flavor, in contrast to the sharpness of fresh lemon zest and pulp, they are marvelous in sauces and salad dressings. I've been known to put a section or two into beef stew, and the lemons are an optional ingredient of the Quick Citrus Coleslaw on page 129.

Makes about 1 ½ cups

2 fully ripe, bright-skinned lemons
6 tablespoons coarse (kosher) salt or sea salt
½ cup fresh lemon juice, more if needed
Olive oil, optional

Scrub the lemons and wipe them dry. Cut them lengthwise into 8 wedges apiece. Toss with the coarse salt, then pack into a small jar; add enough lemon juice to cover. Close the jar with a tight lid and leave it at room temperature, shaking it daily. Be sure that the salty juice covers the pieces well; add more lemon juice if it subsides enough to expose them.

The lemons are ready when translucent, about a week (or less, as noted, if they are sliced thinner.) Refrigerate for storage; make sure the pieces remain well covered with liquid. If you like, a layer of olive oil may be poured in to exclude air, but I don't bother.

The lemons keep for months. You can tell they're beginning to sneak over the hill when their fresh, lemony scent begins to remind you, a little, of varnish; then it's time to fix up another jar.

RICHARD'S RECAPTURED ANGEL CAKE

uarantee: Make this cake exactly the way Richard directs and it will be taller, silkier, and incomparably more comely than garden-variety angel cakes. Richard's way (whose publishing history, so to speak, is outlined after the recipe) has been put to the test over a lot of years and by many cooks. The secret (it's no secret, actually) is putting the cake together carefully; there's not much variation between angel-food recipes, or much room for improvement in their details.

Makes a tall 10-inch tube cake

1½ cups egg whites (from about 12 large eggs)
1 cup cake flour, sifted before measuring
1⅓ cups sifted superfine sugar
½ teaspoon salt
1 teaspoon cream of tartar
1 tablespoon strained fresh lemon juice
1 teaspoon cold water
2 teaspoons excellent vanilla extract
¼ teaspoon almond extract, optional
Optional topping:
  Favorite thin icing
Optional accompaniment:
  Sugared fruit, fruit sauce, whipped cream, or combination

First, scrub a 10-inch loose-bottomed tube pan, your mixing bowl or the large bowl of your mixer, and the mixer whisk or beaters, using detergent and hot water; rinse and dry them well (the point is to be sure there's no trace of grease on the equipment).

Place the egg whites in the now spotless beating bowl and let them come to room temperature (about 70°).

Preheat the oven to 350°.

Sift the flour and sugar separately onto sheets of waxed paper, then check the measurements again; the flour should be spooned lightly into the cup and leveled. Add the salt and ⅓ cup of the sugar to the flour and sift the mixture 3 or 4 times again, holding the sifter high for maximum aeration.

Beat the room-temperature egg whites at slow speed until they are foamy; add the cream of tartar, lemon juice, water, and flavoring and beat the whites at high speed without stopping until they will form peaks but are still moist and glossy, not dry.

Add 2 tablespoons of the remaining sifted sugar and beat it in at moderately low speed until incorporated; repeat the additions of sugar, incorporating each completely, until all sugar has been added.

USHERING IN THE ANGELS: The history of angel-food cake begins and ends with a question—who actually devised it? No real answer as yet, wrote Meryle Evans in that magazine piece, but she notes that an 1883 cookbook claimed "the latest and best" recipe for angel food, indicating that other versions had been around for a while.

What started the cake on its lightfooted way? The Dover rotary beater, Meryle concludes; the Dover, patented in 1869, took the aching muscles out of making cakes and meringues, which had previously involved hours—that's a plural—of beating eggs by hand.

RICHARD'S RECAPTURED ANGEL CAKE (CONTINUED)

Sift about one-fourth of the flour mixture over the whites and fold in lightly with a spatula; repeat, making four additions in all and being careful not to overfold.

Pour the batter lightly into the dry, scrubbed-out tube pan; circle a thin metal spatula or knife blade twice through the batter, once near the tube and once near the rim of the pan. Smooth the top.

Bake the cake 45 minutes, or until it has shrunken very slightly from the sides of the pan and springs back when the top is pressed lightly.

Invert the pan on its supporting legs (or support the central tube in a narrow-necked bottle) and let it cool, hanging in its pan, until completely cold, which will take about 1½ hours.

Release the cake by running a long knife blade around the sides of the pan and, if necessary, around the central tube. Turn it onto a serving plate.

If you like, glaze the cake with any favorite thin icing, or serve it with sugared fruit, a fruit sauce, whipped cream, or any combination that appeals.

To serve, slice the cake gently with a finely serrated blade, or use a toothed cake divider made for the purpose. Angel-food cake keeps for days if protected from the air.

RECAPTURING A RECIPE: The merits of this formula were established a few years ago when an extremely chic food-and-drink magazine I worked for was in need of an angel-food recipe to embellish an article by food historian Meryle Evans. The test-kitchen crew wasn't at all pleased with the recipes they were testing, and the copy deadline was close when I recalled that my husband, a book publisher by trade, had rather eccentrically mastered the art of the angel cake in his youth. Over the weekend he baked a sample, which turned out to be the fairest cake of all, and obligingly wrote out the directions. The recipe, which was published without credit to the modest chap, must have been admired, judging from the number of times I've seen it since, printed verbatim, in other publications. (It has also appeared, with credit, in the *New York Times*.)

THE BEST POT ROAST

Platter of crudités—*sweet red pepper strips, sliced fennel, celery, scallions, or other raw vegetables, with Dipping Vinaigrette (page 101)*

Pristine Pot Roast and Gravy (below)
Hot curly egg noodles sprinkled with pan-toasted sesame seeds (stir seeds briefly in a skillet over low heat until golden and fragrant)

Red Cabbage Braised with Cranberries (below)

Pumpkin Brûlée (below) or Frozen Maple Mousse (page 187)

🌷

To drink: Red wine, preferably a full-bodied one—Burgundy, a fine Rioja, or a Cabernet Sauvignon

Here you are, "the best pot roast" . . . as simple and savory and perfect as pot roast can get, at least in my experience. With it, hot noodles to be blessed with the deep-bronze gravy and, on one side, a beautiful, deep-red, tart-sweet compound of red cabbage and cranberries devised one crisp winter evening for just such a dinner as this.

For dessert, there's a pumpkin pudding topped, *brûlée*-fashion, with crusty caramelized sugar. Alternatively, the pudding can be glazed with honey and a sprinkling of candied ginger.

PRISTINE POT ROAST AND GRAVY

ulinary historians could pile up dozens of distinctive recipes for pot-roasted beef, which has been seasoned somewhere in the world, by someone, with everything from anchovies to the zest of an orange.

There have been many regional, ethnic, and family claims to "the best" pot roast, but for this partisan, the best pot roast is the simplest—a solid cut of beef, long gentle cooking, and no fuss. The gravy is burnished bronze, silky-sheer but meaty and concentrated. Need more be said?

Serves 8 or more

A solid cut of beef, 4 pounds or slightly more (see The Beef for the Pot, right)
Salt and freshly ground pepper, as needed
Beef fat, oil, or other fat for the pot
1 large onion, peeled and halved

GRAVY:
Water or beef broth
Optional: *Bay leaf; pinch of thyme; drops of onion juice (from onion slice squeezed in a garlic press)*
1 tablespoon cornstarch per cup of gravy, stirred with a little cold water
Salt and pepper, as needed

Preheat the oven to 300°.

Wipe all surfaces of the meat dry with paper towels. Rub roast generously with freshly ground pepper and rather lightly with salt.

Spread a little fat or oil in a heavy Dutch oven or other thick pot with a tight cover. Set the pot over medium-high heat until the fat is almost smoking. Sear the roast on all sides, turning it often with tongs, until it is lightly and evenly browned all over; if necessary, lower the heat as you sear the meat.

Put the onion halves face down on the bottom of the pot; cover the pot tightly and bake the meat in the oven for about 3 hours (allow 45 minutes per pound, in general), turning the meat occasionally. When the meat is very tender—investigate it with a long fork—move it to a platter, cover it loosely with foil, and let it rest for 15 minutes or so. (It may be held, lightly covered, in the turned-off oven if the door is left open.)

Gravy: Skim the fat from the liquid. Gradually add water or beef broth to the pan juices to make 2 to 3 cups, depending on how strong the flavor of the juices may be. Add, if you like, the optional bay leaf, thyme, and onion juice.

Bring to a boil over direct heat, scraping up and dissolving any brown bits clinging to the pan. Stir in enough of the cornstarch and water mixture to thicken it lightly; simmer for a few minutes after the gravy boils. Taste and add salt as needed, and add plenty of pepper. Strain into a warmed gravy boat.

Serving: For family-style presentation, carve the meat, arrange the slices overlapping on a hot platter, and pour some of the gravy around and (sparingly) over the meat. Pass the remaining gravy at the table.

A NOT-SO-PRISTINE POT: For anyone unpersuaded of the peerlessness of pot roast with very few seasonings, here's an in-between version: After the beef is brown, stir 1 cup chopped onions in the pot with the meat until golden. Add 1 or 2 garlic cloves, minced, and 2 cups high-quality drained canned tomatoes, a bay leaf, ½ teaspoon dried thyme, and ½ cup beef broth. Cook in the oven as described, basting the meat with the vegetables occasionally and adding more broth if needed. At the end, thicken the chunky gravy or not, as you prefer.

THE BEEF FOR THE POT

Pot-roasting can tame pretty sinewy meat, so the cuts to use come from the chuck or the round, not the gold-coast regions that yield porterhouses and tenderloins. The best bet is a solid chunk of meat, although bone-in cuts, or boned, rolled, and tied meat, are often "potted." A rump or bottom-round cut would be my choice. I like especially the one that's called "tip of the rump," at least in some areas; if you know a living, breathing butcher, ask him what it's called locally. Whatever the cut you use, it should not be overladen with fat.

How much to buy: Allow at least ⅓ pound per person, better ½ pound. The hidden agenda here is leftovers, which you should be able to count on unless the original eaters are carnivores famished by long abstinence. In which case, you'll need the larger allowance, and forget about the sequel.

Leftovers: Open-faced hot beef sandwiches are the highest and best use of the bits and pieces. Heat pot roast slices or scraps in left-over gravy; arrange on toasted bread; ladle the gravy over the top.

AROUND THE WORLD OF POT-ROASTING BEEF:
Boeuf à la Mode, French, but known everywhere; *sauerbraten,* German; *sweet-and-sour pot roast,* a sort of sauerbraten with sweetening, known in many renditions; *all the versions of "braised beef,"* from many countries; *pot-roasted brisket,* a notably good dish in Jewish cookery; *carbonnade flamande,* Belgian pot roast with beef, often made with cut-up meat; *Swiss steak,* actually a pot roast; *Hungarian pot roast,* with caraway and paprika; *Southwestern-style "barbecued" pot roast; Italian pot roasts,* sometimes braised in white wine; *Swedish slottstek,* seasoned with anchovies, brandy, and cream; *Catalan pot roast* with vegetables, red wine, and white beans; and more—many more.

RED CABBAGE BRAISED WITH CRANBERRIES

lazing red in color, vividly sweet-and-tart in its palatal impact, this uncommon vegetable and fruit combination is a perfect match for baked ham, or roasted or grilled red meat, or the traditional main-course dishes for Thanksgiving dinner. It's perhaps best of all, though, with a pristine, deeply beefy pot roast, as here. *A bonus:* Because it's quite keepable, the crunchy red cabbage can be kept on hand and dispensed straight from the refrigerator as a relish with sandwiches, or chicken salad, or cold meat.

The dish came into being when I was thinking of the unappetizing blue-purplish color of red cabbage that has been cooked without the big slosh of acid—usually wine or vinegar—called for in standard recipes for the vegetable. It was an autumn evening as I mused about the chameleon nature of the crimson cabbage I was cutting up, so I reached into the freezer for cranberries and tried combining the two. A delicious dish was created by the pairing, and the cabbage stayed a deep, deep red in the fruity sauce made by the berries.

Vinegar isn't essential to the looks of the dish if a sufficiently large measure of cranberries is included, but I find it functions as a puller-together of flavors as well as a color preserver, so I pour in a little.

If you'd like to braise the cabbage and cranberries "straight," without including vinegar, increase the berries to 3 cups; cook them with the water until they pop, then toss in the cabbage and the remaining seasonings, except the vinegar, and complete the cooking as described.

CRANBERRIES AS KEEPERS: Cranberries in the freezer are an inspiration the year around—you can have this relish or other cranberry dishes in spring or even midsummer if you've tossed a few bags into the freezer, just as they come, during the short cranberry season. They'll keep perfectly for at least a year. To use, rinse quickly while still frozen, pick out the occasional stem or mashed specimen, and the berries are ready to go.

Serves 6 as a vegetable, more as a relish

Small head (around 1
  pound) red cabbage
2 to 3 tablespoons white-
  wine or Oriental rice
  vinegar
1 cup water
⅓ to ½ cup (packed)
  light-brown sugar
Salt, to taste
2 cups (½ pound)
  cranberries, fresh or
  frozen
Unsalted butter, optional

Quarter, core, and shred the cabbage, the finer the better; you should have about 8 cups.

Toss the cabbage shreds with 2 tablespoons of the vinegar and the water in a nonreactive metal pot (stainless steel or enamel). Cook over high heat until wilted, tossing with a fork. Add ⅓ cup of the sugar and a little salt; cover and braise over low heat until tender-crisp, 10 to 15 minutes; add a little water if sticking threatens.

Add the cranberries, toss, re-cover, and cook until the berries have popped and the sauce has become syrupy and deep red, 7 to 10 minutes.

Taste; add sweetness or tartness with remaining vinegar and sugar, if needed; adjust the salt.

Serve hot as a side dish, adding a little butter if you like, or allow to mellow in the refrigerator overnight. (This reheats well.)

If served as a relish, taste after chilling and add more wine vinegar and/or sugar if you think they're needed—chilling may inhibit the flavors.

Keeps, refrigerated, for weeks.

PUMPKIN BRÛLÉE

f this were baked in a pastry shell it would be our family's traditional Thanksgiving pie, which we make from a recipe we've had quite a while. Latterly, Thanksgiving appetites that seem to be dwindling (or more prudent) have prompted me to bake the filling alone in a handsome dish, topped off by a crisp lid of broiled sugar borrowed from the crème brûlée of classic chefdom. The dessert then offers most of the pleasures of a pie but involves less work for the cook and imposes fewer calories on the company.

The top of the pudding can be glossed with honey and sprinkled with candied ginger, as described in the recipe, if you'd like that better than the caramelized topping.

Serves 8 or more

4 eggs
Scant 2 cups puréed
pumpkin (1-pound can)
or sieved fresh pumpkin
(see Preparing Fresh
Pumpkin, below)
2 teaspoons ground
cinnamon
2 teaspoons ground ginger
¾ teaspoon ground
cardamom, optional
¾ teaspoon salt
1¾ to 2 cups granulated
sugar
5 tablespoons all-purpose
flour
3½ cups whole milk, or
combined milk and
cream
Unsalted butter or cooking
spray for the baking dish

TOPPING:
Light-brown sugar, 1 to
1½ cups; or a little
honey and 3 tablespoons
minced candied ginger
Optional accompaniment:
Sour cream, or whipped
cream, or vanilla ice
cream

TORCH SONG: Some chefs
fire up a small blowtorch for
browning or caramelizing the
top of certain foods. You
might want to try this for
Pumpkin Brûlée, if there's a
blowtorch in the family
toolbox.

PUMPKIN BRÛLÉE (CONTINUED)

Preheat the oven to 325°, with a shelf placed in the center.

Beat the eggs well in a mixing bowl; add in order, beating after each addition, the pumpkin, spices, salt, sugar, flour, and liquid. Whisk well.

Butter or coat with cooking spray a shallow baking dish that can go to the table; an oval about 13 inches long and 2 inches deep is about right. Pour the pumpkin mixture through a sieve into the dish. Set the dish on a baking sheet, then put the whole business into the oven.

Bake for 45 minutes, then check for doneness; the pudding is ready when its center shakes only slightly when the dish is jiggled.

If you're going to add the caramelized topping, cool on a rack, then cover and refrigerate the pudding for several hours or overnight.

Alternative topping: Glaze the top of the hot pudding with a little honey and scatter the minced candied ginger over it. This version can be served without chilling.

Caramelized topping: Within 2 or 3 hours of serving time, preheat the broiler. Sieve light-brown sugar over the top of the pudding to make a layer ¼ inch deep. Broil the topping a few inches from the element until it is browned and brittle; stand right there and watch, because the sugar can scorch in a twinkling. If necessary, move the pudding dish to caramelize the topping evenly. Refrigerate again.

Serve directly from the dish, adding to the servings, if you're having sauce, a dab of sour cream or whipped cream, or a spoonful of soft vanilla ice cream.

PREPARING FRESH PUMPKIN: If you can buy a "pie" pumpkin—not a jack o'lantern type—here is how to prepare the flesh for use in recipes. (Winter squash is also fine—some piemakers prefer it to pumpkin.)

Wash and split the pumpkin (or squash) and scrape out the seeds. If it's large, cut it into chunks. Bake the pieces at 325° in a covered dish until they are completely tender; allow an hour at least (this is a job to do when you need to be around the kitchen for something else). Cool the pieces, then scrape the flesh from the skins and sieve it.

Any surplus sieved pumpkin can be frozen for the future; just pack it in a plastic container or heavyweight freezer bag and store it away.

WADDLING INTO DUCK HEAVEN

Iron-Pot Duckling (below)

Red-Cherry Rice Pilaff (below)

Celery & Sweet-Corn Salad with Lemon & Cumin (below)

Honey-Pecan Pie (below) or its Maple-Walnut variation, with Cultured Cream (Crème Fraîche) (page 269); or Cream-Filled Boston Stack Cake (page 196)

To Drink: A rich and tangy red wine, perhaps a Zinfandel or a Petite Sirah, or an excellent Bordeaux

I t's not hard to understand why people order duckling more frequently in restaurants than in butcher shops—ducks, which are both very bony and very fat, aren't especially easy to cook perfectly, and usually they *aren't* cooked anywhere near perfectly. Which is why I treasure and use the foolproof and fussless method outlined in the recipe below. Try; you'll believe.

To complement the duckling there is a dish of rice cooked with sour cherries—a savory combination that goes remarkably well with the bird—and an unusual crunchy celery and corn salad. For dessert it's hard to choose between Honey-Pecan Pie and a truly stacked version of Boston cream pie, so I've included both recipes.

IRON-POT DUCKLING

It is to be regretted that domestication has seriously deteriorated the moral character of the duck. In a wild state, he is a faithful husband . . . but no sooner is he domesticated than he becomes polygamous, and makes nothing of owning ten or a dozen wives at a time.

—MRS. ISABELLA BEETON, *THE BOOK OF HOUSEHOLD MANAGEMENT*, 1861

few fat white Peking ducks that came from China in clipper days were the start of vast flocks here on Long Island, flocks that until recently went off to market, proudly labeled as to origin, from saltwater farms on our East End bays. Duck raising has almost vanished under pressure of new marinas and vacation homes, and "genuine Long Island duckling" has been largely supplanted by Midwestern birds.

A memento of the days of the great white flocks is a little recipe book from the duck farmers' co-op; my copy came from the Mecox Bay Poultry Farm, whose location on a salt-water creek in the midst of "the Hamptons" doomed it to disappearance in favor of condominiums.

This recipe is adapted from that little book. It yields succulent and almost fatless duckling; I've simply replaced the farmers' packaged poultry seasoning and paprika with other choices. (Their seasonings are quite good, though, if you're fond of sage.)

A duckling weighing 4½ to 5 pounds will serve only 4 modest eaters or 2 or 3 hungry folks, as a good deal of its weight is fat and bone. So, to serve 6 you'll need to allow 2 ducklings, no two ways about it. (If there should be leftover duck, cut it up for a salad with celery, mayonnaise, and apple.)

BESIDES THE IRON POT...
If there's an electric skillet in your cupboard, it's ideal for this job; start with a cold pan and set the control at 350°. The duckling can also be braised in the oven; put it into a cold heavy pot and the covered pot into a preheated 350° oven. The turning intervals and cooking time are the same.

Serves 6

2 domestic ducklings, 4 to
   5 pounds each,
   quartered (see Cutting
   Up a Duck, right)
2 tablespoons coarse
   (kosher) salt
1½ teaspoons freshly
   ground coarse pepper
2 teaspoons crumbled
   dried sweet marjoram
   (thyme leaves may be
   substituted)
4 large bay leaves,
   crumbled

Wipe the duck pieces, sprinkle the skin side with half of the salt, pepper, and herbs, and place the pieces skin side down in a single layer in two heavy cold 10-inch skillets or Dutch ovens (or a single big pan, if it will hold them). Sprinkle the remaining seasonings over the duck. (Don't worry about too much seasoning—there's a strategy here.)

Cover the pan(s) and cook the duckling over medium heat for 20 minutes at a slow pace (you'll hear gentle sizzling). Turn the pieces, re-cover, and cook for another 20 minutes; finally, turn the pieces skin side down again and cook for a final 20 minutes, or until there is no fat to speak of under the skin and the tender pieces are handsomely browned. During cooking, don't drain off the fat at any point, although there will be a lot of it.

Drain the duckling quarters and arrange skin side up on a platter; serve promptly, or hold for a few minutes in a warm oven.

Strain and refrigerate the leftover fat, which is a savory asset for use in cooking.

CUTTING UP A DUCK: Most ducks are frozen whole, with the cutting up left to the cook. If fresh duckling—better yet, cut-up fresh ducklings—aren't available, thaw frozen ducklings in their wrappings in the refrigerator; allow 24 hours. (Or do the thawing in a microwave according to the oven manufacturer's directions.)

Cut each duckling into 4 portions, using a sharp boning knife, utility knife, or poultry shears. First cut out the backbone: if using a knife, stand the beast on its bottom and cut straight down each side of the backbone; if using shears, lay the duck on its breast for the operation. Cut the legs away from the body; press on the breast piece to flatten it, then halve the breast lengthwise (this is not difficult, as duckling bones are soft). Cut off the wing tips.

You'll have 4 quarters for cooking, plus the backbone, wing tips, gizzard, heart, and neck for the stockpot, and the liver. The liver can be frozen until enough poultry livers (chicken, turkey, duck, goose) have been accumulated to make a pâté. A screwtop jar makes a good organ bank for the collection.

DUCK BROTH: Put wing tips, neck, backbone, and giblets (but not the liver) into a pot with onion, bay leaf, celery, parsley, a little thyme, and a pinch of salt; simmer with water to cover until the broth tastes rich, about 1-½ hours. Strain and refrigerate for up to 2 or 3 days, or remove the coagulated fat and freeze the broth for longer storage. Fully as useful as chicken broth.

RED-CHERRY RICE PILAFF

 his fruited rice was inspired by one-half of a recipe by cookbook writer Marian Tracy, a lady who got around the cuisines of the world on behalf of stay-at-homes long before Julia Child hit France. Although she didn't say so, the pattern must have come from the Middle East.

During my student days at Columbia the complete dish, topped with chops and baked, was served to guests more than once. Since then I've adapted the rice half of Marian's recipe by adding savory seasonings and switching the cooking method. The resulting "pilotto" is halfway between a risotto and a pilaff.

Serves 6

3 tablespoons rendered
  duck fat or unsalted
  butter
1 medium red onion,
  chopped (about ⅔ cup)
1 cup long-grain or
  converted (parboiled)
  rice
16-ounce can red sour
  cherries, with their juice
½ cup dry red wine
2½ cups, or as needed,
  strong chicken or duck
  broth
Grated zest (colored rind
  only, no pith) of half a
  lemon
3-inch cinnamon stick,
  broken once or twice
1 medium bay leaf
Salt, to taste
Freshly grated nutmeg

Melt the fat in a heavy nonreactive pot; add the onion and stir over medium-low heat until the onion is soft, which will take from 5 to 7 minutes, depending; don't brown it. Add the rice and cook it, stirring it often with a wooden spoon, until the grains are translucent, perhaps another 8 to 10 minutes.

Add the cherries and juice, red wine, about a cup of the chicken broth, the lemon zest, cinnamon stick, and bay leaf. Stir briefly with a fork, bring to a boil, lower the heat, and simmer uncovered until most of the liquid has evaporated.

Add about half a cup of broth, cover partially, and continue to simmer, adding a little more broth as needed to prevent sticking, until the rice is done, about 25 minutes in all. Don't stir the rice as it cooks or it may become gummy; instead, shake the pan vigorously from time to time.

Stir the pilaff lightly with a fork, taste, and season with salt (the quantity will depend on the saltiness of the broth) and a pinch of nutmeg. Fork the rice lightly again, cover it, and let it rest and compose its flavors for a few minutes before transferring it to a warm serving dish, preferably one with a cover.

CELERY & SWEET-CORN SALAD WITH LEMON & CUMIN

iltproof, crunchy and subtly flavored, this salad is an ideal make-ahead for a buffet. If the celery is tender, there's no need to "string" it; if it's slouching toward maturity, I'd remove the strings with a swivel peeler before chopping it. Either way, include as many of the celery leaves as possible, if they are fresh and perky. In seasoning, follow your tastebuds: the measurements are guides, not rules.

Combine the celery and corn in a serving bowl. In another bowl, whisk together the oil, lemon juice, salt, mustard, and cumin. Taste the dressing, then add more of anything that seems to be needed—the flavor should be quite vivacious.

Pour the dressing over the salad, toss it, and let it marinate until serving time. Toss the salad again with the chives and parsley, taste it one last time, and make any needed adjustments in the seasoning.

TOASTING CUMIN: Stir whole cumin seeds in a skillet over moderate heat until the seeds smell toasty and have browned lightly, a matter of a couple of minutes. For use, grind in a small mortar or spice mill. Whole, toasted seed may be shelf-stored in a sealed jar, so it's sensible to toast more seed than you need while you're about it.

CELERY & CABBAGE SLAW: No, not a slaw made with "celery cabbage" (another name for napa or Chinese cabbage), but a variation on the theme of the preceding recipe. Just replace the corn with about 2 cups, well packed, of finely shredded young cabbage. Omit the cumin but increase the mustard a little, and add a pinch or two of sugar.

Serves 6

3 cups thinly sliced or diced celery, including leaves

1½ cups golden whole-kernel canned or frozen corn, drained

¼ cup vegetable oil

3 tablespoons, or more, fresh lemon juice

1 teaspoon salt

1 teaspoon, or more, mustard powder

½ teaspoon, or more, ground toasted cumin seed (see Toasting Cumin, right)

1 tablespoon, or more, snipped chives

2 tablespoons, or more, minced parsley, preferably Italian (flat-leaf) parsley

HONEY-PECAN PIE

verybody is entitled to a helping of pecan pie once a year, and this is the pie. It's less sweet than most—which gives the tastebuds a better chance to perceive its charms—and it has a higher ratio of nuts to filling than some people's pies.

Unless the pecans are outstandingly crisp and flavorful, I toast them to improve both taste and texture. The honey should have an attractive character—it should be flowery, resinous, herbal, "dry," or otherwise distinctive, not just sweet.

A variation made with maple syrup and walnuts follows the main recipe. More Northern in its ingredients and outlook, it's equally nummy.

Preheat the oven to 375°.

Beat the eggs with the brown sugar to mix them well. Beat in the honey, corn syrup, melted butter, salt, and vanilla.

Strew the pecans in the pie shell and pour the filling over them; "dunk" any exposed nuts to coat them.

Bake the pie in the center of the oven for 35 to 40 minutes, or until the filling has set (the center will barely jiggle when the pan is nudged) and the top has browned.

Cool the pie on a rack for several hours to let the texture settle. Serve in narrow slices with the traditional blob of whipped cream.

MAPLE-WALNUT PIE: Replace the pecans with walnut chunks or halves (toasted, if you'll take my advice; see page 276) and use ¾ cup maple syrup and ¼ cup dark corn syrup in place of ½ cup honey and ½ cup corn syrup. Halve the vanilla. Dark maple syrup, if you can find it—look for Grade B—has a deeper and more maply flavor than Grade A or AA, and that's what I'd use if I had a choice.

Makes an 8- or 9-inch pie; serves 8

3 large eggs
2 tablespoons (packed) light-brown sugar
½ cup full-flavored honey
½ cup dark corn syrup
2 tablespoons melted unsalted butter
½ teaspoon salt
1½ teaspoons vanilla extract
2 cups pecan chunks or halves, toasted (see page 276)
Unbaked 8- or 9-inch pie shell (page 277)
Optional accompaniment: Whipped cream

SLOW FOOD, FOR A CHANGE

Creamy Tomato Aspic (page 156), served with Masa Cheese Sticks (below); or Tapenade (page 165), accompanied by the cheese sticks

Beanpot Chicken (below), the version with noodles

Steamed snap beans, broccoli, or asparagus sauced with Classic Vinaigrette (page 273) or Butter & Lemon Sauce (page 106)

Pepper hash or another tart relish, or room-temperature Red Cabbage Braised with Cranberries (page 174)

Frozen Maple Mousse (below), with Old-Fashioned Sugar Cookies (page 232); or Rummy & Raisiny, Topless & Bottomless Sweet-Potato Pie (page 131)

To drink: A medium rosé wine, if you like rosés; otherwise, a Chablis or a Johannisberg Riesling from California

Making haste shouldn't be your aim if you want "stewed" chicken with real flavor, so this method takes time but not trouble—the bird simmers along in the oven with practically no attention from the cook. You can choose to serve it with its own gravy, or with noodles cooked in the juices.

MASA CHEESE STICKS

hese nibbles aren't just cheese flavored: they also have the savor of a good tortilla because they're made from masa harina, a special flour prepared from lime-treated corn and used, most famously, for making tortillas and tamales. Gringos with a taste for nominally Southwestern foods also use masa harina for the crust of tamale pie, a delicacy, I'm fairly sure, that's unknown south of the border.

Preheat the oven to 375°.

Make the dough. Food processor: Combine the masa harina, salt, baking powder, red pepper, and cheese in the bowl and pulse the motor on and off a few times until the cheese is chopped fine and distributed through the dry ingredients.

Measure the water, add the egg yolks and oil without mixing, and pour the liquids through the feed tube of the processor while the motor is running. Run the machine until the dough coheres into a soft mass above the blades.

By hand: Sift the dry ingredients together and mix in the finely grated cheese thoroughly; combine the liquids as directed above, add to the drys, and complete the mixing with a wooden spoon, beating the dough thoroughly.

Scrape the dough into a pastry bag fitted with a fluted or plain tube with an opening about ¼ inch across. Pipe 2 or 3-inch sticks onto a nonstick baking sheet, placing them ½ inch apart.

Bake 10 minutes at 375°, then lower the oven setting to 325°. Bake 10 minutes longer. (The sticks should not be allowed to brown more than faintly—the baking lets them puff a little and become firm.) Pull out the shelf, turn the sticks upside down on the pan, and return the pan to the oven. Bake 5 minutes longer, then turn off the oven, open the door a little, and leave the panful to dry until completely cool.

(Alternatively, the cheese sticks may be served while

Makes 4 to 5 dozen

1 cup masa harina (tortilla flour)
½ teaspoon salt
½ teaspoon baking powder
Pinch of ground hot red pepper, optional
1 cup grated sharp Cheddar-type cheese (about ¼ pound)
1 cup warm water (115°)
2 large egg yolks
1 tablespoon vegetable oil

TORTILLAS: Once you have caught your *harina,* you needn't settle for using it in this recipe alone; it's quite feasible (and enjoyable) to make tortillas from scratch. A press for shaping them (helpful but not essential) is a standard offering of kitchen shops and mail-order equipment specialists. The tortilla recipe is on the box, and very simple it is.

tender and soft, immediately after baking; but a bit of crispness improves them.)

Stored in a closed canister, the sticks keep for at least a week. If they soften, they may be recrisped in a 300° oven.

———

MASA MATTERS: Moist, fresh-ground *masa*—ready-to-use tortilla dough—isn't something that can be found just anywhere, so masa flour, a fairly modern development, is a boon to those on both sides of the Mexican border for whom tortillas are daily bread. The flour is good for other foods, too—I've experimented with using a portion of it in yeast bread, to which it contributes a distinctive flavor, and in crepes, which are most delicate and delicious. (Masa crepes filled with creamy chili-seasoned chicken, blanketed in bechamel, and baked until hot under a sprinkling of cheese are a cross-cultural phenomenon worth knowing about.)

Quaker—the company known for its cylindrical cartons of rolled oats—is the best-known packer of masa harina; however, I've come across one or two other labels.

IN THE BAG: If a pastry bag isn't at hand, a cookie press fitted with the plate that produces a tubular or half-round shape will do for shaping the sticks. If the sticks are thicker than a quarter-inch, they'll require longer baking. Just keep an eye; don't let them brown, and allow end-time for drying and crisping with the oven off.

BEANPOT CHICKEN

 est described as an unbrowned fricassee, this savory dish is happy to bubble along peaceably while you do or think of other things. The recipe is one to use when you have a big bird—a fowl that has had a chance to acquire enough flavor to be interesting. If the chicken has also had a chance to acquire a lot of fat, pull out as much of it as you can.

The best cooking vessel for this is a covered beanpot holding about 3 quarts; such a pot, designed for slow cooking, really helps cosset the fowl into tenderness. If you lack a beanpot, any fairly deep covered casserole will serve.

The rich cooking juices can be finished as gravy or used in preparing Chicken with Noodles, for which directions follow the main recipe.

Serves 6 to 8

5-pound chicken, cut into
 serving pieces
Salt and pepper, preferably
 white pepper, to taste
All-purpose flour for
 dredging
1 medium onion, sliced
 thin
2 carrots, scraped and
 sliced thin
1 large rib celery, sliced
 thin, or a handful of
 chopped celery tops
1 bay leaf, broken up
¼ teaspoon crumbled
 dried thyme
3 large sprigs parsley
1 quart, or as needed,
 boiling-hot chicken broth
 or water
For Chicken and Gravy: 1
 tablespoon cornstarch
 mixed with 1 tablespoon
 cold water
For Chicken and Noodles:
 8 ounces broad curly egg
 noodles
Garnish: Minced parsley
 leaves

Preheat the oven to 350°.

Rinse the chicken pieces and pat them dry with paper toweling. (The neck, gizzard, and heart can go into the beanpot to enrich the juice, but reserve the liver for a grateful cat.)

Salt and pepper the pieces generously (but salt sparingly if salted chicken broth will be the cooking liquid). Put 1 cup flour into a paper or plastic bag; drop in 2 or 3 pieces of chicken at a time and shake them, holding the neck closed, to coat every nook and cranny with flour. Flour the rest, adding more flour if needed.

Put a slice or two of onion and a scattering of carrots and celery in a 3-quart beanpot. Add floured chicken to make a close layer, then repeat the layers of vegetables and chicken, tucking in the bay leaf, thyme, and parsley here and there.

Pour in enough boiling broth or water, or a mixture, to cover the chicken well; cover the beanpot; bake 2 to 3 hours, depending on age and quality of the bird (old bird, longer time); the chicken should be meltingly tender when done. Reduce the oven setting to 325° after the liquid has begun to bubble; check the liquid level occasionally and add boiling water sufficient to keep the pieces covered.

When done, the chicken can be held for up to an hour in the oven at the "keep-warm" setting. Complete the dish in either of the two ways described below.

CHICKEN WITH GRAVY: Drain the liquid from the beanpot through a strainer into a saucepan; return the pot of chicken to the turned-off oven to keep warm.

Skim surplus fat from the juices, then boil the liquid briskly to reduce by about half. Mix 1 tablespoon cornstarch with 1 tablespoon cold water and add gradually to the liquid, using just enough of the cornstarch mixture to thicken the gravy lightly. Simmer the gravy a minute or two, until it becomes clear, then check for seasoning; add salt as needed and plenty of white pepper.

To serve, either pour the gravy over the pot of chicken and carry the pot to the table, or arrange the chicken in a deep platter and pour the gravy over it. Garnish with parsley.

CHICKEN WITH NOODLES: Strain the juices from the pot of chicken into a saucepan, skim off the fat, and simmer the liquid to reduce it slightly. Meanwhile, keep the chicken warm. Reset the oven, if it has been turned off, to 325°.

Cook 8 ounces of broad curly egg noodles in lightly salted boiling water until half done, bite-testing a noodle after one-third of the cooking time suggested on the package. Drain the noodles.

Arrange the noodles and chicken in a deep ovenproof platter or shallow casserole. Taste the reduced cooking liquid, season well with pepper and more salt if needed, and pour it into the dish; the liquid should not quite cover the noodles. (If there isn't enough liquid, add boiling water; if there's too much liquid, stop pouring before the dish is drowned.) Cover the dish with foil and bake 15 to 20 minutes, or until the noodles are tender enough to suit you. Uncover and garnish with parsley.

This juicy combination is best served in wide soup plates, with a spoon as well as a fork.

FROZEN MAPLE MOUSSE

 his is among the loveliest of frozen desserts, and it's one with deep Northern roots. The barebones recipe was given me by a friend, who told me it had come from her great-grandmother. (That lady would have had to pack the mold in ice and salt to freeze the mousse.) I like Great-Grandmother's method of putting the dessert together, which you see below; the alternative, which also works well, is cooking the eggs and syrup into a preliminary custard in a double boiler before adding the other ingredients.

I've added a garnish of toasted pecans, an optional fribble but one that tastes good. Additional nuts could perfectly well be folded into the mousse, if the combination of North Country maple and Southern pecans is your particular pleasure.

MAPLE MUSINGS: Darker syrup is richer in flavor than the pale stuff, other things being equal; so it follows that Grade B is preferable to Grade AA or even Grade A for this dessert, if you have a choice. (Grading is based on color, not quality, in case you were wondering.)

Serves 8 to 10

4 large eggs, separated
¼ teaspoon salt
1¼ cups pure maple
  syrup, as flavorful as you
  can find (see Maple
  Musings on the
  preceding page)
1 teaspoon vanilla extract
2 cups very cold heavy
  cream, preferably not
  ultrapasteurized
Garnish: ⅓ to ½ cup
  finely chopped toasted
  pecans, optional

FROZEN MAPLE MOUSSE (CONTINUED)

In the large bowl of an electric mixer, beat the egg yolks with the salt at high speed until the mixture is thick, pale, and fluffy.

Boil the syrup in a roomy saucepan over high heat until it spins a very short thread when poured from a spoon; how long this takes depends mostly on the humidity of the atmosphere—watch the boiling and test often by pouring a drop or two from a spoon. With the mixer running at medium speed, pour the syrup slowly into the beaten yolks; then beat at medium-high speed until the mixture has cooled to tepid. Beat in the vanilla, then scrape the mixture into a large metal bowl and chill it.

Beat the egg whites to the soft-peak but still glossy stage. In another bowl (no need to change the beaters), beat the cream just until it will hold a soft peak on the lifted beater.

Stir about one-fourth of the whites and one-fourth of the cream thoroughly into the chilled maple mixture to lighten it; then scrape the remaining cream into the bowl of egg whites and pour the maple base over both. Fold everything gently together with a large rubber spatula, folding just until the streaks vanish.

Pour the mousse into a 6- to 8-cup soufflé dish (or a metal mold if you plan to unmold the dessert). Cover the mousse with plastic wrap or foil and set it in the deep-freeze to stay for at least 8 hours; it freezes slowly because of its richness.

Once frozen, the mousse can be held for several days. To protect its flavor during storage, enclose the container in a well-sealed freezer bag, or overwrap it airtight with plastic or foil.

To serve from the soufflé dish: Move the mousse to the refrigerator about half an hour ahead of time to let it soften slightly. Garnish the top, if you like, with pecans and serve the mousse from its dish at the table.

If the mousse has been molded: The best bet is to do the unmolding well before it's time to serve dinner. Invert the mold onto a chilled serving dish, then wrap it in a cloth wrung out of hot water. Leave the cloth for 20 to 30 seconds, then try lifting the mold off the dessert; if it won't come off, try the warm cloth again, but don't overdo the warming or the mousse will look smooshy rather than shapely. Once it has been unmolded, return the mousse to the freezer, cover it lightly, and leave it until near dinnertime. Then, if it's still quite hard, move it to the refrigerator for half an hour to mellow to eating consistency. Garnish the top with the nuts just before serving.

STEAK & ALL THE TRIMMINGS

Orange & Lemon Salad with Mint (page 119), or its Orange & Onion variant

Pan-Seared Sirloin (below)

Swiss-Style Skillet Potato Cake (Rösti) (below)

Panned Cherry Tomatoes (below) or Sautéed Red & Green Tomato Slices (page 113) or steamed broccoli, served with An Excellent Hollandaise (below)

Cream-Filled Boston Stack Cake (below) or Upside-Down Fruited Ginger Cake (page 158)

To drink: A full-bodied red wine— Burgundy, Rhône, or Zinfandel

We all seem to know quite well how to grill meat over charcoal, but dealing with a large, luscious (and inevitably expensive) beefsteak indoors can be baffling and disappointing. The fault isn't always the cook's.

Range broilers, with rare exceptions—such as the intensely hot units in the professional-type ranges sometimes installed in private houses—just aren't capable of doing the best job of broiling steaks, though they're fine for chicken and fish. Gas-fired units do better than electric elements, but on the whole a thick cast-iron skillet or griddle will turn out a more succulent steak than any oven broiler, if the steak for you should have a seared surface and a juicy center. So that's how the steak for this menu is done.

The rest of the menu plays second fiddle, but it's a well-tuned fiddle: A citrusy salad prepares the palate for the steak, then there's a crisp potato cake, panned tiny tomatoes (or steamed broccoli), and a perfectly luscious dessert. It all deserves a good bottle of red wine, perhaps a full-bodied red of the Burgundy persuasion.

PAN-SEARED SIRLOIN

an broiling, so-called, is a dry-heat method, so it's suitable for most tender steaks (the key word is *tender*); but the method and the meat come together to best effect when the cut is a bone-in sirloin, a naturally tender steak with more "beefy" flavor than such cuts as the filet mignon. (Boneless sirloin cuts tend to be iffy as to suitability because it's hard to tell what part of the steer's sirloin section—between the short loin and the round—they come from.)

Choosing a sirloin: Of the several sirloin steaks, among the choicest, according to experts, are the pin bone, which resembles a porterhouse with an additional bone—the pin bone—lying below the base of the T-bone; the flat-bone sirloin, with a single bone resembling the sole of a tiny sneaker; and the round-bone sirloin, with, of course, a small round bone serving as its mark of identity. For pan broiling, steaks shouldn't be much over 1 inch thick.

Amount to buy: For each person, calculate ¾ to 1 pound of bone-in steak, according to the carnivorousness of the crowd; that's not as much as it seems, considering that the weight includes the bone and the bordering fat, which can be abundant in the highest grades of beef.

Before cooking: Remove the steak from the refrigerator an hour before cooking will begin and leave it, lightly covered, on a plate; the meat will be more tender at the finish than if it's left in the icebox until the last minute. Just before cooking begins, pat the steak dry with a paper towel to be sure it will brown beautifully.

Pan-broiling the steak: Set a heavy cast-iron skillet over medium-high heat. (Use a thick iron griddle that fits over two burners for a steak too large for your pan, or for more than one steak.) Leave the pan until it is hot enough to sizzle when an edge of the steak is touched to the surface. Rub the pan with a scrap of trimmed-off steak fat.

Slap on the steak and let it sear until well browned, usually 5 minutes or so. Turn it (use tongs or a fork thrust into the fat, not the flesh) and sear the second side. Continue to cook for a few minutes, lowering the heat a

---

STRIPING YOUR STEAK LIKE A TIGER: Besides the plain heavy iron pan—either a skillet or a griddle—suggested in the recipe, a most desirable pan for stovetop grilling is a skillet with a ridged bottom. The ridges raise the meat above its drippings, and they also char handsome stripes into its surface when the pan is adequately preheated.

Look for a grill pan made of plain cast iron, or, if you want a nonstick pan, choose one of seriously heavy iron or other metal and be sure the coating is one highly rated for durability. Enameled iron is third choice; the porcelain enamel isn't the best conductor of the high heat you want for good grilling, and the surface is rather easy to chip.

little, until the meat is done as you like it; it's okay to turn it once or twice. Remove from the pan any fat that can be spooned or blotted up as the steak cooks if you'd like a surface that has been seared, not fried.

Checking doneness: An instant-reading thermometer inserted into the center of the steak at a long slant will read 120° when it's time to take the meat from the heat if you want it rare. (These readings are according to me, not to some standard tables, which recommend 140°, which is too high, for rare); for medium-rare, 130° on the thermometer is about right. If you go much beyond that you're on your own—a "medium" steak is tricky to achieve, and "well-done," is likely to be "well-toughened."

The finger test: People who broil steaks for a living check them for doneness by poking a stiff finger into the meat—if it feels soft it's rare, if there is slightly more resistance it's medium-rare, if it's firm, it's either well done or at the "forget it" stage, depending on how you like your steak. If you'd like to perfect this skill, which is also useful when grilling outdoors, use the touch test together with the instant thermometer until you get the hang of it.

Serving the steak: The meat will go on cooking for a bit after it comes out of the pan, which is why it's a good idea to stop the cooking a few degrees below the degree of doneness you want. Place the steak on a warmed platter or a carving board, season it with coarse salt and a few grinds of pepper, add a pat of butter if you like, garnish it minimally (a tuft or two of parsley), and serve it forth.

A pan sauce: The steak will have produced a bit of brown crustiness in the pan if the job has been done right. Dissolve the crust with a little hot water or red wine, stirring up the bits; season the liquid with salt and pepper; swirl a tablespoonful of butter around in it to thicken it slightly, and pour the sauce—there won't be much—into a warmed gravy boat.

Carving: There's no special protocol about this—just cut around the bone(s) to free them, then cut inch-wide slices across the body of the steak.

———

WHERE IS, INDEED, THE BEEF? Government grading has been revised to upgrade beef of a given quality, ostensibly because leaner meat is better for us, and we'll buy it more readily if it bears a grade once given to well-marbled meat. (Lean beef also costs less to produce, so there's a money incentive for the industry, too.) A steak that would have once been graded "choice"—the second level of quality—is now marked "prime." *Real* prime beef is almost all reserved for restaurants.

TAKING THE TEMPERATURE OF STEAK: There's a knack to using an instant-reading thermometer to check a relatively thin chunk of meat like a steak. Poking the probe straight down will take the temperature of the pan, or of the seared bottom of the meat at best. If you slide the probe into the meat at a flat angle, so its tip rests midway between the top and bottom surfaces, the reading will reflect what's going on in mid-steak.

SWISS-STYLE SKILLET POTATO CAKE (RÖSTI)

he down-to-earth Swiss know how to value potatoes, having sometimes been obliged to live on them in hard times; my favorite Swiss cookbook, rich in regional specialties, gives as much space to potatoes as to all other vegetables combined. Among potato dishes from Switzerland, rösti is the one I like best and the one that's guaranteed to make a hit with all spud-lovers. The recipe here is for basic *rösti*; cooks sometimes add cheese, bacon, or onions.

One point of *rösti* know-how: The best skilletful—a crisp-crusted, golden-brown round, tender and steaming and fragrant with butter inside—is made from half-cooked potatoes that have been refrigerated overnight. However, the dish *can* be made with leftover boiled or baked potatoes, or even from grated raw potatoes if the cooking method is modified (see Last-Minute Rösti, on the following page).

These potatoes are a natural with sauced dishes, but they also go beautifully with such unsauced meats as the steak in this menu.

Serves 6

2 to 2½ pounds baking or all-purpose potatoes, scrubbed (about 6 medium)
About 1 teaspoon salt
4 to 6 tablespoons unsalted butter or Clarified Butter (see page 268)
A little milk

Boil the potatoes in their skins until they're half done, about 10 minutes; drain, cool, and refrigerate overnight.

Peel the potatoes and grate them onto a platter, using your coarsest shredder; sprinkle with salt and toss gently with a fork.

Melt 4 tablespoons of the butter in a large skillet over medium heat (a nonstick pan makes the cooking simpler). When the foam begins to subside, add the potatoes and press them into a compact cake with a spatula. Sprinkle the top with about 2 tablespoons milk, cover tightly, and cook for a moment or two. Reduce the heat to its lowest point and cook the potatoes 20 minutes, shaking the pan once or twice to prevent sticking. (If the potatoes stick in spite of this, loosen the cake with a spatula and add more butter to the pan.)

After 20 minutes, check the browning of the underside and the doneness of the potatoes; if necessary, recover and cook for up to 10 minutes longer. Cover the pan with an inverted platter, hold pan and platter together, and turn out the *rösti*. Serve very hot.

———

LAST-MINUTE RÖSTI: Peel the raw potatoes and grate them fine. Melt ⅓ cup (¾ stick) butter in the skillet, add the potatoes, sprinkle them with salt, and stir them in the butter for a few moments over medium heat. Press the potatoes into a cake, add more butter to the pan if needed, cover, lower the heat to its lowest point, and cook the *rösti* until done, about 30 minutes.

PANNED CHERRY TOMATOES

 leave the skins on when I cook cherry tomatoes this way, just as I would if they were to be consumed raw. Two reasons: The skins are thin and not unpleasant to eat; and, although they will split during the brief "panning," they help the juicy little tomatoes keep their shape and good looks. (To skin cherry tomatoes, scald them about 20 seconds in boiling water, cool them in ice water, drain them, and strip off their skins.).

This quick vegetable course (which is also a handsome garnish for important platters) can be enjoyed most of the year, because cherry tomatoes marketed in winter are quite good. In fact they're the only *edible* tomatoes (barring an occasional greenhouse specimen) available out of season; that they are good to eat is, no doubt, due to an oversight on the part of the industrial farming cartel—I won't remind them if you don't.

TAMER TOMATOES: Here is a milder-mannered version of Panned Cherry Tomatoes for a menu in which the emphatic flavors of olive oil and garlic aren't wanted.

"Pan" the tomatoes in the same way, but use half vegetable oil and half butter in place of olive oil, and toss in a little minced scallion (if you like) in place of garlic. Season the finished tomatoes with salt, pepper, and a big pinch of dried sweet marjoram or basil; swirl them with a chunk of additional butter and about 2 tablespoons of fine dry bread crumbs.

Serves 6

1 pint basket ripe cherry
   tomatoes
3 tablespoons olive oil
1 teaspoon minced fresh
   garlic
Salt and pepper, to taste
Squeeze of lemon juice, if
   needed
¼ cup minced parsley
   leaves, preferably Italian
   (flat-leaf) parsley
A little fresh basil,
   rosemary, thyme, or
   other herb, optional

Stem, rinse, and dry the tomatoes well.

Heat the oil in a wide skillet over high heat just until it looks watery. Add the garlic, stir it around the pan once, and put in the tomatoes. Shake and roll the tomatoes constantly about in the pan until they are well heated through, the work of 2 or 3 minutes; don't let them overcook unless you want tomato mush. Remove the pan from the heat.

Season the tomatoes with salt and pepper and, if they lack tartness, a little lemon juice. Add the parsley and any other herb being used, swirl and toss to mix, and serve at once.

AN EXCELLENT HOLLANDAISE

ou will find this foolproof hollandaise is superior to a blender-made sauce—which is the easiest for an inexperienced cook to tackle—and absolutely equal in lusciousness to the classic top-of-the-stove hollandaise, which is trickier to make than this, my pet version. Another virtue: The sauce can be made hours or days ahead and rewarmed as the recipe describes.

Makes about 1½ cups

5 large egg yolks
½ teaspoon salt, or more
   to taste
½ cup water
12 tablespoons (1½
   sticks) unsalted butter,
   cut into 1-tablespoon
   slices
2 tablespoons, or to taste,
   strained fresh lemon
   juice
Pinch of white pepper or
   ground hot red pepper,
   optional

Whisk the egg yolks, ½ teaspoon salt, and water together in a small, very thick saucepan (or do this in the top of a double boiler).

Whisking constantly, heat the mixture over very low heat (or over, not in, simmering water in the double-boiler base) until the mixture begins to feel quite warm to a probing fingertip; the temperature will be about 125° on an instant-reading thermometer.

Continuing to whisk, add butter one slice at a time, blending in most of each before adding the next. When all the butter has been added, remove the sauce from the heat at once and stir in the lemon juice and pepper. Taste and add more lemon, salt, or pepper if needed. Strain the sauce, if you want absolutely flawless texture.

The sauce will be warm enough to serve for up to 15

FURTHER INTO HOLLANDAISE: This lovely sauce isn't for hot vegetables only. Spoon some over poached eggs for a touch of gilding; or pass the sauce with poached fish of any sort; or toss a little with hot noodles for a suave and lemony finish.

minutes; to hold it longer, set it over hot tap water (no more than 140°). If it's to be served hours later, let it cool, then rewarm it (below). The sauce may be refrigerated for three days or more.

Rewarming: Set the container of sauce in a bowl of hot tap water (no more than 140°); whisk it occasionally until it is warm, replacing the hot water as necessary.

CREAM-FILLED BOSTON STACK CAKE

f all the Boston cream pies I've tasted since youth (that dessert was considered wholesome enough for children), here is the best version I've met, better even than my own recipe developed from what James Beard used to call "taste memory."

With its four layers and lavish filling, this cake is taller than the two-layer prototype baked in a piepan, and I think it's better, although it's less rich and less sweet. Its pattern is Ann Batchelder's Silver Lake House Cream Pie, a two- or three-layer confection found in a Batchelder cookbook rescued from a second-hand bookshop.

In food history, the cakes called "Boston cream pie" belong to the type known as "jelly cake" or "Washington pie," which were often filled with preserves instead of a creamy filling like the one here. Another dessert, called "stack cake," had many layers, typically separated by applesauce; I've borrowed the name in honor of our four layers.

The filling was made with heavy cream back when cholesterol didn't count; part cream and part milk seems more prudent now. After sugaring the top, I like to add strawberries or other pretty fruit shortly before the cake is served.

JAM-FILLED STACK CAKE: Bake, cool, and split the cake layers as described. Instead of making the cream filling, spread raspberry (or other berry) jam lavishly between the layers; you'll need about 1½ cups. Dust the top with the sugar.

_ _

Serves 8

CAKE LAYERS:
Unsalted butter or oil and
*   all-purpose flour for*
*   coating the pans*
2 large eggs
¾ cup granulated sugar
1½ teaspoons finely
*   grated lemon zest*
*   (colored rind only, no*
*   pith)*
1¼ cups all-purpose flour
2 teaspoons baking
*   powder*
½ teaspoon salt
3 tablespoons melted
*   unsalted butter, cooled*
*   slightly*
¾ cup milk
1 teaspoon vanilla extract

FILLING:
¾ cup granulated sugar
⅓ cup all-purpose flour
½ teaspoon salt
2 large eggs
2 cups light cream, or half
*   cream and half milk*
1½ teaspoons finely
*   grated lemon zest*
*   (colored rind only, no*
*   pith)*
1 teaspoon vanilla extract

TOPPING:
Sifted confectioner's sugar
Optional garnish:
*   Strawberries or other*
*   fresh fruit*

Layers: Line the bottoms of two round 8-inch layer pans with aluminum foil, trimmed to fit; butter or oil the foil and the sides of the pans, dust with flour, knock out excess, and set aside. (If preferred, four pans may be used to bake the layers.)

Preheat the oven to 360°, approximately halfway between the 350° and 375° control markings.

Beat the eggs with a mixer at high speed until fluffy, then gradually beat in the sugar; add the lemon zest; beat the mixture until thick and pale.

Meanwhile, sift together the flour, baking powder, and salt.

Beat the melted butter into the eggs and sugar, then beat in the dry ingredients and milk alternately at slow speed, starting and finishing with dry ingredients. Beat in the flavoring.

Spread the batter in the pans, bang each pan on the counter twice to level the batter, and bake 15 to 18 minutes, until the cake shrinks slightly from the sides and is light gold on top. Cool the layers briefly in the pans, then turn onto cake racks, remove the foil, and cool.

Filling: Whisk together the sugar, flour, and salt.

In a saucepan, whisk the eggs to mix well; whisk in the cream, then the dry ingredients. Add the lemon zest.

Cook the custard, stirring constantly, over medium heat until it thickens; boil it for a minute or two, stirring.

Cool to lukewarm, whisking now and then; add the vanilla.

Assembling the cake: With a serrated knife, split each layer in two (if you've made four layers, don't split them). Place a layer on a serving plate; spread one-third of the filling over it in a thick layer, keeping the filling ½ inch from the edges; add the remaining layers and filling, topping the cake with the best-looking top surface. Press the top lightly to encourage small swags of filling to emerge between the layers.

Sift confectioner's sugar over the top. To make a lacy pattern—a classic prettification—first lay a paper doily on the cake, sprinkle with sugar, press the sugar lightly, then lift off the doily.

The fruit garnish, if it's added, should be put in place just before serving time.

WHAT *IS* A SUPPER, ANYWAY?

Supper must come together simply and easily out of what is at hand and by whoever has the chore or gets home first...
—JOHN THORNE, *SIMPLE COOKING*

"What shall we have for supper?" Mama would ask. A long pause and then "I know—a lightly boiled egg."
—NICOLAS FREELING, *THE KITCHEN*

Poor Mama. She was evidently the one who got home first ...Perhaps we can do better than a lightly boiled egg. (Freeling records that his Papa was driven to go out and buy cookbooks for self-preservation; he himself became a classically trained professional cook before establishing himself as a writer.)

Once we have settled what supper *is* these days, we can consider what to serve. Supper used to be simple to describe—it was what everyone ate in the evening after having had "dinner" at midday; thus it was a smaller and simpler meal. (Some suppers were milk and crackers.) But as lunch became more of a meal and less of a snack it began to replace noon dinner, which in turn was forced to a later and later hour (it started out, in Britain, at around 9 A.M. back in the days when barons feasted). Except for the few folk who cherish and use the old term, we hardly ever say "supper" now unless we mean a light meal on Sunday evening (note that we still often have an earlier "Sunday dinner"), or a collation after the theater or a concert, or the refreshments at an evening party. So much for semantics and the migration of meal hours.

Of the menus in the other sections of this book, many are convertible into suppers; just check the Index (and see the Seasonal Recipe Lists) for such dishes as Corn Oysters, Savory Chicken & Veal Loaf, Scrapple, Finnan Haddie in Cream, Lobster Salad, Chipped Beef in Cream (perhaps in a baked potato), Classic Chicken Salad, Pre-Pasta Macaroni Salad, Slunk, Buttered Lobster, Eggs à la Hotrod, Beanpot Chicken, Old New England Corn Pudding, and Pretty Good Chili con Carne. Those are some of the possibilities, and there are more, such as pancakes, or a hot pot-roast sandwich, and we haven't even mentioned the desserts yet . . . .

HAMMING IT UP

Baked smoky ham, either home-cooked (below) or the delicatessen's best

Salad of Chinese Cabbage, Fruit & Nuts (below)

Blueberry Corn Muffins (page 141) or the Blueberry Version (page 217) of Cinnamon-Capped Apple Muffins

Very Chocolate Ice Cream (below) with White Chocolate Marshmallow Sauce or Two-Berry Sauce (both below)

To drink: Beaujolais, a fresh Bordeaux, or another moderately light red wine

A lighthearted meal of one or two dishes that can be rustled up quickly, with a nibble of something sweet to finish, describes this supper that can be offered to potluck guests without a blush or a qualm.

Cold baked ham always seems to taste better than hot ham (my theory is that its molecules have had a chance to settle down after their violent disruption by cooking); and, despite Dorothy Parker's definition of eternity as "two people and a ham," a ham is a comfortable thing to have on hand.

The crisp salad of Chinese cabbage is quick to assemble; the muffins, if you have baked them earlier, rewarm very well; the dark chocolate ice cream is, by definition, in the freezer; and the two dessert sauces keep contentedly in the refrigerator until wanted.

FRINGE BENEFITS FOR THE HAM-BAKER: Besides the succulent fresh slices to serve hot or cold, a home-baked ham is lavish with gustatory bonuses.

The ham juices: If baked under foil, most hams will release into the pan, in addition to fat, wonderfully flavored concentrated juices. Drained into a jar and refrigerated, the ham essence is sealed airtight by the fat, so it can be stored for as long as two weeks. Nobody needs to tell the canny cook about adding ham juice to half-cooked lentils or black beans, or to minestrone; or about making use of the delicious fat, lifted off when the essence is used, in any cooking that will be enhanced by its flavor.

The ham skin, which should be refrigerated until needed, is also rich in flavor, so it's useful in the same ways as ham juice—for seasoning dried beans, long-cooked vegetables, for sauces, and for soups. (Fish out the pieces of skin before serving the dish.)

The ham bone stars in Red-Wine Beans with a Ham Bone (page 139). It can do the same jobs as those mentioned for ham essence or skin when simmered long enough.

WORDS ABOUT HAM, & HOW TO BAKE IT

his isn't a blow-by-blow recipe, but rather a compilation of a few things to think about before, and to do after, acquiring a whole or half ham of the types discussed.

Country hams—the real thing, full of flavor due to slow and complete curing and lengthy smoking—must be soaked and simmered according to the packer's instructions; this is absolutely essential to rehydrate the meat and remove some of its excess salt. After simmering, a country ham is usually skinned and its fat is scored decoratively and coated with a sweet or spicy glaze or with crumbs—general cookbooks have many glazing suggestions. Wonderful country hams are still produced in (of course) Smithfield, Virginia, and also in Kentucky, Tennessee, and Vermont, among other states.

Common or garden-variety hams are more lightly cured, partly because of changing tastes and partly because refrigeration now makes a heavy cure unnecessary. They range from carefully produced "premium" hams (priced at the costlier end of the range) to everyday brands, many of which have been cured by pumping a solution of salt, sugar, saltpeter, and flavorings into the meat.

The main distinction between non-"country" hams appears on the label. If the label says "Cook before eating," plan to bake the ham on a rack under a light tent of foil for 20 minutes per pound in a 325° oven until an instant-reading thermometer records 160° to 165° when inserted into the center of the lean meat. The ham is then ready to skin, score, and glaze, or just to skin and slice.

"Ready to eat" and "fully cooked" are labels

that are technically true but not to be taken literally. Such hams taste better and have better texture if they are baked as described above. The "done" temperature for these hams is 140° to 145°, which should be reached in a little over 15 minutes per pound.

Sizes: Whole hams usually weigh between 10 and 15 pounds; a butt half (the rounded section) or the shank end (with the long bone) will weigh about half as much. A nominal half-ham will weigh less if the butcher has subtracted a center slice or two to sell separately.

Serving: You'll carve about 3 servings per pound of ham, uncooked weight.

Storage: Refrigerate leftover ham. Later servings will taste best if allowed to return to room temperature.

SALAD OF CHINESE CABBAGE, FRUIT & NUTS

he delicate crispness of Chinese cabbage, which is also called napa (and used to be called "celery cabbage") is set off by apples, raisins, and nuts in this cheerful salad that's a distant cousin of the Waldorf tribe. It will prove particularly agreeable with the ham in this menu.

Chinese cabbage isn't absolutely required by the salad—you can use another cabbage if it's tender (Savoy is fine) and has been shredded paperthin. Orange sections, small cubes of pineapple, or halved grapes can be tossed into the bowl instead of (or in addition to) apples and raisins. If the fruit is increased by more than a little, the amount of dressing will need to be increased proportionately.

THE OTHER HALF OF THE HEAD: Chinese cabbage heads are either long and slim or roundish and often enormous. If you've bought a large head and have cabbage left over after making the salad, wrap and refrigerate it for another meal. Slice and steam the cabbage lightly (it cooks fast), then sauce it with salt, pepper, butter, and drops of lemon juice.

Serves 6 to 8

2 quarts fine-shredded
Chinese cabbage (napa),
about 2 pounds
2 firm red-skinned apples
3 tablespoons, or as
needed, fresh lemon or
lime juice
½ cup raisins, golden or
dark
½ cup broken-up walnuts
or pecans
½ cup mayonnaise
2 teaspoons, or to taste,
granulated sugar
½ teaspoon, or to taste,
salt

Makes 2 quarts

3 large eggs
1¼ cups granulated sugar
4 ounces (4 squares) high-
quality unsweetened
chocolate
¼ cup Dutch-process
cocoa powder
1 quart half-and-half, or 2
cups each heavy cream
and milk
¼ teaspoon salt
1 tablespoon vanilla
extract

SALAD OF CHINESE CABBAGE, FRUIT & NUTS (CONTINUED)

Put the Chinese cabbage in a glass or ceramic salad bowl. Scrub, core, and dice the apples, skins and all, and sprinkle them with half the lemon or lime juice. Add the apples, raisins, and nuts to the cabbage.

Whisk together the mayonnaise, sugar, and salt with the remaining citrus juice; toss with the salad. Taste-check to discover whether more citrus juice, mayonnaise, sugar, or salt would be an improvement.

VERY CHOCOLATE ICE CREAM

Anyone who's passionate about chocolate will want to try this seriously dark and dense ice cream made with a custard base that contributes great body to match the intensity of a double-chocolate hit. Ordinary cocoa won't do as well by this recipe as Dutch-process cocoa. If you're interested in the why's and wherefore's, see Cocoa: Going Dutch (right).

Beat the eggs and ½ cup of the sugar in a mixer at high speed until very thick and fluffy.

Meanwhile, whirl to a powder in a food processor or blender ¼ cup of the remaining sugar, the chocolate, and the cocoa. Reserve.

Heat to simmering the half-and-half or combined cream and milk, the salt, and the remaining ½ cup sugar. Beat about half of the hot cream into the eggs, then pour the egg mixture into the pan of cream and stir steadily over low heat just until the mixture will coat the spoon. Remove from heat.

Add the chocolate blend; beat until the chocolate has dissolved. Cool to lukewarm; add the vanilla.

Chill well, then freeze according to manufacturer's instructions for your ice-cream maker. Store in the freezer for a few hours before serving.

COCOA: GOING DUTCH.
Dutch-process cocoa gives better results than run-of-the-mill cocoa in certain recipes because less of the natural fat (cocoa butter) has been removed from Dutch cocoa than from regular types, and the flavor and color are more intense.

In the mid-nineteenth century, a Netherlander named Conrad van Houten, whose family name still appears on cocoa canisters, devised a way to remove some of the overabundant fat from chocolate so it could be converted into cocoa powder; he also devised the "dutching" process in which an alkali is used to reduce the acidity of the powder, darken its color, and mellow its flavor.

Makes about 2½ cups

1½ ounces white
   chocolate
1 tablespoon unsalted
   butter
½ cup plus 1 tablespoon
   water
⅔ cup white corn syrup
1 cup granulated sugar
2 large egg whites
Pinch of salt
½ teaspoon vanilla extract
3 or 4 drops almond
   extract

WHITE CHOCOLATE MARSHMALLOW SAUCE

s luscious and light as the inside of a toasted marshmallow, this snowy sauce devised during a recent dessert-making spell is a "keeper," despite its seemingly fragile texture. I like to have a jarful in the refrigerator, ready to dollop over bittersweet chocolate ice cream (or deep, dark coffee ice cream) when nostalgia for a "sundae" treat gets the upper hand with any denizen of the house. (The white chocolate is the difference between this compound and the soda-fountain sauce beloved of kids.)

The sauce has yet another use: If there's a tart salad of fresh fruit, a spoonful, blended into lemony mayonnaise, makes a light-hearted dressing.

Melt together the white chocolate, butter, and 1 tablespoon water in a small heavy pan over low heat, stirring constantly. Cool.

Measure ½ cup water into a saucepan; add the corn syrup and sugar. Bring to a boil and boil briskly until a little of the syrup forms a firm ball when dropped into ice water and tested with the fingers. Boiling will take several minutes—on a dry day the boiling time is shorter than in damp weather.

Meanwhile, beat the egg whites with the salt in the large bowl of an electric mixer until almost stiff but still glossy. When the syrup is ready, pour it slowly into the egg whites with the beaters running at high speed. Beat until the sauce is very fluffy, one or two minutes. Beat in the flavorings, then the cooled white chocolate mixture.

Scrape the sauce into a storage jar, cool it, then store it, covered, in the refrigerator. It will keep indefinitely.

BUT IS IT CHOCOLATE? Well, no, but white chocolate is a kissing cousin, more or less, of the dusky-toned real thing.

The luscious ivory-colored white stuff with the honorary designation of chocolate is based on cocoa butter, the fat found abundantly in the fruit of the cocoa tree, *Theobroma cacao*, which is retained in various percentages in all processed forms of chocolate, including cocoa.

To make white chocolate, cocoa butter is mixed with sugar and milk solids and lo, a sweet, milky confection that has a chocolate-like aroma and a less chocolate-like flavor.

TWO- BERRY SAUCE

 hen I can lay hands on both raspberries and strawberries, either from farmstands in summer or from the freezer the rest of the year, I like to combine them in a sauce that dresses up such plain-Jane simplicities as rice or vanilla pudding, sliced fruit, or vanilla ice cream. The combination of this sauce with a chocolate dessert seems unlikely until its tasted.

Makes about 2 cups

2 cups fresh or frozen
    unsweetened raspberries
2 cups fresh or frozen
    unsweetened
    strawberries
⅔ cup superfine sugar
Optional: 2 tablespoons
    Framboise or orange-
    flavored liqueur

If the berries are fresh-picked, rinse them briefly if they seem dusty or otherwise in need of cleansing; if not, don't bother.

Purée the berries in a blender or food processor until they are as smooth as possible. (Frozen berries need not be thawed first.)

Push the purée through a fine sieve to remove as many seeds as you can. (You may need to do this twice if your sieve is coarse, or if you're determined to get rid of every last seed.) Add the sugar and stir until it has dissolved. Add the liqueur if it's to be included. (You might postpone adding the liqueur until near serving time, if the sauce is to be frozen for future use.)

Serve the sauce without further chilling, or refrigerate it in a covered jar for a few days' storage. The sauce may be frozen for up to a year.

AUTUMN'S BOUNTY

Large bowls of Superb Lobster Stew (below)

*Fresh Corn Popovers (page 43) or Cornsticks (below), or split
and toasted Angel Biscuits (page 266)*

*Cranberry, Raisin & Nut Pie (below) or A Tart of Amber
Apples (page 231)*

To drink: Black Velvet (page 259) or chilled stout

Composed for October or November, we have here a supper
to celebrate the glorious time of year when lobsters have
recovered from their summer doldrums, the new crop of
cranberries is glowing at the greengrocer's, and apples—if you
choose to make the Tart of Amber Apples instead of the cranberry
dessert—are also at their best. If fresh corn can still be had—it's
often still around in October—I use it in the popovers.

Ah, lobster. It's my view that not everyone *deserves* lobster (any
lazybones who won't tackle a steamed specimen in the shell probably isn't entitled to it, either in or out of the shell), but so long as the
family and/or guests are all eligible, lobster stew is one of the most
satisfying ways to serve this delicacy to a whole tableful of eaters.

For one thing, lobster stew *must* be made ahead; it's absolutely
a next-day dish that needs to rest overnight in order to develop its
briny and complex character. On the day of the feast, it's ready.

SUPERB LOBSTER STEW

n opulent supper for 6 is achieved this way from 3 smallish lobsters, which would feed only half that number if served *au naturel*. Not a few lobster fanciers would prefer the stew, and it's easy to agree with this school of thought, once you've experienced this ambrosial brew.

If lobsters are plentiful and appetites are generous—or if you feel like splurging—you can add another small lobster to the pot. Just be sure the extra chunks have sufficient swimming room to qualify this as a stew, not a casserole; if there's not enough of the creamy liquid, add a bit more milk and/or cream and recheck the seasonings.

Slice the butter into a large stewpot and melt it over low heat just until it foams. Add the crumbled lobster coral, if you have it, and the fat scraped from the lobster shells. Cook gently, stirring often, until the coral is just hot through, perhaps 2 minutes.

Add the lobster meat, toss to coat it with the butter, and heat it gently, still over very low heat, turning the pieces from time to time, until they're heated through; this should take less than 10 minutes.

Meanwhile, heat the milk and cream in another pot to just below simmering (there will be beads around the edge). Add the mixture to the lobster, taste the budding stew, and season it judiciously with salt, white pepper, and a few grains of mace.

Cool the stew uncovered, then refrigerate it, closely covered, overnight or for up to 24 hours.

At serving time reheat the stew very slowly, stirring it gently from time to time, until it's piping hot; don't let it boil or even come close to boiling. Taste it again and add anything you think it needs.

Ladle the stew into a heated tureen or heated individual bowls and top it with the additional butter.

Serves 6

10 tablespoons (1¼ sticks) unsalted butter
Lobster coral and any fat from the lobster shells
Meat (about 4 cups) of 3 small lobsters, cooked and picked as described in Basic Lobster (page 60)
1 quart whole milk
3 cups heavy cream, or 2 cups cream and 1 additional cup milk
Salt and white pepper, to taste
Few grains ground mace
Garnish: 3 tablespoons additional unsalted butter, cut into thin slices

CORNSTICKS

or cornsticks you need to use special cast-iron pans that turn out extra-crusty corn bread; they come in various sizes. These cornsticks are made with the batter for Blueberry Corn Bread or Muffins (page 141), without the blueberries.

Makes about 12

Preheat the oven to 425°.

Grease cornstick pans (bacon fat is fine for this) and preheat the pan(s) in the oven for 5 minutes.

Spoon the batter into the sections, filling them two-thirds full. Bake the cornsticks until firm and well browned, about 15 minutes for average-size sticks.

CRANBERRY, RAISIN & NUT PIE

ne of the great-grandmothers of our children used to make a fine autumn pie of cranberries only, with no other fruit. (Her grandchild remembers it.) Other grandmas in other families, as food history shows, combined raisins with the cranberries in various proportions. There ain't no such thing as a poor pie made either way, but the confection described below raises the whole concept a notch, thanks to its subtle spicing (see Cardamom & Cranberries, page 210) and the crunch of the nuts.

This pie is a good thought for Thanksgiving dinner, especially if some of the thanks-givers don't adore the usual mincemeat or pumpkin finale for the feast.

CRANBERRIES, BY HAND: The ancestral cranberry pie mentioned in the text was truly a labor of love—the berries were cut in half one at a time, with a paring knife, before they were sugared and piled into the crust. A far cry from today's mechanized chopping; and who knows? Maybe Grandmother's pie was all the better for her patience and care...

Serves 6 to 8

*Pastry for a two-crust pie
(page 277)*
*2 cups (about ½ pound)
fresh or frozen
cranberries*
2 cups dark raisins
*½ to 1 cup coarsely
chopped walnuts or
pecans, preferably
toasted (page 276)*
2 tablespoons water
*2 teaspoons fresh lemon or
lime juice*
1⅓ cups granulated sugar
*2 tablespoons all-purpose
flour*
*½ teaspoon freshly ground
cardamom seeds*
*Glaze: A little cream or
evaporated milk*

CRANBERRY, RAISIN & NUT PIE (CONTINUED)

Line a 9-inch piepan with a bit more than half of the pastry. Roll out the remaining pastry for the top; reserve the lined pan and the rolled pastry in the refrigerator.

Preheat the oven to 450°.

Chop the cranberries and raisins slightly (this is easiest to do with a few on-off pulses of a food processor). Add the nuts to the cranberries and raisins; stir in the water and lemon or lime juice. Combine the sugar, flour, and cardamom with a whisk, then stir the mixture thoroughly into the pie filling.

Fill the pastry-lined pan, cover with the top crust, and trim, seal, and crimp the edges (if you need pointers, see page 281). Cut vents in the top crust, then brush the crust lightly with the cream or evaporated milk.

Bake the pie 10 minutes at 450°, lower the oven heat to 350°, and continue baking the pie for about 40 minutes more, or until the top has browned sufficiently and a little clear juice has bubbled up through the openings in the top crust.

Set the pan on a rack to cool the pie. It will have the liveliest flavor if it's served at room temperature or while still slightly warm.

CARDAMOM & CRANBERRIES

Cardamom is a most ancient Eastern spice that's much used in Indian and Middle Eastern cooking and also in certain Occidental baked goods, especially in Scandinavia and northern Europe. Cardamom is also, I've discovered, a wonderful enhancement for cranberries—its warm flavor gives depth and compexity to their chill and slightly one-dimensional acidity. I put cardamom into oven-baked cranberry preserves, and I spice a favorite cranberry cake with it; and it takes another role in this pie. It can be omitted from the pie filling, or coriander can be substituted, but the real thing is worth searching for. Indian or Middle Eastern food shops are your best bet.

Cardamom seeds are encased in little papery pods that are white if they have been bleached, light green or brownish if they haven't. There are several varieties, so the pods vary in size. Jars of ground cardamom are included in supermarket spice displays, but I advise against them, as the spice loses its flavor rapidly after it has been ground.

To grind cardamom: Chuck the whole pods into a mortar, flatten them enough to free the seeds, remove the bits of pod, then crush the seeds fine with the pestle.

TWO BAKED BEAN SUPPERS

Better-Than-Yankee Baked Beans (below)

Chinese-Cabbage Coleslaw with Pimientos & Blue Cheese (below)

Toasted and butter-brushed French or Italian crusty bread

Plum Velvet (below), with English Pouring Custard (below) and a crisp cookie or two

To drink: *Ale*

Vermont-Style Baked Beans (below)

Cinnamon-Capped Apple Muffins (below), or store-bought Boston brown bread, well warmed

Home-made or home-style chili sauce, corn relish, and sweet pickles; a bowl of large-curd creamed cottage cheese

Upside-Down Fruited Ginger Cake (page 158), with English Pouring Custard (below); or Frozen Maple Mousse (page 187)

To drink: *Hard cider for grownups, sweet cider for children*

The bean that is baked is the bean that is right. Boiled beans are just a poor relation.

—ANN BATCHELDER'S COOKBOOK

We could call these two hearty repasts dinners, but "supper" is the term that has survived from a simpler day for an evening meal of all-American baked beans; so supper menus these are and will remain for our present purposes, which include the possibility of sharing the occasion with a few friends.

Like the proof of the pudding, the test of baked beans is in the eating, and these, I promise, go down extremely well. I've taken both kinds to covered-dish gatherings and hope to do so again, and in season I serve one or the other at home to the sort of guests who enjoy chili more than a lamb chop (the best kind of guests, according to me).

Both the beanfeast menus include dishes that add up to a savory melting pot if looked at with an international eye. The coleslaw is made from an immigrant Chinese vegetable, the crusty loaves used to be exclusively European (that was a while back), and the custard sauce for the dessert remains to this day as much British as American.

However, the rest of the dishes are true-blue Yankee, like the beans. Among them are apple muffins—the best I've ever tasted were baked in the Green Mountains of Vermont—Boston brown bread, gingerbread made into an upside-down cake, and a frozen mousse based on maple syrup—New Englanders all, or as close to it "as makes no difference."

Serves at least 10, depending

2 pounds dried navy or
  pea beans
2 medium onions, peeled
4 whole cloves
1 large bay leaf
½ teaspoon crumbled dry
  thyme
½-pound chunk slab
  bacon, rind removed
½ cup unsulphured
  molasses
2 tablespoons dry mustard
2 tablespoons tomato
  paste or ¼ cup canned
  tomato sauce
¼ to ½ teaspoon black
  pepper
2 teaspoons balsamic or
  other mild vinegar
Salt, as needed

BETTER-THAN-YANKEE BAKED BEANS

fter evolving this recipe over a fair stretch of time I've ended up making only slightly subversive changes in the classic New England baked-bean formula. I'm convinced they're worth making.

Some bean-fanciers may put in more molasses than I do, and others may be doubtful about bacon in place of salt pork, or about including the bay leaf, thyme, or tomato paste, not to mention the secret drops of vinegar. All fine by me—just try this recipe for a slow-baked potful, then decide for yourself whether, and how, it could be improved on.

Sort and rinse the beans, then bring them to a boil, covered with 2 inches of water. Boil the beans 1 minute, then cover them and leave them to stand 1 hour.

Drain the beans, cover them with fresh water, and add the onions, each stuck with 2 cloves, plus the bay leaf and the thyme. (No salt at this stage.) Bring them to a boil, lower the heat, and simmer them just until the skin of a sample bean splits when it's blown upon. This will take anywhere between 30 minutes (for fresh-crop beans) to much longer for really old stock. If in doubt, undercook the beans to prevent them from turning mushy later.

Preheat the oven to 275°.

Drain off and reserve the bean liquid. Put one-third of the beans, one of the onions, and the bay leaf into a large beanpot or a heavy casserole, preferably a tall one. Cut the slab of bacon into thick slices and lay one-third of the pieces over the beans. Repeat with a layer of beans, another onion, more bacon, more beans, and finally the last of the bacon, which should be pushed down into the top layer.

Mix the molasses, mustard, tomato paste, pepper, and vinegar with 3 cups of the bean liquid (save the rest).

CHOOSING TO SOAK:
Parboiling the beans as described in the recipe gets the beanfeast off to a fast start. If there's no rush, soak the beans overnight in cold water to cover by several inches; drain and proceed with the recipe.

WHERE'S THE SALT PORK? Where I live and bake my beans, this one-time staple is still easy to find because clam chowder calls for salt pork and we're in clam country. It's also easy to buy slab bacon, which is my own choice because of its smoky character. Some of the unctuous fat of either salt pork or bacon cooks into the beans with wonderful effect on their flavor and texture, and the meat becomes translucent and most delicious after its long cooking.

BETTER-THAN-YANKEE BAKED BEANS (CONTINUED)

Add only a little salt—perhaps ½ teaspoon—to the mixture, as the bacon will add saltiness. Pour enough of this mixture over the beans to barely cover the top layer.

Cover the pot and let the beans bake until they're very tender but still shapely, 2 to 6 hours, again depending on the relative maturity of the beans. (Baking can always be done in two sessions if it turns out to be lengthier than you expect. Refrigerate the beans if final baking is postponed.) As the beans bake, keep the top layer moist by adding some of the molasses mixture as long as it lasts, then use the plain cooking liquid or boiling water. When baking is well along, taste for salt; if it's needed, add some salt to the next addition of liquid. Toward the end of baking, remove the cover and let the beans crust over.

Let the finished beans rest and mellow overnight in the refrigerator no matter how much your mouth may water. Before serving the beans, add a little boiling water if they have absorbed all their sauce, then reheat until piping-hot throughout in an oven set at about 350°.

VERMONT-STYLE BAKED BEANS: Flavored with maple syrup in place of molasses, these beans follow the same recipe pattern as Better-Than-Yankee Baked Beans. In brief:

Soak and cook 2 pounds of beans as described, but omit the onions and herbs. Bake the beans with ½ pound of salt pork, 2 teaspoons dry mustard, 1 cup of full-flavored maple syrup (dark syrup, grade B or even Grade C, is best for this purpose, if you can find it), a little white pepper, a little salt (added late in baking), and the bean cooking liquid.

YANKEE-MEX BEANS: Now that Tex-Mex dishes aren't just Border-country food in the United States, everyone seems to know about refried beans, *frijoles refritos*, which can even be bought in cans. The very notion of Yankee beans *refritos* would make a Texan groan, but never mind, here is a good way to deal with the last of a beanpotful.

Slice 2 or 3 slices of bacon crosswise and cook until crisp in a big skillet. Remove and reserve half of the fat. To the bacon and remaining fat add 2 or 3 cups of leftover baked beans; cook over medium heat, mashing the beans and turning the mass whenever a crust forms on the bottom. Add more bacon fat if it's needed, and cook until the mass of beans is studded with crusty bits.

Scoop the beans onto beds of shredded crisp lettuce on individual plates and strew some grated mild Cheddar cheese on top. Home-style chili sauce goes with this. (And cold beer.)

CHINESE-CABBAGE COLESLAW WITH PIMIENTOS & BLUE CHEESE

 eginning as an improvisation to round out a bean supper (when you live eight miles from the village, you try to be creative with what's in the larder), this savory salad has since become a favorite alongside other main dishes as well. If everyone is fond of "hot stuff," you may want to increase the number of peppers.

Serves 8 to 10

2 to 2½ quarts shredded Chinese cabbage (napa), about 2 pounds
½ to ⅔ cup coarsely chopped bottled pimientos or roasted sweet red peppers
¾ cup mayonnaise (low-calorie is fine)
¼ cup fresh or bottled unsweetened lime juice
¼ cup white wine vinegar or Oriental rice vinegar
½ teaspoon salt
¼ teaspoon granulated sugar
Freshly ground pepper, to taste
½ cup crumbled blue cheese

Toss the Chinese cabbage and pimientos or roasted peppers together in a salad bowl. Whisk together the mayonnaise, lime juice, vinegar, salt, sugar, and pepper until smooth. Pour the dressing over the vegetables, add the crumbled blue cheese, and toss the salad. Taste it for seasoning and adjust as necessary.

The slaw is ready to serve, but it is all the better for a few hours' standing at room temperature. If there is too much liquid at serving time, spoon off the surplus.

Any leftovers can be refrigerated for up to 3 days. You'll need to drain off the extra liquid given off by the cabbage before serving the salad again.

COLESLAW WITH JALAPEÑOS & BLUE CHEESE: Use the preceding recipe, but use tender green cabbage, preferably Savoy. Replace the pimientos with 2 (or 3, if more piquancy is welcome) slivered jalapeño peppers, which can be fresh, canned, or pickled.

This is especially good with chili, or alongside a hamburger.

CINNAMON-CAPPED APPLE MUFFINS

he better the fruit, the better the muffins. Firm, tart, almost winy apples are the kind to choose—nippiness counts. We use this batter to make blueberry muffins, too; see The Blueberry Version, after the main recipe.

Preheat the oven to 400°. Butter (or fit paper liners into) the cups of 1 or 2 muffin pans of the desired size.

Toss the apples with the lemon juice and the optional lemon zest; set aside.

Whisk together in a mixing bowl the all-purpose flour, whole-wheat flour, light-brown sugar, baking powder, salt, and cinnamon, if using.

Whisk together the milk, egg, and melted butter; pour over the dry ingredients, then add the chopped apples and fold everything together gently, just until the dry ingredients have been dampened but are not completely mixed; the batter should be thick and decidedly lumpy, apart from the chunks of diced apple. Spoon the batter into the prepared muffin cups.

Stir the topping ingredients together and sprinkle a share over each muffin.

Bake the muffins 25 to 30 minutes, or until they are firm. (Smaller muffins will take a little less time.) Remove from the pan.

Serve the muffins hot, or cool them on a wire rack and store them, wrapped, at room temperature for a day or two. To keep them longer, bag them airtight in heavy plastic and freeze them; they'll keep for several weeks in the freezer.

Reheating: Wrap loosely in foil and heat the muffins in a 350° oven until they are hot through, about 15 minutes; for still-frozen muffins, this will take perhaps twice as long.

Makes 12 large or 16 average muffins

Unsalted butter for coating
1½ cups diced pared and cored apples
1 teaspoon fresh lemon juice
1 teaspoon grated lemon zest (colored rind only, no pith), optional
1⅓ cups all-purpose flour
1 cup whole-wheat flour
½ cup (packed) light-brown sugar (use more for sweeter muffins)
4 teaspoons baking powder
1 teaspoon salt
¼ teaspoon ground cinnamon, optional
1 cup milk
1 large egg, lightly beaten
¼ cup melted unsalted butter

TOPPING:
3 tablespoons granulated sugar
1½ teaspoons ground cinnamon

THE BLUEBERRY VERSION: Add 1 teaspoon vanilla to the milk mixture; substitute 1½ cups rinsed and dried fresh or frozen blueberries for the apples; omit the lemon juice. Stir the blueberries briefly with the dry ingredients before adding the liquid.

PLUM VELVET

 eal fruit, jelled and molded into a "shape" that's dense, dark, and delectable, is startlingly good if you're acquainted only with the sparkly but fake-flavored jelled desserts that begin in a cardboard box.

Dark-skinned July plums, either yellow- or red-fleshed, are used in this recipe, but many other fruits will make lovely jellies, as noted below the recipe.

Rinse and slice the plums. Simmer them, pits and all, with the wine in a covered saucepan until they are soft, which takes about 20 minutes.

Press the plums through a food mill to get rid of the seeds (or just fish out the seeds); measure 3 cups of the pulp and juice.

Purée the pulp until it's velvety and shows no visible particles, using a blender or food processor. Add sugar to taste, stirring to dissolve it. Add the vanilla; taste the mixture and add drops of lemon juice if a touch of pleasant tartness is needed. (This depends on the plums.)

Sprinkle the gelatin over the water in a metal measuring cup and soak it until soft, about 5 minutes. Melt the gelatin, stirring, over very low heat, then stir it into the purée.

Pour the mixture into a 4-cup mold rinsed with cold water, or divide it among individual molds. Chill the Plum Velvet until it's firm, 2 hours or more. (The jelly can be made up to 2 days ahead.)

To serve, unmold the jelly (see Unmolding a "Shape," on the following page); garnish the dessert with mint or other green leaves. Pass the sauce separately.

Serves 6 to 8

1½ pounds dark-skinned plums, fully ripe
¾ cup ruby Port or medium Marsala
½ to ⅔ cup, or to taste, granulated sugar
1 teaspoon vanilla extract
Fresh lemon juice, if needed
4 teaspoons (about 1½ envelopes) unflavored gelatin
¼ cup water
Garnish: *Mint or other green leaves*
Sauce: *English Pouring Custard (page 218), lightly whipped cream, sour cream, or Cultured Cream (Crème Fraîche) (page 269)*

UNMOLDING A "SHAPE":
Dip the mold up to its rim in quite warm water for a few seconds, wipe the outside, then invert it onto the serving dish and shake both together, holding them at an angle to encourage the jelly to release from the mold. If the jelly doesn't drop out readily, dip the mold again, but cautiously—you don't want to melt the surface, just warm it enough to persuade it to slip out.

Alternatively, invert the mold onto the dish without dipping it and cover it with a towel wrung out of very hot water; leave the cloth in place for a moment, remove it, and try to lift off the mold. Repeat if necessary.

OTHER FRUITS TO JELL: Try such summer fruits as apricots, cherries, nectarines, or berries, cooked until soft with a little water or wine (red, white, or pink). Purée and sweeten the fruit, then jell it in the same fashion as plums. In early autumn, use blue (prune) plums or Damsons; later in the fall, full-flavored grapes of the Concord type make a delicious velvet. At any season, thick pulpy fresh orange juice (blood oranges make an especially beautiful dessert) can be jelled without cooking, but I'd increase the gelatin by about a teaspoonful because of the high acidity of the fruit. Canned purple plums, drained, are a good bet in winter; reduce the wine a little to compensate for their moistness. Fresh pineapple to be jelled *must* first be cooked to deactivate an enzyme that would otherwise prevent the gelatin from jelling.

PROPORTIONS: The recipe illustrates the proportions of gelatin to fruit—1 envelope (about 2½ teaspoons) of unflavored gelatin to 2 cups of sweetened pulp and liquid, including the soaking liquid for the gelatin. Taste the purée before adding sugar, and follow your taste, remembering that chilling will decrease the apparent sweetness of the fruit.

ENGLISH POURING CUSTARD

 pitcherful of this velvety golden sauce is perfect with a real-fruit jelly like Plum Velvet, with Amber Apples, and with several other desserts in this book, or with apple tart or almost any pudding. Add a tot of Bourbon to the sauce if it accompanies bread pudding made with or without raisins.

This sauce is the genuine article, unlike the "custard" often encountered in Britain nowadays, which gets its start in a packet of something called "custard powder."

Serves 6 or more

*1½ cups whole milk or
  mixed milk and cream*
*¼ cup, or more to taste,
  granulated sugar*
Pinch of salt
*3 large egg yolks, whisked
  to mix well*
1 teaspoon vanilla extract
*2 or 3 drops almond
  extract, optional (see
  Flavor Synergism, left)*

Heat the milk (or the milk and cream) to scalding—just below simmering—in a heavy saucepan over low heat (see Cautious Custard-Making, below, for tips.) Add the sugar and salt and stir until dissolved.

Whisk about one-fourth of the hot mixture into the egg yolks, then return the yolk mixture to the saucepan. Cook the custard over low heat, stirring it constantly, just until it has thickened lightly—the sauce will coat the back of a spoon when it has cooked enough. Don't let it reach the point of bubbling, much less boiling.

Immediately pour the sauce into a cold bowl and cool it, stirring occasionally. Add the flavorings, then strain the sauce into a storage jar or serving pitcher and refrigerate. It will keep for several days.

CAUTIOUS CUSTARD-MAKING: Cooks who are custard novices may want to use a double boiler, at least the first time out, to ensure the slow cooking that helps prevent overcooking. (A custard can turn into a mass of tiny curds in an instant if it's cooked at too-high heat or too long.)

If you're using a saucepan, try the old trick of rinsing the pan with cold water before pouring in the milk; it won't be so likely to stick to the pot.

However you cook the custard, you'll still have to stand right there, stirring, as you watch for the instant when it has thickened just enough.

FOOLING AROUND: Delectable versions of the classic fruit desserts called "fools" can be made with this custard instead of the usual whipped cream.

For 6 servings of a custard-based fool, you'll need a batch of cooled English Pouring Custard and 2 cups, give or take, of crushed or lightly puréed fruit or berries, not too juicy. Sweeten the fruit lightly, allowing for the sugar in the custard, and let it stand for a few minutes. Fold the components together with a rubber spatula, leaving a few streaks of color showing. Chill in a serving bowl or individual dishes.

A few uncooked fruits to fool with are strawberries, raspberries, and well-ripened mangoes; suitable stewed fruits include dried apricots, tart apples, and sieved blackberries.

THE BIG FREEZE—A CUSTARDY ICE CREAM: To use the custard to make 2 quarts of ice cream, cook and cool it as described, but use 3 whole eggs instead of yolks alone and 1 cup sugar instead of ¼ cup; increase the vanilla to 3 teaspoons. Add 3 cups of half-and-half (or part milk and part heavy cream) and freeze the mixture as instructed by the freezer maker.

FLAVOR SYNERGISM: The almond extract enhances the vanilla flavor without announcing its own presence. Good strategy for cakes and puddings and icings, too, and also good strategy for sweets flavored with chocolate.

SOUP'S ON

In cool or cold weather:
*A Big Soup of Beef & Okra (below) or Wild Rice & Porcini
Soup (below)*

In warm weather:
Sorrel Egg-Flower Soup (below)

*Garlic Version of "Barbecued" or Pulled Bread (page 51) or
Buttery Breadsticks (below)*

Winter dessert:
*Ambrosia (below) or Very Chocolate Ice Cream (page 204)
with Old-Fashioned Sugar Cookies (page 232)*

Summer dessert:
Strawberries and cream with cookies

To drink: *Sherry at the start and, if you like, with the soup*

No two ways about it, soup means supper whether we're talking word origins or cuisine, and here is a three-way menu built around supper choices for various seasons.

There is a soup of beef and okra that's closely related to gumbo, one that is earthy with the savor of wild rice and wild mushrooms, and one made with sorrel in a broth enriched with egg "flowers." Each makes a most satisfying meal when you add a good bread (or the breadsticks below) and follow up with a generous dessert.

A Big Soup of Beef & Okra

lthough it's a form of gumbo, thanks to the okra that establishes its character and to the optional filé powder whose inclusion I recommend, this hearty soup-stew is a good deal simpler to construct than classic Southern gumbos. (It is also less rich in the fat that's essential to the roux-based real thing, an observation which may or may not be of interest.)

At our house we enjoy this soup as a one-bowl meal once in a while in nippy weather, making it with the packaged frozen okra that's easier to find than the fresh vegetable, at least up North. The soup can be made more substantial (although it's already pretty substantial) by ladling it, as recommended, over a scoop of hot rice in a big soup plate.

At the risk of joining the broken-record chorus —I know I've mumbled about this before, writing about other foods—let me remind you again of the advantages of making dishes like this one ahead of time—even two days ahead if that's more convenient than cooking them the day before. If the soup can rest at least overnight before it's served, the flavors come together and mellow most magically. (Undoubtedly the reason for the existence of covens of secret leftover-lovers.)

For this dish there's one caution, however: The filé powder (see Filé File, page 222), which is listed as an optional ingredient, should be added, if it's used, just before the hot soup is served. (Some filé fanatics sprinkle it in the bowl before ladling in the soup, instead of adding it to the pot.) Care is necessary because this particular herbal seasoning turns ropy if the soup, gumbo, or other dish is cooked or heated after it is added. Although the flavor doesn't change, the altered texture won't greatly appeal to the fastidious.

Serves 6 as a main dish

*About 3 pounds bone-in
    shin of beef or 2 pounds
    boneless chuck*
*2 tablespoons bacon
    drippings or vegetable oil*
*1½ cups each diced onion,
    celery, and sweet red
    peppers*
3 cloves garlic, minced
*3 cups sliced fresh okra or
    2 10-ounce packages
    frozen okra, sliced*
*2 cans (1 pound each)
    whole Italian-type
    tomatoes, chopped, with
    their juice*
¼ cup tomato paste
*Herbs: 2 bay leaves, 1
    teaspoon crumbled dried
    thyme, and ½ teaspoon
    each crumbled dried
    basil and sweet
    marjoram*
Salt and pepper, to taste
*Tabasco or other hot
    pepper sauce, optional*
*Tomato juice or canned
    beef broth, if needed*
Filé powder, optional
Accompaniment: *Hot
    cooked rice*

A BIG SOUP OF BEEF & OKRA (CONTINUED)

Cover the meat with about 2 quarts of water in a pot; bring it to a boil and boil briskly, skimming off the foam until no more rises, 10 to 15 minutes. Reduce the heat and simmer the meat, partly covered, for 1 hour.

Remove the meat and dice it; skim most of the fat from the broth and return the meat to the broth, along with any marrow that can be extracted from the bones.

Meanwhile, heat the fat in a heavy soup pot; add the onions and stir and cook them until they are light golden brown, about 8 to 10 minutes. Add the celery, sweet peppers, and garlic; stir, cover the pot, and "sweat" the vegetables until they're limp, stirring once or twice, about 5 minutes.

Pour the broth and meat over the vegetables and bring everything to a brisk simmer. Add the okra, tomatoes and their juice, tomato paste, and herbs. Season everything lightly with salt and a little pepper. Return the soup to boiling, lower the heat, cover it partially, and simmer until the meat and vegetables are very tender and the soup is quite thick, about 1 hour. Season the soup to taste with salt and pepper; add a few dashes of hot pepper sauce, if desired. Remove the bay leaves.

If the soup is to be served at once, add the filé powder (see Filé Proportions, below) and serve it promptly. If time permits, it's best to cool the soup, uncovered, then refrigerate it at least overnight. If the soup is too thick after resting, thin it with added beef broth or tomato juice; reheat it and add the filé when it is piping hot. Don't continue heating it after the filé goes in.

Ladle the soup over hot rice in each soup plate.

FILÉ FILE: Filé powder is the most distinctive of Louisiana seasonings, a native herb that was introduced to European newcomers by the Native Americans. It's the dried and powdered leaves of the sassafras tree, which is commonly seen in shrub size as well. Filé is available commercially, but preparing it is a simple project.

Dry the mitten-shaped sassafras leaves like any other herb—in a dry, shady spot, in an oven at "warm" setting, in a food dehydrator, or in a microwave—then remove the stems and whirl the leaves in a spice mill or a blender. Sift the powder through a fine sieve and bottle it airtight. It keeps well for a year or more.

FILÉ PROPORTIONS: Add ½ to 1 teaspoon of filé powder to each quart of hot soup after it comes off the fire; stir and let the soup stand for a few minutes before it's served.

THE BOLETUS TRIBE:
You'll find dried boletus mushrooms labeled in various languages, but they're botanical siblings. Look for porcini, cèpes, funghi secchi, Steinpilze, Polish mushrooms, boletus, boletes, and "dried European mushrooms." If I come across Chilean dried mushrooms I snap them up, as they're closely related. They are always less expensive.

WILD RICE & PORCINI SOUP

Serves 6 to 8

½ ounce (⅓ cup) to 1
 ounce dried porcini,
 cèpes, or other boletus
 mushrooms (see Porcini
 and Others of the
 Boletus Tribe, above)
2 cups very hot tap water
¾ cup wild rice
Salt, to taste
2 tablespoons unsalted
 butter
1 medium-small onion,
 chopped
1 rib celery, chopped
4 cups chicken broth
1 bay leaf
¼ teaspoon crumbled
 dried thyme
¾ cup to 1 cup, to taste,
 dairy sour cream
¼ cup medium sherry
Freshly ground pepper, to
 taste

sumptuous pottage, both fragrant and earthy, with some slightly chewy grains of wild rice studding a velvety purée of wild rice and wild mushrooms that have been cooked in broth. Half an ounce of porcini makes a fine version; an ounce makes it superb.

Half an hour to several hours before starting the soup, put the porcini to soak in the hot tap water. Squeeze and rub the pieces once or twice as they soften; this helps release any clinging grit, which will fall to the bottom of the liquid.

Place the wild rice in a sieve and hold it under the hot water tap until the grains are quite hot. Let it drain.

Bring 3 cups of water to a boil, salt it lightly, and sprinkle in the wild rice. Stir, cover, and simmer the rice 30 to 40 minutes, or until the grains have split or "flowered" but remain a little chewy. Drain the rice.

Melt the butter in a soup pot. Add the onion and celery, stir to coat, cover the pot, and "sweat" the vegetables over low heat until they are soft, about 5 minutes.

Lift the mushrooms from the soaking liquid and add them to the vegetables. Strain the soaking liquid through a strainer lined with close-woven cloth to remove the inevitable grit. Add the mushroom liquid to the pot.

Add half of the wild rice (reserve the rest), the chicken broth, bay leaf, and thyme. Bring the soup to a boil, lower the heat, and simmer it, covered, until the mushrooms and rice are very soft, about 45 minutes. Remove the bay leaf.

Purée the soup in a food processor or blender until it is smooth; return it to the pot. Add the reserved wild rice and reheat to simmering.

Whisk in the sour cream and sherry and let the soup reheat again just to simmering, but don't let it boil. Taste and add salt and pepper as needed. Serve the soup while it's still piping hot.

SORREL EGG-FLOWER SOUP

ost sorrel soups of the Western European persuasion are doused with a lot of heavy cream, but to my palate, at least, the cream interferes with the clean, tart taste of the greens. So, using perennial sorrel from my small garden, I've devised this soup made without added butterfat; it's a leafy broth with Chinese-style egg "flowers" blooming in it.

We like it a lot at our house, as a bowlful is just satisfying enough for a light lunch or supper, and it's a quick soup to put together. In smaller servings, it can be a stimulating starter for dinner. If you're offering it as a one-bowl meal for half a dozen, you should double the recipe.

The soup is equally good made with fresh sorrel or with a stash from the freezer (see Freezing Sorrel, right).

Makes 1 quart

3 cups full-flavored
  chicken broth, any fat
  removed
2 cups (packed) shredded
  fresh French sorrel, or ½
  cup frozen sorrel (see
  Preparing Sorrel and
  Freezing Sorrel, right)
1 large egg
1 teaspoon cornstarch
  mixed with 2 teaspoons
  water
¼ teaspoon, or as needed,
  Oriental (roasted)
  sesame oil, optional

Heat the broth to simmering; add the sorrel and simmer it briefly until the shreds are olive-green, a matter of moments. (If frozen sorrel is used, it need not be thawed—just heat the sorrel in the broth until it simmers again.)

Beat the egg a little to mix it, then beat in the cornstarch and water mixture and, optionally, ¼ teaspoon of sesame oil (which I recommend for the elusive hint of nuttiness it contributes.)

Drizzle the egg mixture slowly into the simmering soup, looping it about as you pour; don't stir it at all after adding the egg, but turn off the heat, cover the pan, and let the egg flowers "blossom" for 2 or 3 minutes. (The soup can rest longer, for up to 10 minutes, if that's more convenient.)

Serve while hot, adding 2 or 3 drops of additional sesame oil to each bowl if you like.

THE TWO SESAME OILS:
The oil to use for aromatizing this soup is the tawny, fragrant Oriental kind made from roasted (or toasted) sesame seeds; it's used as a finishing seasoning in many Chinese and some Japanese dishes, and it should be in the international-foods section of any good supermarket.

Its flavor is quite different from that of sesame oil pressed from unroasted seeds; that kind is yellow in color and bland in taste, and it won't do as a replacement.

PREPARING SORREL: As noted, the sorrel to use is the French variety, with long leaves shaped like lance heads in a medieval painting. (There are wild kinds, too, and a successful forager could no doubt make good soup with them.)

Cut off the sorrel stems, stack the leaves, and slice them crosswise into ¼-inch shreds. (Crosswise cutting keeps the leaf veins from asserting their natural stringiness.) When measuring, pack the cup somewhat firmly; this green shrinks amazingly when cooked.

FREEZING SORREL: When sorrel is flourishing or can be bought at the greengrocer's, I like to freeze a supply to use in future sauces for fish as well as for this soup.

First blanch the sorrel by steaming the shreds (see above) in a steamer basket until they turn olive-green (it takes only a moment); or drop them into abundant boiling water and scoop them out with a slotted spoon at once. Drain, cool, and freeze the sorrel in ½-cup batches. I use small zip-top freezer bags, being sure to press out all air before zipping them.

BUTTERY BREADSTICKS

 all, twisty, airy, and crisp, these buttery batons are among the best breadsticks you can make. Maybe the best. They keep perfectly in a canister, so a recipe's worth is a good investment of time.

Makes at least 3 dozen, depending on length

Divide the ingredients for Angel or "Riz" Biscuits, Rolls, or Cookout Buns (page 266) in half—you'll use 1 cup buttermilk, 1½ tablespoons (or envelopes) yeast, 1½ teaspoons salt, 1 teaspoon granulated sugar, ¼ teaspoon baking soda, about 3 cups all-purpose flour (plus a little more for kneading), and 3 tablespoons melted and cooled butter, either regular or unsalted.

Separately, melt and reserve another 3 to 4 tablespoons of butter for brushing the breadsticks.

I won't repeat the steps of the basic recipe for making the dough, but once it has been kneaded and rested for 5 minutes, pat or roll it out about ¼ inch thick (you may wish to divide it in half first). Using a pizza cutter (the easy way) or a very sharp knife, cut it into strips no more than ½ inch wide. They can be long or short—your choice.

One at a time, twist the strips a few times (precision doesn't matter) and lay them an inch apart on a nonstick or lightly greased baking sheet. If any strip tries to untwist, press each end firmly against the pan to discourage wriggling.

Brush the dough generously with the melted butter, using a pastry brush, and let the sticks rise until they're twice as fat as they were, 30 minutes or so. (Test the degree of rising by pressing the side of a strip—a finger mark will remain in the dough when the breadsticks are ready to bake.)

Meanwhile, preheat the oven to 400°.

Bake the breadsticks 5 minutes, then brush them with butter again and continue baking until they're delicately browned and firm, perhaps 20 minutes' baking in all. If there is any butter left, brush it over the finished breadsticks.

Cool the breadsticks on a rack and store them in a canister at room temperature.

AMBROSIA

This more-than-meets-the-eye dessert seems very Southern, but it has never been a stay-at-home; its status as a special treat goes way back, all over the country. It's worth reviving where it's been forgotten, and it doesn't need such furbelows as the liqueurs sometimes added in all innocence.

Ambrosia is best in the season when oranges are best—winter, when California navel oranges are to be had. (Yes, I know, oranges also come from—what's the name of that place, again?) Fresh coconut makes better ambrosia than the sweetened stuff that comes from a package, so there's guidance at the left on how to reduce a hairy brown coconut to sweet, snowy shreds.

CRACKING AND SHREDDING A COCONUT: A medium-size coconut will yield about 3 cups of shreds. A good nut will contain liquid (shake and listen). Puncture the "eyes" of the coconut and drain off the water. (The cook is allowed to quaff it as a bonus.) Bake the coconut 15 minutes in a 325° oven; the shell will then crack easily when tapped with a hammer. Pull out the chunks of meat, pare off the brown skin, and grate or shred the coconut. To store, wrap the coconut airtight and freeze it.

Serves 6

*6 or more seedless
oranges, depending on
size*
*About 3 cups shredded
fresh coconut (see
Cracking and Shredding
a Coconut, left) or best-
quality commercial
coconut*
*Superfine or confectioner's
sugar, if needed*
*Optional garnish: Candied
cherries and/or more
slices of orange*

Peel or pare the oranges, removing every scrap of membrane on the outside. If the oranges are small, slice them paper-thin crosswise; halve larger oranges lengthwise, then slice them into half-moons.

Sprinkle a little coconut in a crystal or glass serving bowl, then make alternate layers of oranges and coconut, ending with coconut. Sprinkle the oranges lightly with sugar as you go, unless the fruit is quite sweet or the coconut has been sweetened.

Chill the ambrosia for up to 3 hours—it shouldn't be icy-cold, for the best flavor. At serving time garnish the bowl, if you like, with the cherries, or with additional slices of orange, or with both. (Fresh mint leaves are also pretty.)

———

REMEMBERING WHEN: Maraschino cherries used to be the garnish of choice for this and many other gala desserts, but that was before it was discovered that the dye used to color them that improbable shade of red should be a cause of concern to the health-conscious. Perhaps they'll have a comeback one day, in a more wholesome guise, but meanwhile candied cherries, homemade or store-bought, are a decent alternative.

A SUPPER FOR ANY SEASON

*Hearty Cornbread Skillet with Bacon & Whole-Kernel Corn
(below), served with Thick Yogurt (page 270), Whipped
Cottage Cheese (page 270), or dairy sour cream*

*A steamed green vegetable—snap beans, summer squash,
broccoli, or slant-cut asparagus—with
Butter & Lemon Sauce (page 106) or
Classic Vinaigrette (page 273)*

Amber Apples (below)

*Old-Fashioned Sugar Cookies (below) or Twice-Baked Orange
& Nut Cookies (page 93)*

To drink: Hot or iced tea; or beer

The absence of a substantial meat component in this menu has no great social significance; it's just that sometimes a little- or no-meat meal is refreshing to both spirit and palate. In other words, you don't need to have vegetarian convictions to enjoy this supper.

The smoky bacon in the main dish is there as a flavoring rather than a major source of protein. (However, through a happy synergism, the two forms of corn plus the dairy sauce, taken together, provide dietarily complete protein.) With an added vegetable and dessert, no one will leave the table hungry.

HEARTY CORNBREAD SKILLET WITH BACON & WHOLE-KERNEL CORN

hole-kernel corn adds enough texture and substance to this bacon-flavored version of crackling bread to transform it into a main dish.

Crackling bread used to be a staple on farms where porkers were routinely made into hams, sausage, salt pork, lard, and other good things besides chops and roasts. The cracklings were the flavorful scraps remaining after the lard had been slowly cooked out of the pig's fat. In off-season times when no cracklings were on hand, the farm cook would substitute crisp-fried salt pork. Salt pork is replaced in this recipe by smoky bacon, which gives a more rounded flavor to the dish.

This skillet casserole evolved from an eggy cornbread we used to make on country weekends, using fresh stone-ground cornmeal from the Hook Mill in East Hampton, on New York's Long Island, where we now live the year around; we followed a "yaller bread" recipe from a vintage issue of a now-forgotten farm magazine.

Most supermarkets carry stone-ground meal, and natural-food stores and specialist grain suppliers are good sources if the grocer fails you. Choose a coarse grind if it's offered; you can make wonderful polenta with it, too.

A HOT PAN MAKES CRUSTY CORNBREAD: Schools of thought about cornbread aren't limited to the debate about yellow meal *versus* white meal; baking methods differ, too.

Most recipes instruct the cook to start the baking in an ordinary, cold baking pan. However, using a preheated heavy skillet, as for this dish, rewards the cook with a crustiness that can't be won in any other way.

The hot skillet, in case you were wondering, is a legacy of hearth-baking days, when cornbreads and other breadstuffs were baked in a three-legged iron "spider" over the coals on the open hearth.

Serves 6 to 8

Bacon fat or neutral
vegetable oil for coating
the pan
About ⅓ pound slab or
thick-cut bacon, cut into
¼-inch dice
1½ cups stone-ground
yellow cornmeal,
preferably coarse
½ cup all-purpose flour
1 teaspoon salt
1 teaspoon baking soda
½ teaspoon baking
powder
Freshly ground coarse
black pepper
2 large eggs
2 cups buttermilk or
substitute (see Pinch-
Hitter for Buttermilk,
below)
3 tablespoons vegetable oil
or reserved liquid bacon
fat
¾ cup drained whole-
kernel corn, fresh-
cooked, canned, or
frozen
Sauce: *Thick Yogurt (page
270), Whipped Cottage
Cheese, (page 270), or
dairy sour cream*

HEARTY CORNBREAD (CONTINUED)

Preheat the oven to 375°. Set a lightly greased 9-inch iron skillet on the center shelf of the oven to heat thoroughly; allow about 5 minutes.

Cook the bacon in a second skillet over low heat, stirring, until the bits are crisp. Drain; reserve the bacon pieces, and reserve the fat, if you wish—some of it can be used in the batter.

Whisk together thoroughly the cornmeal, flour, salt, baking soda, baking powder, and pepper in a mixing bowl.

Beat the eggs; stir in the buttermilk and the oil or liquid bacon fat. Pour the liquid over the dry ingredients and stir lightly, just until the "drys" are dampened; don't overmix the batter or the finished texture of the cornbread will be as tough as an overmixed muffin.

Pull out the oven shelf and pour the batter into the hot skillet; instantly scatter the bacon and corn over the top. Bake for 30 minutes, or until the top is browned and firm and the sides begin to shrink away from the pan.

Serve the cornbread piping hot and directly from the skillet; cut it into wedges for serving and top each helping with your sauce of choice.

Leftovers: Heat leftovers in foil in a 350° oven for about 15 minutes, or until well warmed, and serve.

Or you can split wedges of the bread, slip a generous slice of sharp Cheddar, Monterey Jack, or other cheese that will melt readily into each, wrap the bundles individually in foil, and place them in a 350° oven to heat for about 15 minutes. A good lunch. (If plastic-wrapped the sandwiches are also microwavable.)

CONFETTI CORN SKILLET: If the batter is embellished with a handful of diced red and/or hot peppers, this farmstyle dish takes on a pleasing touch of Southwestern flavor. Reduce the corn kernels by ¼ cup and add ⅓ to ½ cup of drained and diced bottled jalapeños and/or roasted red peppers.

PINCH-HITTER FOR BUTTERMILK: Genuine buttermilk—the tangy thick liquid that remains after real butter has been churned from real cream—has vanished from the market; the "buttermilk" in dairy cases is low-fat milk that has been fermented and thickened by a lactic culture. Good, but not quite the same.

If a recipe calls for buttermilk and there's none in the fridge, you don't need to head for the store. Just measure 2½ tablespoons of white vinegar into a 2-cup measure; fill the cup with low-fat or regular sweet milk, stir it, and let the milk thicken for a few minutes.

AMBER APPLES

haker applesauce is one of the most delectable dishes created by the almost-vanished Shaker communities, whose women were very good cooks indeed. Made by boiling gallons of sweet cider down to a syrup in which sliced apples are then cooked, it is intense in flavor and color, a pure pleasure for apple lovers.

As I didn't own a pot big enough to boil gallons of cider, in past apple seasons I scaled down the original recipe to fit the *batterie de cuisine* at my command. Later I streamlined the process further by starting off with frozen apple-juice concentrate, which works very well if pot watching isn't high on the list of things there is time for.

Serves 6 to 8

*2 cans (6 ounces each)
frozen apple juice
concentrate, thawed
2½ pounds firm-fleshed
tart apples (Greenings,
Granny Smiths, Mutsu,
etc.)
Granulated sugar, if
needed
Drops of fresh lemon juice,
if needed
Accompaniment: Cultured
Cream (Crème Fraîche)
(page 269) or sweet
fresh cream*

Pour the apple-juice concentrate into a wide skillet or sauté pan made of nonreactive material.

Peel and core the apples and cut them into sixths or eighths, according to their size, dropping them into the skillet as you go. Shake the pan occasionally to persuade the apples into a single layer; if they won't all fit, deploy a second pan and use a share of the liquid in the first pan.

Bring the liquid to a simmer, then lower the heat and cook the apples very slowly, basting them often with their syrup, until they are translucent and amber-colored. The total time depends on the type and ripeness of the apples, but about 45 minutes would be par for the course. (If the syrup threatens to scorch at any point, add a little water.)

When the apples are almost done, taste a slice and add sugar and/or lemon juice if needed for a good tart-sweet balance. Transfer the slices to a shallow serving dish, pour the syrup over them, and chill. (They will keep for several days.)

Serve with a pitcher of fresh cream or Cultured Cream.

The fruit also makes a handsome apple tart (below).

A TART OF AMBER APPLES: For this somewhat more

formal presentation of Amber Apples, make and bake completely a 9-or 10-inch tart shell, using your favorite recipe or the directions for making pastry dough and baking shells that begin on page 277.

Drain a batch of cooled Amber Apples (on the preceding page) very well, saving the syrup. Arrange the fruit in rings in the baked shell, overlapping the slices to make an attractive pattern.

Unless the reserved apple syrup is already thick enough to serve as a dense glaze, transfer it to a saucepan and reduce it further by brisk boiling, stirring it often. When you judge it's thick enough, brush it over the apples to glaze the top of the tart.

Serve the tart at room temperature, accompanied by cream in some form—whip about ½ cup heavy cream until quite fluffy but not stiff; or serve Cultured Cream (Crème Fraîche, page 269), or allow vanilla ice cream to soften until it's pourable enough to pass in a pitcher.

OLD-FASHIONED SUGAR COOKIES

The recipe below has been adapted from an earlier book of mine called, for the sake of the joke, *Mrs. Witty's Monster Cookies.* (Although, I hasten to add, it has recipes for cookies of all sizes.)

You can make enormous sugar cookies if you like (the how-to's are in that book), but the recipe here is for your choice of mid-size mouthfuls or mini-monsters—not as big as actual monsters—which are molded with the help of a coffee can.

Smaller cookies shaped by hand as directed in the recipe can be transformed into Snickerdoodles, which are especially good with that glass of milk. Just roll the shaped balls of dough in granulated sugar that has been blended with enough cinnamon to tint it pale rosy-brown. Snickerdoodles are flattened and baked the same way as sugared but unspiced cookies.

SHORTCUT SHORTCAKES:
Here's a quick dessert caper that starts with sugar cookies made large enough to be served as individual "shortcakes." (You might mold them in a middle-sized fruit can, or go to the coffee-can size for truly impressive cookies.)

At serving time, spread each cookie with Uncooked Lime or Lemon Curd (page 130) and top the "shortcake" with berries, sliced peaches, nectarines, or ripe apricots, making a pleasant pattern. Lovely, with or without a tuft of whipped cream.

*Makes about 3 dozen
3-inch cookies*

1 cup (2 sticks) unsalted
   butter
1 cup granulated sugar
½ cup (packed) light-
   brown sugar
2 large egg yolks
½ teaspoon finely grated
   lemon zest (outer rind
   only, no pith)
1 teaspoon vanilla extract
2½ cups all-purpose flour
2 teaspoons baking
   powder
¾ teaspoon salt
About 2 teaspoons water,
   if needed
Unsalted butter for
   coating the baking sheets

TOPPING:
*Coarse decorating sugar,
   or additional granulated
   sugar*

Cream the butter until soft; cream in the two sugars gradually; beat in the egg yolks one at a time, then stir in the lemon zest and vanilla.

Sift together the flour, baking powder, and salt; stir the dry ingredients thoroughly into the creamed mixture. If the dough is too stiff to mix easily, sprinkle on and mix in enough drops of water to make a smooth but not wet dough.

For hand-shaped cookies: Wrap and chill the dough until it is firm, 2 hours or so.

To mold the dough for slicing: Pack it into one or more well-cleaned and dried food cans (soup to coffee-can size, according to the diameter of the cookies you want) whose tops have been smoothly removed. Cover the surface of the dough with plastic wrap and chill the can(s) until the dough is firm, from 2 hours to overnight. (The dough may be kept in the refrigerator for 2 days or so if that's most convenient.)

At baking time, preheat the oven to 350°. Butter 1 or 2 cookie sheets lightly.

For molded dough: With a can opener that makes a smooth cut, cut out the bottoms of the tin-can molds, but leave them in place. Then, using the bottom as a pusher, shove a quarter-inch thickness of dough out of the can; slice it off with a sharp knife and transfer the slice to a baking sheet. Repeat, arranging the slices 2 inches apart on the pan, until all the dough has been dealt with. Sprinkle the cookies with coarse or regular granulated sugar. Brush surplus sugar from the pans.

For hand-shaped cookies: Pinch off rounded table-spoonfuls of chilled dough and shape them into balls. Roll them in sugar and arrange them 3 inches apart on baking sheets. Press each ball out to 2-inch diameter with the bottom of a drinking glass dipped in extra granulated sugar.

However the cookies have been formed, bake them on the center shelf of the oven for about 6 minutes (for smaller cookies), longer for larger ones, depending on their thickness and their diameter. They are done when the centers have puffed and fallen again and the edges are golden-brown.

Cool the cookies on their pans until they are firm, about 5 minutes, then remove them with a spatula and allow them to cool completely on a wire rack before storing them.

The cookies will store well in a canister for up to 2 weeks. If they soften in storage, warm them in a low oven (300°) and cool them again to restore crispness.

READY-AHEAD SUPPER

Large bowls of Six-Seafood Chowder (below)

Cornsticks (page 209), Buttery Breadsticks (page 225), split and toasted Angel Rolls (page 266), or purchased pilot crackers or sea toast

Summer dessert: Gingery Melon Mold (below)
Winter dessert: Pecan or Black-Walnut Graham Torte (below)

Any season: Fresh apples with Cheddar, or any blue cheese

To drink: Beer or ale; or a chilled Chablis, Muscadet, or Riesling

A luxurious dish for all its simplicity, Six-Seafood Chowder is a special treat to celebrate with when the fishman's shop is superbly stocked and appetites at home are ravening for seafood. It's a chowder to cherish, too, because it's best when made a day ahead, and it can be put together at whatever pace best suits the cook. I'm tempted to dub it the best of all the chowders I know and love.... But no. No favoritism.

For dessert after this bowlful of briny bliss, choose either Gingery Melon Mold or Pecan or Black-Walnut Graham Torte, made with wondrous native American nuts plus graham-cracker crumbs.

SIX-SEAFOOD CHOWDER

 ix-Seafood Chowder doesn't call for any exotic or difficult cooking techniques, but it does require a number of orderly steps; the final brimming bowlful will reward careful attention to each.

The recipe looks more complicated than it is, because the cooking steps, though simple, add up to a lengthy description. The chowder-maker who marches along from each to the next will savor the dish at its best, without such blemishes as gritty mussels or chunks of fish overcooked to porridge.

The finished chowder is distinguished by several varied textures. It is studded with firm chunks of shrimp, monkfish, and scallops, buttery mussels, semifirm flakes of cod, and fragile bits of flatfish, all of which show to advantage in a base made along classic lines, with bits of salt pork, diced potatoes and onions, and rich milk.

Timings: To preserve these textures, try to precook the shrimp, mussels, and scallops according to the timings specified in the recipe. The several kinds of fish, though, must be cooked more watchfully in the first stage. Exact timings will depend on the type of fish (there's guidance in the recipe) and the thickness of the pieces and will require you to keep a careful eye on the proceedings to avoid overcooking. Bear in mind that the chowder will be cooked further after it has been assembled, and you don't want the fish in your lovely potful to turn to mush. (If in doubt, undercook.)

For suitable replacements for any unavailable ingredient, see Sending in the Substitutes (page 237). Like most chowders, this one is flexible; you can always substitute, or increase the quantity of one or two of the others, just so the total bulk of ingredients remains more or less the same.

Serves 6 generously as a main dish

2 pounds (about 2 quarts) scrubbed and bearded mussels (see Bearding a Mussel, right)

2 cups water (or light fish stock, if you have some on hand; see Chowder Choices—Liquid, page 238)

½ pound medium shrimp, in the shell

Additional water, fish stock, bottled clam juice, or chicken broth, as needed

1 bay leaf

2 generous slices onion

2 or 3 sprigs parsley

Sprig of fresh thyme, or pinch of dried thyme

½ pound sea or bay scallops

½ pound monkfish

½ pound codfish

½ pound flounder or other flatfish

¼ pound salt pork, diced small

2 medium onions, diced (about 1 cup)

3 cups diced peeled all-purpose potatoes

4 to 6 cups whole milk, or combined milk and half-and-half or cream

Salt and white pepper, to taste

Pinch of freshly grated nutmeg or ground mace, optional

Dash or two of paprika

Garnish: About 4 tablespoons (½ stick) unsalted butter, sliced, and a little minced parsley

SIX-SEAFOOD CHOWDER (CONTINUED)

Combine the mussels with the 2 cups of water or other liquid in a pot, cover, and cook over high heat, shaking the pan often, just until they open, 2 to 5 minutes. Lift the mussels from the broth with a slotted spoon; reserve the shellfish and the broth.

Strain the broth (see Bearding a Mussel, right), rinse out the pot to remove any lurking grains of sand, return the broth to the pot, and reheat it to simmering.

Simmer the shrimp in the mussel liquid until they turn decisively pink, about 3 minutes. Lift out the shrimp (again, save the broth) and reserve them.

Strain the broth again and measure it; add one of the listed liquids (water, fish stock, clam juice, or broth) to make a generous 4 to 5 cups. Return the liquid to the pot and add the bay leaf, onion slices, parsley, and thyme. Bring to a boil and simmer 5 minutes.

Drop the scallops into the broth and poach them (see Poaching, page 238) for 5 minutes for sea scallops, 1½ minutes for bay scallops; remove and set aside the scallops.

Add the monkfish to the broth after returning it to simmering and poach the fish for 12 minutes for each inch of thickness at the thickest part of the piece; if any thinner parts are done before the thick part, lift them out. (Monkfish requires longer cooking than most fish.) Remove and reserve the monkfish.

Add the codfish and poach it for 7 minutes for each inch of thickness at its thickest part; remove and reserve.

Add the flounder or other flatfish and poach it very briefly, especially if the fillets are thin—1 to 2 minutes will do it; remove and reserve the fish as soon as it turns opaque. One last time, strain the broth, discard the vegetable debris, and set the broth aside.

Now it's time to change pots. In a soup pot or other heavy-bottomed pan, cook the diced salt pork, stirring, over low heat until the bits are crisp and golden but not brown. Add the chopped onions and cook them, stirring, until they are translucent, about 5 minutes. Add the potatoes and stir them constantly until the pieces are hot. Stir in the reserved liquid, bring the chowder base to a boil, lower the heat, and simmer it uncovered until the vegetables are tender, perhaps 10 minutes.

Meanwhile, flake the codfish (it will fall into natural chunks); cut the monkfish or other firm fish into generous chunks; break fragile fish into large pieces; shell the mussels and cut the meats in half if they are large. Shell the shrimp, devein them (this is optional among shrimp lovers; see Cleaning Shrimp, page 238), and cut them into ½-inch chunks. Slice sea scallops crosswise in half, then cut the slices into quarters; if you have used bay scallops, halve them crosswise unless they're small enough to leave whole.

Add all the fish and seafood to the chowder base and reheat everything to simmering; don't stir the chowder at this point.

Meanwhile, bring to a simmer 4 to 6 cups of milk, the amount depending on how juicy the chowder base seems to be. Pour the hot milk over the solids and heat everything for a moment or two more, turning the seafood and vegetables gently with a spatula once or twice.

Remove the chowder from the heat, taste it, and correct the seasonings; how much salt the chowder needs will depend on how the cooking liquid(s) were seasoned, but be fairly generous with the white pepper and frugal with the nutmeg or mace (an optional addition). A little paprika will warm up the color of the chowder, but it won't do much actual seasoning.

Set the pot aside, partly covered, to let the chowder mellow for whatever time is available—from half an hour to overnight. When it's cool, refrigerate it, covered, if it's to be held for more than 2 or 3 hours.

At serving time, reheat the chowder to just short of the boiling point, turning the ingredients over gently with a spatula once or twice to insure even heating; avoid actual stirring.

Pour the hot chowder into a warmed tureen or warmed individual chowder bowls and top it with slices of butter and the parsley.

SENDING IN THE SUBSTITUTES: Fresh mussels—especially cultivated mussels raised on rafts, which are wonderfully free of sand and grit—are always the first choice, but canned mussels (which usually come from Scandinavia) will do. Buy enough canned mussels to provide about 1½ cups of meats. The broth from the canned mussels can be used in the recipe instead of clam broth.

Monkfish (a.k.a. goosefish and angler fish) is highly desirable for its firm lobsterlike character, but tilefish or halibut are fine substitutes. Haddock or hake can replace cod. Any other flatfish—fluke, or any of the so-called "soles"—can take the flounder role. Any salt-water bass can replace any one of the other fish.

BEARDING A MUSSEL: These bivalves latch on to their underwater supports by means of a clingfast, a mass of fibers called a "beard," which often incorporates bits of

ALSO FROM THE CHOWDER POT: Chowders almost certainly take their name from the Breton fishermen's cauldron, the *chaudière,* in which the first New World fish stews were cooked.

In the centuries since then, American chowders have been made in great variety (and with much argument about what's a "real" chowder) from every kind of seafood (and fresh-water fish) and from chicken and countless vegetables as well. There's *corn chowder,* which can also contain potatoes; everything-in-the-garden *vegetable chowder; chicken chowder; potato chowder; bean chowder,* often containing tomatoes; and chowders of *parsnips, salt fish,* and even *mushrooms.* The lid, it would seem, is the limit to inventions for the chowder pot.

CHOWDER CHOICES—
LIQUID: This recipe "builds" its own rich seafood stock as it goes along if you start with water, but it's all the better if fish stock starts off the proceedings. Chowders can be made with fish or shellfish stock from the freezer, or with bottled clam broth combined with water, or even with chicken broth, which should be relieved of all fat before it's used.

There are dehydrated fish-stock cubes, too, that aren't at all bad—Knorr is one brand I've used.

seaweed and gravel. Mussel shells frequently carry hitch-hikers, too—clinging barnacles or other kinds of small mendicant shellfish.

To clean mussels, wait until you're ready to cook them. (Store them in an uncovered bowl or open bag, preferably not plastic, in the refrigerator; don't exclude air.) Dump them into a sinkful of cold water and pull them apart if they are clumped together. Check each shell to make sure it's inhabited by mussel, not mud: to do this, try to slide the shells apart with strong sidewise-slipping pressure—a "mudder" will open and reveal its guilty secret, but a good mussel can't be induced to open this way.

Using a knife blade, scrape off any barnacles or other creatures clinging to the mussel's shell. Tug hard on the "beard" and pull it out by its roots, which extend inside. Rinse the mussels well by sloshing them in fresh water, rinsing them more than once if sand is in evidence at any point. (Some cultivated mussels are sand-free; some wild ones are anything but.)

If you find mussels are sandy as you clean them, after precooking them (for this or any other recipe), shell them, then swish them thoroughly through their own broth (which should first be strained, as described below) and lift them out with a slotted spoon.

Before using the broth, strain it again—I pour it through a sieve lined with close-woven cheese muslin, which is finer-textured than the very loosely woven "cheesecloth" that seems to be the only kind available now; such "cheesecloth" is pretty useless for most kitchen purposes, but it's okay for polishing furniture, I suppose.

POACHING: This way of cooking food very gently in liquid is not for seafood only. What poaching *is not* is boiling. In poaching, the liquid is brought just to the boiling point, the food is added (it should be covered by the liquid), and the heat is kept high just until the barest simmer begins again (small bubbles will appear around the edges; an occasional bubble may rise). At that point, before even gentle boiling can begin, the heat should be lowered to maintain the gentlest of simmers. Timing of the poaching begins at this point, not when the food is first added to the liquid.

CLEANING SHRIMP: There are gadgets that remove the shell and the vein from cooked shrimp in one swoop; if you have one of these, you know how to use it.

Otherwise, cut off the tail fins and peel off the shell in segments. Using a small knife, make a lengthwise cut about ¼-inch deep along the curved back of the shrimp. If the intestinal vein can be seen (often it can't be found), pry it out with the tip of the knife and discard it. If you want to rinse the shrimp, do it quickly to preserve the flavor.

BUYING A MELON—THE NOSE KNOWS: When choosing a melon, it's a good idea to go beyond poking, which is not much use unless the melon is far gone, and also to go beyond just looking. The skin color isn't always significant, but upstanding netting indicates more ripeness than flat netting. Above all, *sniff.* A ripe melon smells good when a deep breath is taken at the blossom end (the end without the stem scar). A fruity scent, even if faint, is promising; let such a melon ripen further in the fruit bowl.

Serves 6 to 8

3¼ cups ginger beer
 or strong ginger ale
¼ cup honey
2 tablespoons fresh lemon
 or lime juice
2 envelopes unflavored
 gelatin
3 cups balls or cubes of
 ripe cantaloupe or
 muskmelon (about 1½
 medium melons)
Garnish: *Fresh mint or
 grape leaves*
Optional accompaniment:
 *¾ cup chilled heavy
 cream, whipped;
 optionally, stir the
 whipped cream with 2
 tablespoons minced
 candied ginger*

GINGERY MELON MOLD

 inger beer, which rejoices in more character and body than ginger ale, makes the most flavorful version of this shivery "shape." However, if the "beer" (nonalcoholic) can't be found on the fancy-food shelves, very good ginger ale will do. If a premium brand or a local specialty is available, by all means use it; bargain bottles just don't have enough gingery pizzaz for this dessert.

The melon can be either cantaloupe or muskmelon, so long as it's ripe and fragrant.

Not for supper only, this spicy but cooling dessert is offbeat but nice to serve, perhaps without the whipped cream, for a warm-weather late breakfast or early lunch.

Blend together the ginger beer, honey, and citrus juice. Measure ½ cup of the mixture into a small saucepan or metal measuring cup. Sprinkle the gelatin over the liquid and let it soak 5 minutes.

Set the pan or cup over very low heat and stir until the gelatin has melted. Whisk the mixture into the remaining ginger beer, honey, and juice, stirring vigorously to explode as many bubbles as possible. Chill until slightly thickened, about the consistency of egg white. At the same time, chill the melon balls or cubes.

Shake the melon pieces in a sieve to drain them of all possible liquid, then fold the melon into the chilled gelatin. Rinse a 5- or 6-cup mold, or 6 individual molds, with cold water, then pour in the gelatin; if individual molds are used, distribute the pieces of fruit equally.

Cover the mold(s) and chill the dessert until firmly set, allowing several hours. (It will keep for 2 or 3 days, unmolded, in the refrigerator.)

Unmold the dessert onto a chilled serving dish or dishes and garnish it, if you like, with mint or other green leaves. Serve it with the whipped cream, if desired.

BLACK WALNUT LORE: If you live far from black-walnut country, you'll have the best chance for good nuts if you mail-order them from a reputable dealer.

Nut shops often don't supply the cold storage needed for these nuts, which are so rich in oil they easily turn rancid at shelf temperature. Once purchased, store them in the freezer, airtight (best for all nuts, actually).

Serves 8 to 12

Unsalted butter and all-purpose flour for coating the pan(s)
1½ cups graham-cracker crumbs, preferably made from honey grahams
½ cup black walnuts or pecans
½ cup all-purpose flour
2 teaspoons baking powder
½ teaspoon salt
8 tablespoons (1 stick) unsalted butter, at room temperature
1 cup granulated sugar
3 large eggs, separated
1 teaspoon vanilla extract
¾ cup milk
TOPPING:
1 cup heavy cream, chilled
Confectioner's sugar
Garnish: A few additional nuts

PECAN OR BLACK-WALNUT GRAHAM TORTE

hether it's called a torte or a cake, this hybrid confection does full justice to the two distinguished nuts with which it can be made. Black walnuts are a weakness of mine, and the torte was devised to show them off; but pecans are excellent, too.

Preheat the oven to 350°.

Butter generously and flour a deep 10- or 11-inch loose-bottomed pan with either plain or fluted sides.

Combine the crumbs and nuts in a food processor (or do this in batches in a blender) and pulse the machine on and off until the mixture is uniformly fine. Add the flour, baking powder, and salt to the crumb mixture; mix by pulsing the food processor, or whisk everything together.

Cream the butter and sugar together until fluffy; beat in the egg yolks one at a time; beat in the vanilla. Stir in a third of the crumb mixture, then half of the milk, another third of the crumbs, and so on.

Beat the egg whites until they hold a soft peak but remain glossy. Stir a fourth of the whites thoroughly into the batter, then fold in the remaining whites just until no streaks can be seen.

Spread the batter evenly in the prepared pan. Bake in the center of the oven for about 40 minutes, until the cake has shrunken very slightly from the pan and a cake tester emerges clean after probing the center.

Cool the pan on a rack for 15 minutes, then remove the rim and let the cake cool completely on the pan base. Remove the cake from its base onto a serving platter.

Shortly before serving, whip the cream in a chilled bowl, gradually adding 1 to 4 tablespoons confectioner's sugar, to taste. Spoon or pipe the cream onto the cake in swirls or rosettes and garnish the top with nuts.

Refrigerate any leftovers.

SHORTCAKE SOLO

Summer Fruit Shortcake (page 68), with the best fruit of the season—strawberries, peaches, nectarines, raspberries, or blackberries

Pitcher of heavy cream, or bowl of lightly whipped cream

Supper: *Add a first course of Sorrel Egg-Flower Soup (page 224), served with croutons or oyster crackers*

To drink: *Tea, coffee, or other beverage*

Shortcake—that's all, folks, or nearly all, you need to serve for a supper (or why not a weekend breakfast?) that's delightfully different from any other family or company occasion of the year. Depending on which fruit is at the peak of its season, you can sponsor your own personal strawberry festival, or perhaps a celebration of any of the other fine shortcake fruits— peaches, nectarines, raspberries, and the several kinds of blackberries and their hybrid versions.

To serve whatever number of guests you expect for a supper or breakfast, make one recipe of the shortcake on page 68 for each six eaters or so. I say "or so" because you may want to lean toward the generous side in calculating helpings; people *have* been known to take second helpings of shortcake on festive occasions, and even "small thirds" aren't unheard of.

If the meal is supper, it might be rounded out by an opener of soup. I'd favor Sorrel Egg-Flower Soup (page 224), but a chowder, A Big Soup of Beef & Okra (page 221), or Wild Rice & Porcini Soup (page 223) are other possibilities, especially for hearty appetites.

A LITTLE MORE THAN A SNACK

Richard's Celtic Soda Bread with Raisins & Caraway (below)

Sweet butter and mild Cheddar, Monterey Jack, Bel Paese, or another unassertive and mellow cheese, or cream cheese

Raspberry or other jam (below), or honey

To drink: *Tea, or hot cocoa*

Few of the things we enjoy eating at odd moments are as heartwarming as those intended to go with a cup of tea as a light meal or supper—a repast somewhat along the lines of what the British call "high tea" to distinguish it from afternoon tea, which, as we Yankees are often reminded, is the domain of paper-thin sandwiches and dainty pastries.

For such a super-snack, the soda bread my spouse turns out when the mood is upon him is most satisfactory. (It's called "Celtic" here because his recipe is neither Scottish nor Irish but has characteristics of breads from both places.) It's fancier than some, with its enrichments of egg and butter, but those ingredients help it to hang on to its freshness longer than basic soda bread. So it needn't be made at the last minute, although it perfectly well can be, as it's quickly put together. To go with the bread, see the directions for a few preserves which appear on the opposite page.

OTHER SPREADS: Another delectability to serve exactly like a fruit preserve is Uncooked Lime or Lemon Curd, page 130. And on page 54 you'll find a way to make a pretty and delicious tomato jam that's especially good when made with a touch of fresh ginger.

A FEW PRESERVES

 erewith two small preserving projects to consider when there's space in the refrigerator for a jarful of something good to have with Richard's Celtic Soda Bread, or with hot biscuits, corn bread, or just everyday toast.

APRICOT JAM WITH PEACH SCHNAPPS

To make about 3 cups: Soak ¾ pound (about 2 cups) dried apricots overnight in water to cover, about 2½ cups.

Chop the fruit coarsely, by hand or by pulsing a food processor on and off. Combine the fruit and its liquid in a heavy saucepan with 3 tablespoons of lemon juice; bring to a boil, then simmer 10 minutes, stirring often.

Add 1½ cups of granulated sugar, stir to dissolve, and cook the jam, stirring it often, at a moderate boil until it is quite thick and ploppy, about 20 minutes.

Remove the jam from the heat, cool it slightly, then stir in 3 tablespoons of peach schnapps (or choose apricot liqueur). Put the jam into 3 half-pint jars that have been boiled 10 minutes to sterilize them, then drained. Cool, cover, and refrigerate the jam; it keeps for 3 months.

FALLBACK RASPBERRY PRESERVES

Once the berries and sugar have rested together for a couple of hours, this ultra-fast jam takes less than 10 minutes to cook. It *must* be cooked in small batches, no more than 2 pints of berries at a whack. That amount will make about 3 cups of jam.

To each pint of fresh raspberries (picked over, but rinsed only if dusty), add 1½ cups sugar and 2 tablespoons fresh lemon juice. Stir; let rest 2 hours (or longer is okay, if it's more convenient), stirring once or twice more.

Boil the sugared berries rapidly in a wide skillet,

stirring constantly with a wooden spatula, until the jam has thickened, about 5 minutes. To test, remove from the heat and pour a few drops onto a chilled saucer; let cool 2 minutes. If the sample wrinkles but doesn't run when the saucer is tipped, the jam is done. Put it into jars and store it as for apricot jam.

RICHARD'S CELTIC SODA BREAD WITH RAISINS & CARAWAY

his cross-slashed loaf, rugged and crusty, is splendid just as is, in thick slices spread with sweet butter, but it can be made even more beguiling by a slither of honey, marmalade, or jam. To move right along to a more substantial snack than bread-and-jam, serve soda bread with a gentle-mannered cheese such as Longhorn, a mild Cheddar or Munster, an Edam, or a Bel Paese, or have it slathered with good cream cheese. (By "good" I mean pure cream cheese made without the several gummy additives that diminish the charm of most versions.)

Soda breads, the more free-spirited members of the family of quick pan loaves called "tea breads," are made variously with wheat meal, whole-wheat flour, ordinary flour, or a combination. They can be studded with currants or raisins, or even (why not?) with dried cherries or blueberries (see Instead of Raisins, right). They are often flavored with caraway, and they may or may not be enriched with butter and egg (this one is). These loaves are made the way our family likes them, but nowhere is it written that you can't change, or leave out, such ingredients as the dried fruits and the caraway

SHAPING A ROUND LOAF: Philologists tell us that the word "lady" derives from a term meaning "loaf-giver" in one of the several language-ancestors of English. Here's an appropriately ladylike way to shape a round loaf of soda bread:

Curve your hands around the piece of dough, fingers together. Rotate the dough between your cupped hands, using light downward pressure to form the turning dough into a ball that's smooth on top and sides and gathered together underneath where it will rest on the pan. Keep turning the shape until it suits you; for best looks it should be a little higher than it is wide.

Transfer the loaf to the baking sheet before slashing it, and use a long, very sharp knife in a decisive way to make ½-inch cross-cuts extending a little down the curving sides of the loaf.

seeds. (You could even add nuts.)

It's feasible to make this bread several hours or even one or two days before it's to be served, as it keeps fresh longer than most versions. If it's made ahead, it benefits from being refreshed, as described in the recipe, before it's sliced.

Preheat the oven to 375°. Butter and flour a baking sheet.

Whisk together the two flours, sugar, salt, baking soda, baking powder, and caraway seeds in a mixing bowl.

Cut in the butter, using a pastry blender or two knives. Mix in the raisins.

Beat the buttermilk and the egg together; stir into the dry ingredients just until moistened.

Turn the dough onto a lightly floured work surface and knead it briefly, just until it is firm, perhaps 2 minutes. Halve the dough and form each half into a high round loaf (see Shaping a Round Loaf on the facing page).

Place the loaves well apart on the baking sheet; cut a large cross ½ inch deep in the top of each.

Bake the bread 40 minutes, or until a thump on the bottom of a loaf produces a hollow sound. Remove the loaves to a wire rack.

Serve the bread slightly warm or at room temperature, with plenty of sweet butter. Wrap any remainders and store at room temperature for up to 3 days.

Leftovers: Sliced thick, left-over soda bread makes splendid toast. A cooled loaf (or leftovers) will be all the better for being refreshed before serving: Wrap the bread in foil and warm it in a 350° oven, which should take about 10 minutes.

If leftover bread has been frozen for storage, rewarm it the same way, but at least twice as much oven time will be needed.

_____

INSTEAD OF RAISINS: Dried cranberries, sour cherries, or dried blueberries aren't usual in this bread—far from it—but they're a delightful replacement for the traditional currants or raisins. Dried cranberries have appeared only lately in fancy shops; dried cherries and blueberries are also specialty-store items. If you'd like to try drying your own cherries or blueberries, how-to's are in my book *Fancy Pantry.*

Makes 2 free-form loaves, about 1¼ pounds each

Unsalted butter and all-purpose flour for coating the pan
2 cups fresh whole-wheat flour (see Flour Freshness, below)
2 cups all-purpose flour
2 tablespoons granulated sugar
1 teaspoon salt
1 teaspoon baking soda
1 teaspoon baking powder
1 tablespoon caraway seeds, bruised in a mortar or coarsely ground
2 tablespoons unsalted butter
1 to 1½ cups raisins or currants (we like lots)
1½ cups buttermilk (see Pinch-Hitter for Buttermilk, page 230)
1 large egg

FLOUR FRESHNESS:
Whole-wheat flour, especially if it's stone-ground, loses quality much faster than white flour because of its relatively high oil content. Unless it can be used up within a couple of weeks, store it in a glass jar or heavy plastic bag in the freezer.

THREE GATHERINGS, AND GOOD NIGHT

When the subject of parties comes up, no one needs to ask what to do about birthdays (that is, if the family is an affectionate one), or about wedding anniversaries, or graduations, or a few other occasions that just naturally get celebrated without fuss or, usually, much formality. For most of us the really hard social decisions are about such problems as having business or professional colleagues—yours or a spouse's—to dinner without risking nervous exhaustion. Can we consider such occasions "parties" at all?

Well, you'll just have to ask the peerless Miss Manners, who is sure to be correct in whatever she decides. For myself, I've been much taken with Miss M's comment to the effect that business entertaining is an oxymoron. Like her, I'm in favor of entertaining at home only if it's going to be enjoyable—if it's for actual friends, or to honor an occasion when family duty calls to us in a pleasant voice, or to mark an event that really turns you on, from the return of a prodigal to winning a sweepstakes. If getting out a twelve-foot tablecloth, hunting up the extra leaves for the table, and polishing the family silver just for the sake of shining up a business relation-ship sounds like the start of a fun evening, I'd say, do it. Otherwise, take 'em to a restaurant. You'll do yourself a favor and earn brownie points with the restaurateur, who has to live, too.

If you really like to invite people to your house out of a feeling of warm, fuzzy friendship, I'm with you all the way. Far in the past for me—and for a lot of other people these days—is the giving of large miscellaneous cocktail parties with what James Beard called "doots" to eat (why did we ever do it?). Behind us, too, is all that fussing with just-so dinners. At some point in our social lives such stiffish evenings, no doubt all very well in their way, have become clearly not our way.

Which leaves us with the homey occasions for which the menus in the preceding pages are intended. Guest-friends can be welcomed with a late weekend breakfast (let's not say "brunch" unless we have to), or a relaxed lunch—which must also be on a weekend, unless full-time leisure is available to everybody concerned—or with one of the unpretentious dinners or suppers planned around all manner of beasts, birds, and fish. Now, in this chapter designed to fill gaps in the social calendar, we have menus for three pleasant gatherings.

There is a Thanksgiving feast rooted in but not enslaved to tradition, with far more than enough dishes listed so your favorite foods may be selected. (The roast turkey is stuffed with a few good things that aren't found in every other turkey on the block.)

Next, there's a dessert buffet, proposed as an enjoyable way to entertain when a sit-down dinner or full buffet is out of the question. The desserts can be changed or added to by consulting the Index.

Finally there is our family supper for Christmas Eve, a simple meal that seems just right for a night when unfancy but excellent light dishes are in order. *Confession:* The oyster stew hasn't been served every Christmas of our family life of thirty-some years. In recent years particularly we've sometimes had our best "bicoastal" clam chowder, which couldn't be crammed into this book. Next year we just may have bowls of Six-Seafood Chowder, which you can find on page 235.

Merry Christmas, and God bless us every one. Mrs. Witty is going to bed.

LET'S GIVE THANKS

Starters:
Consommé, or oysters or clams on the half-shell, with lemon and fresh pepper

Table Trimmings:
Celery, black and green olives, radishes; cranberries in jelly, sauce, or relish, or pickled cranberries; salted nuts

The Main Event:
Turkey for Thanksgiving (below), with Wild Rice & Black Walnut Stuffing (below) and Giblet Gravy (below)

Vegetables:
The Real Mashed Potatoes (page 103)
Orange & Honey Spicy Sweet-Potato Sticks (page 135)
Red Cabbage Braised with Cranberries (page 174)
Remolded Broccoli (or Remolded Purple & White Cauliflower) with Butter & Lemon Sauce (page 105), Onions in Sage Sauce (below), Poached Radishes in Marjoram Cream (below)

Dessert:
Mince pie and/or pumpkin pie

Finale:
A bowl of seasonal fruits and nuts to admire, if not to eat
Coffee; brandy; a snooze

To drink: *A fine red wine or a full-bodied white*

Thanksgiving is, and should be, a feast of abundance; to my mind it's the only gastronomic occasion of the year when "spa" cooking is a wretched idea. At our house the menu is always traditional in its outlines but not necessarily in its details—we don't think "tradition" means binding the cook with hoops of steel. But we do like dishes whose earthy roots are perceptible, dishes without new-fangledness displayed for its own sake.

This well-rooted menu is meant to be chosen from according to each family's customs, tastes, and capacity—to include every suggestion would be to set up the noisiest of groaning boards. For any recipes not given in these pages—for consommé, for instance, if you'd like to make your own—see some such kitchen bible as *Joy of Cooking*, one of the absolute best.

You'll notice that the Thanksgiving choices here include some foods that weren't available to the Pilgrim Parents—New England didn't and doesn't produce wild rice, nor does history record the settlers' early use of black walnuts, but these native American foods are surely as appropriate to a harvest feast today as cranberries, turkey, and pumpkin.

As Thanksgiving dessert, at our house, we have both pumpkin pie and mince pie because we're thinking of the feast after the feast—the day after, when the delicious leftovers will be served as "another Thanksgiving dinner that can't be beat," as Arlo Guthrie sang about Alice's Restaurant. We use homemade green-tomato mincemeat—the "scratch" recipe is in my book *Fancy Pantry*; other homemade or store-bought mincemeat may be your preference. Our pumpkin-pie filling—a family recipe—is the same as the custard for Pumpkin Brûlée (page 175). Half the quantity in the recipe will fill a standard crust. Glaze the finished pie with honey.

TURKEY FOR THANKSGIVING

For the past two Thanksgivings, the parental Wittys have been bidden to a feast prepared by our young George in the kitchen of the old Suffolk farmhouse that is the headquarters of his plant nursery business. It's something of a reversal of "Across the river and through the woods, to Grandmother's house we go," and we've enjoyed it very much.

There we were, parents, sister Anne come from afar, George's bachelor housemate, and friends of his heart of several ages—from about seven to about seventy—all surrounding a many-leafed table holding a twenty-pound bird and sumptuous trimmings. True to family form, George seems to add guests up to the last minute and still have plenty of leftovers. (Our family's mealtime motto is something like "If you're feeding four, fix for six." For a dozen, I'd say George cooks for twenty.)

This year, George stuffed his mighty turkey with crumbs, sausage, and chestnuts, a "dressing" we're all fond of. (Good versions are in general cookbooks.) For this menu, though, I'm suggesting a crunchy stuffing I've devised with wild rice brought back from Minnesota plus black walnuts gathered along farm roadsides near home.

This recipe shows off those two native American foods to great advantage, and there's a pleasing symmetry in using the stuffing to embellish a third native food, the turkey. (That bird would have been our American avian emblem if Ben Franklin had had his way.)

You'll notice that some brown rice is used with the wild grain. Wild rice alone can be used, but after making the stuffing both ways—starting out with 100 percent wild rice—I think this combination is better.

PREPARING, STUFFING, & ROASTING THE TURKEY (& MAKING GIBLET GRAVY)

Inspect the bird inside and out—if it has been handcuffed with one of those metal gizmos, the first thing to do is to wrestle out the device and throw it away. Remove the neck, gizzard, liver, and heart, which you'll find stashed within. (The liver can go into the stuffing if you like; stew the other giblets lengthily, until very tender, with onion, celery, peppercorns, parsley, and bay leaf, in water to cover well, to make the stock for the giblet gravy that's to accompany the feast.)

Wash the turkey inside and out with plenty of cold water. Remove any loose bits of tissue from the inside, and tweeze out any pinfeathers the processors have missed. Wipe all surfaces dry with paper towels. Rub all surfaces of the inside with about a tablespoonful of coarse salt—no, it's not too much.

Spoon in the stuffing, which should be cool, filling the main cavity. This rice mixture doesn't swell the way a bread stuffing does, so the bird may be filled to capacity. Insert lacing skewers across the abdominal opening and lash them together with crisscrossed string, preferably butcher's twine (endlessly useful around the house). Stand the bird on its tail and fill the neck cavity. Pull the neck skin back over the stuffed cavity and fasten it to the back of the turkey with small skewers and more string.

Trussing: Truss the wings into position close beside the breast with string, passing it across the bird's back; carry the twine down the back and tie the tips of the drumsticks close together, crossing the string between them; finally anchor the drumsticks by passing the string below the tail and tying it securely.

This may seem complicated, but it boils down to doing your best to keep the wings and drumsticks close to the body without allowing the string to cross the breast of the bird. (No holds—or knots—are barred, so long as it works.)

Into the pan: Rub the turkey generously with unsalted butter (or bland vegetable oil) and place it on a rack in a shallow roasting pan.

How to roast & how long: Preheat the oven to 325°, set the roasting pan on a shelf as far above the oven floor as space permits, and proceed to roast the turkey for approximately 20 minutes per pound of unstuffed weight. When calculating when to put your turkey in the oven, allow an additional 30 minutes at the end of roasting for the bird to "rest" before it's carved.

During roasting brush the bird with unsalted butter from time to time; after drippings appear in the pan, brush it with pan fat. If the skin is browning too fast over the neck cavity or the drumsticks, put little tents of aluminum foil over those places as protection. The same can be done later on for the breast if it's threatening to brown too deeply before roasting is finished.

Checking for doneness: The pop-up timers with which some birds are equipped seem to function quite well when checked against a thermometer reading. If there's no pop-up, use an instant-reading thermometer inserted into the inner part of the thigh, not touching the bone; it will read 180° to 185° when the bird is well and truly done. As a double check, probe the stuffing with the thermometer (from the side, not down through the breast); the reading at the center of the stuffing should be at least 165° to indicate that "done" temperature has been reached.

Resting time: Cover the turkey lightly with foil and leave it to settle its juices for about half an hour. (This makes it easier to carve.) Meanwhile, drain off the pan juices for gravy—a bulb baster will remove them from the pan without requiring a wrestling match with a hot bird.

Making the giblet gravy: For old-fashioned, meaty giblet gravy, the cooked meat from the simmered neck, heart, and gizzard is chopped very fine and the cooking broth strained to remove the seasoning vegetables.

Remove most of the fat from the pan drippings; combine the drippings, the chopped meat, and any brown bits you can retrieve from the roasting pan with the broth in a saucepan, simmer to concentrate it if necessary, and thicken the gravy by stirring in gradually a mixture of cornstarch and a little cold water. Allow 1 tablespoon cornstarch mixed with 2 tablespoons of water to thicken each 2 cups of gravy; simmer, stirring, until the liquid is translucent. Taste the gravy and season it with salt, pepper, and a pinch of crumbled dried thyme.

Serving it forth: Shift the turkey to its platter. If any juice has collected in the pan, pour it (and scrape any remaining brown bits) into the pan of hot gravy. Scissor off the string and remove the skewers. Garnish the platter minimally if you'd like to help the carver out; a few tufts of parsley and perhaps a few pickled crab apples or other colorful fruits will do the job without getting in the way.

THE RIGHT THING TO DO WITH LEFTOVERS: To preserve the eating quality and safety of leftovers, don't let them sit around at room temperature, which is the ideal environment for the growth of organisms causing spoilage. Scoop any remaining stuffing from the cavities and refrigerate it separately from the well-wrapped bird.

DECONSTRUCTING A BIRD: Just to prove that taking things apart is not for literary critics only, poultry packers are now practicing their own version of the art, and a very good thing it is, too—a humungous gobbler is a daunting thing except when a feast is on the calendar and a crowd has gathered.

Now that packers are deconstructing the bird for us, we can choose to roast only the breast if we like, or we can use breast meat for veal-like turkey cutlets or turkey tonnato, both toothsome. The legs can be bought separately, and their dark meat is ideal for turkey chili (make it like beef chili, but without actually browning the meat), or for a full-flavored fricassee. Ground turkey is a low-fat and quite tasty replacement for chopped beef or veal in certain dishes—see, for instance, Turkey Sausages in Garlic Cream (page 120).

WILD RICE & BLACK WALNUT STUFFING

here's not much to add about this stuffing beyond what has been said on a previous page, except that, reduced, the recipe is dandy for other poultry besides turkey.

Makes about 10 cups, enough for a 15-pound turkey

1½ cups wild rice
Salt, as needed
1 cup Basmati-type or other brown rice (see The Brown Rices, below)
¼ pound bacon, cut into thin crosswise strips
2 tablespoons additional bacon fat, butter, or oil
Liver of the turkey, optional
1 cup chopped mild onion, or combined leek (white part only) and onion or shallots
1 cup diced tender celery, including some leaves
⅓ to ½ cup dry sherry
1 cup coarsely chopped black walnut meats (or substitute walnuts or pecans—see page 276)
2 teaspoons crumbled dried sweet marjoram
1 teaspoon crumbled dried thyme
¼ teaspoon Powdered Bay Leaves (page 274), optional
Salt and pepper

Rinse the wild rice in a sieve under running hot water until it's thoroughly hot. Bring a large pot of water to a boil, add a little salt, drop in the rice, and simmer it, partly covered, until the grains "bloom" or burst, 30 to 45 minutes, depending on how long ago the rice was harvested. Drain; spread out to cool. (The cooking and cooling can be done ahead for both the wild rice and the brown. Refrigerate the rice if it's held overnight.)

Cook the brown rice in the same way in another pot (but without the preliminary rinse) until it is tender-firm, still slightly chewy, about 30 minutes. Drain, spread out, and cool it.

Cook the bacon in a skillet over medium heat, stirring, until it begins to become crisp; remove and reserve the pieces. Add the extra fat to the pan, set it over medium heat, and sauté the liver, if it's being used, until its surface has become firm. Add the onion and celery and sauté everything, stirring often, until the vegetables are softening, about 5 minutes. Drain off and discard any surplus fat. Dice the liver, if it is included. Cool the mixture.

In a mixing bowl fold together the two rices, the bacon, vegetables, diced liver, sherry, black walnuts, sweet marjoram, thyme, and the optional powdered bay leaves. Taste and add salt and pepper.

The stuffing may be made ahead of time, even the day before, and refrigerated until it's time to roast the turkey. (It's *not* a safe notion to stuff poultry ahead of time, though it's tempting to try it when things are rushed; resist the temptation.)

THE BROWN RICES: From basic (Carolina brown) to

GILDING THE GRATIN: To make creamed onions into a handsome gratin for Thanksgiving or any other dinner, arrange them in a shallow baking dish, add a topping of buttered breadcrumbs, and bake the assemblage in a 400° oven until the top has browned, perhaps 15 minutes.

Serves 6 to 8

1½ pounds tiny white onions ("silverskins"), or substitute 2 14-ounce jars of cooked onions
Salt

LIGHT WHITE SAUCE:
3 cups milk
4 tablespoons (½ stick) unsalted butter
Small bay leaf
2 tablespoons cornstarch mixed with 2 tablespoons water
Salt and white pepper, to taste
2 to 4 dried whole sage leaves, or ½ to 1 teaspoon crumbled dried sage, to taste

designer types, there are a number of these, and they are delicious; they're also pleasing to the tooth because of their substantial texture. The recipe refers to Basmati-type domestic rice, which I've seen labeled "Texmati;" then there's the "wild pecan" type, which is especially flavorful; and natural-food stores offer other kinds of brown rice, too.

ONIONS IN SAGE SAUCE

verybody knows about creamed onions for Thanksgiving, but this recipe rings a small and savory change. The touch of sage is especially harmonious with the flavor of poultry, but the onions would be equally good with fresh or smoked pork.

Cooking fresh onions: Peel the onions (this is easier to do if they're first blanched in boiling water for 1 minute), then cut a deep X across the root end of each to prevent the inner layers from creeping out during cooking.

Cook the onions, covered, in 2 inches of lightly salted boiling water (or steam them in a steamer basket) until they just begin to be tender, about 15 minutes depending on size; avoid overcooking. Drain the onions and set them aside, uncovered.

White sauce: Heat together the milk, butter, and bay leaf in a heavy saucepan over medium heat. When the milk is steaming hot, stir in the cornstarch mixture. Stir the sauce over the heat until smoothly thickened, then cook it for 2 minutes longer.

Season with salt and white pepper. Add the sage, cover the pan, and let the sauce rest for up to several hours to imbibe sage flavor.

Near serving time, remove the bay and sage leaves from the sauce (or leave them in, it's up to you). Drain the onions again (or drain bottled onions thoroughly) and fold them gently into the sauce. Reheat the dish until piping hot over low heat. Before serving, taste again and adjust the seasonings with more salt, pepper, or even a little more.

POACHED RADISHES IN MARJORAM CREAM

e don't think of cooking radishes very often, but we should—they make a delicious vegetable dish, and they are always to be had at the greengrocer's. For Thanksgiving dinner or other cold-weather meals, the rich herbal touch of sweet marjoram is appropriate. Simple creamed radishes *sans* marjoram are good, too.

If you don't want to risk having the radish skins tint the sauce a pretty pink, combine the vegetables and sauce just before the dish is reheated.

Serves 6 to 8

*About 4 bunches
(depending on bunch
size) of small red
radishes
1 cup chicken or beef stock
Light white sauce from the
preceding recipe
¾ teaspoon, or to taste,
crumbled dried sweet
marjoram*

Trim the tops and roots of the radishes and wash them well; if they are quite large, halve or quarter them.

Heat the stock to boiling, drop in the radishes, and simmer them, partly covered, until not quite tender, about 5 minutes; there should be a hint of crunchiness when a radish is tested with a fork. Drain and set aside, uncovered.

Make the white sauce as directed on page 255, substituting the sweet marjoram for the sage. Let the sauce rest, covered, until near serving time, for up to several hours.

Add the drained radishes to the sauce, first removing the bay leaf if you wish. Reheat the dish and adjust the seasoning, adding more marjoram if it seems a good idea.

COME FOR DESSERT

Richard's Recaptured Angel Cake (page 169), with a bowl of chilled fresh berries

Cream-Filled Boston Stack Cake (page 196)

Pumpkin Brûlée with Ginger (page 175)

Berry Bavarian (page 98), garnished with bottled mandarin orange sections, or served with a sauce suggested in the recipe

Dark Chocolate Mousse with Raspberry Sauce (page 142)

Honey-Pecan or Maple-Walnut Pie (page 182)

Plum (or other fruit) Velvet (page 217)

Old-Fashioned Sugar Cookies (page 232), Twice-Baked Orange & Nut Cookies (page 93), or Peppernuts (page 262)

Whipped cream to sauce desserts as desired

To drink: *A dessert wine, and/or after-dinner coffee, brandy, liqueurs*

White grape juice for any children in attendance, or glasses of milk

his party can be given for a handful or a houseful, and it can be thrown for bridge players, or after dinner, or on a weekend afternoon on any pretext whatsoever.

If there are to be children, a sure-fire addition is a glass bowl heaped with scoops of various ice creams. This can be stashed hours ahead of time, lightly covered, in the freezer, to be set out at party time for round-eyed choice by the young. (Don't be surprised if the not-so-young dip in, too.)

Strategy: Offer enough desserts from the menu to allow your guests to yield to temptation a little. In my experience, even the joggers (perhaps especially the joggers) will sample more than one sweet when the party is, like this one, a *banquet*, in the old, original sense of the word—a spread of desserts set out independently from the main meal. So the aim here is "plenty"; leftovers aren't likely to be a problem.

All the desserts may be prepared a day ahead of time; however, the fresh berries and the whipped cream must be dealt with on the actual day.

SUPPER FOR CHRISTMAS EVE

Goblets of Black Velvet—two-thirds chilled Guinness stout, one-third chilled Champagne or other sparkling dry white wine

Big bowls of Christmas Eve Oyster Stew (below) or Six-Seafood Chowder (page 235) or Superb Lobster Stew (page 208)

A positively Dickensian heap of hot buttered toast; or split, toasted, and buttered common crackers; or warmed sea toast or pilot crackers

Platter of several kinds of cheeses —Cheddar or Colby; Gruyère or Emmenthal; Edam or Gouda; Roquefort or Gorgonzola; Brie or Camembert; a good cream cheese or an Explorateur; Port Salut or Munster; a Castello or a Danish blue; or other favorites, with the rest of the crackers and a bowl of apples, pears, and grapes

Peppernuts for Christmas (below), or other Christmas cookies

Brandied black coffee and/or a favorite cordial

 f Christmas fell in midweek when the children were young, the Witty family was obliged to travel on Christmas Eve after office hours had ended for Poor Old Dad and Poor Old Mom (known as POD and POM on such occasions).

We were so obliged, at least, if we wanted (as we did) to celebrate the holiday in our "summer" house on the far end of Long Island rather than in Manhattan.

There the Christmas tree would have been decorated on a previous weekend and there would have been hidden the presents bought between Thanksgiving and Christmas in local shops, especially in the variety store of our delight, which has now been gone for several years and replaced by—what else?—a boutique.

When we set out on the long drive we could look forward to our traditional Christmas Eve supper, which was almost always a creamy, briny, delectable stew made with oysters from Long Island Sound.

When we couldn't arrive early such a supper was possible only because the Vorpahl family, with great kindness, would have the oysters shucked and waiting for us at Stuart's Seafood in Amagansett even though the market itself, tucked behind the gray-shingled Vorpahl family house, would have been closed for hours.

Once we'd arrived, a pail of shucked oysters in hand, at our house in the woods near the bay called Accabonac Creek, the order of business was to turn on the heat and plug in the lights on the Christmas tree, unload the good-natured cats and the luggage from the car, and then get out the big double boiler and start the oyster stew. While the cookery proceeded, POD would pour glasses of Black Velvet for the grownups, something suitable for the children, and bowls of milk for the feline family.

Here is a supper that still says "Christmas Eve" to us.

ANOTHER STEW: Speaking of mussels, which we were doing elsewhere in these pages, these bivalves, which until quite recently have been widely ignored in the U.S., are now being raft-grown and distributed by mussel farms, so one no longer needs to live at the shore to obtain (and learn to love) them.

These richly flavored, tender little shellfish figure in any number of perfectly delicious dishes in cuisines *haute* and low alike, and it's no surprise to mussel fans that they can replace oysters in a stew. Directions are below.

CHRISTMAS EVE OYSTER STEW

*O*ysters have a passport to the soup plate. But having to hunt for the oyster in a stew is bad business.   *—ANN BATCHELDER'S COOKBOOK*

 nectarious oyster stew can be made in many ways and with many seasonings, but I like a tureenful that tastes lavishly of *oysters.* So I recommend using plenty of shellfish and keeping the seasonings in the background. You needn't eliminate all enhancements from the brew, though, as the recipe shows.

One bit of advice: Don't let the oysters overcook either before or after adding them to the milk and cream; if they are heated even a bit too long they'll turn rubbery. Keep an eye on what's going on in the pot—this is no time to trust to luck.

Serves 6 generously

1 quart milk
1 quart cream or half-and-half
2 or 3 slices mild onion
Handful of fresh celery tops, optional
A good-size blade of mace
Small scrap of bay leaf, optional
1 quart shucked oysters, with their liquor
8 tablespoons (1 stick) unsalted butter
Salt and white pepper, to taste
Ground hot red pepper, optional
Paprika

Combine the milk, cream, onion, celery tops, mace, and bay leaf, if using, in a heavy pot (or in the top of a double boiler set over simmering water); heat gently to just below simmering. Maintain the lowest possible heat while infusing the seasonings for 30 minutes, then strain out and discard the seasonings. Keep the stew base hot.

Check the oysters—most easily done with your fingers—to make sure there are no bits of shell. If the oysters are quite large, halve them.

Heat the oysters and their liquor with two-thirds of the butter just until they have plumped up and their edges have begun to ruffle, swirling the pan to move them; watch carefully to prevent overcooking or they will turn tough.

Add the oysters to the hot milk and cream and reheat the stew gently, taking it off the heat before it reaches the boiling point. Season the stew with salt, white pepper, and, if you like, a little ground hot red pepper.

Serve the oyster stew in a heated tureen or individual bowls, topped with paprika and the remaining butter.

TOMORROW'S SUPPER: Oyster stew may be mellowed for several hours or for as long as overnight in the refrigerator—something recommended for lobster stew, too, as you've noticed if that recipe has caught your eye. You cool the stew uncovered, with an occasional stir to speed up the cooling, then cover it tightly before refrigerating it.

When reheating the well-rested stew, don't even think of letting it reach the boiling point. Stir it often over low heat as it warms gently, and remove it from the heat when it's just below an actual simmer.

MUSSEL STEW: For the how-to's of storing, cleaning, precooking, and de-sanding mussels, see the discussion of these bivalves on page 237.

To replace the quantity of oysters in this recipe, you'll need 4 pounds of middle-size mussels in the shell. Steam them only long enough to get them open, shuck out the meats, rinse them in their broth if they seem even slightly sandy, and proceed to make the stew by adding the shelled mussels, the butter, and about 1 cup of the well-strained mussel broth to the seasoned milk and cream. Reheat the stew gently, then let it steep and compose its molecules for a few minutes before it's served.

PEPPERNUTS FOR CHRISTMAS

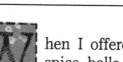

When I offered a recipe for these festive spice balls (called *Pfeffernüsse* in Germany, their land of origin) in a magazine column on seasonal cookery I wrote while my children were small, quite a lot of readers wrote in for it. So this particular recipe is bound to be known to recipe-savers in that group, at least; here it is for the rest of the world.

Since the recipe was originally sent out, the food processor has made a difference; the machine helps a lot with such jobs as mixing and "sifting" the dry ingredients and chopping the nuts, candied fruits, and lemon zest. The chopping can be done in one fell swoop by pulsing the machine on and off if

A SIMPLE FINISH: After a seafood stew and the lavish selection of cheeses and fruits, a finale of simple sweet nibbles is the best way to round off this supper.

Besides the Peppernuts in the menu, you may want to offer some Twice-Baked Orange & Nut Cookies (page 93) and/or, if there are children, some Old-Fashioned Sugar Cookies (page 232) decorated with patterns of colored sugar. To make a stencil, set a small star or Christmas-tree cookie cutter on cardboard, trace around it, cut out the design, and lay the stencil on each unbaked cookie before sprinkling on the colored sugar, either store-bought or tinted by stirring ordinary sugar with drops of food coloring.

Makes about 10 dozen

½ cup vegetable
  shortening
2½ cups granulated sugar
5 large eggs
1 tablespoon ground
  cinnamon
1 tablespoon ground
  cardamom
1 teaspoon ground cloves
1 teaspoon freshly grated
  nutmeg
1 teaspoon anise seed,
  lightly crushed, ground
  in a spice mill, or left
  whole
½ teaspoon freshly ground
  black or white pepper
4 cups all-purpose flour
1 teaspoon salt
½ teaspoon baking soda
1 tablespoon (packed)
  finely grated lemon zest
  (colored rind only, no
  pith)
½ cup chopped toasted
  natural almonds (see
  page 276)
3½-ounce jar candied
  citron, chopped
3½-ounce jar candied
  orange peel, chopped
Vegetable shortening and
  all-purpose flour for
  coating the pans

GLAZE:
2 tablespoons hot milk
  mixed with 1 cup sifted
  confectioner's sugar

you place the nuts, fruits, zest, and about ½ cup of the sifted dry ingredients in the bowl.

It's feasible to halve this recipe, but having the whole big batch on hand is no hardship. The crackly-coated little nuggets keep beautifully and they ship well, if holiday cookie packages go out from your house.

Preheat the oven to 350°F.

Place the cookies on greased and well-floured cookie sheets, spacing them 1½ inches apart (they spread).

Brush each cookie with the glaze mixture.

Bake the cookies 10 to 15 minutes, or until they are crackled and lightly browned.

Cool on wire racks, or loosen the cookies with a spatula and let them cool on their pans. Store them in a closed container. These cookies benefit from mellowing for a few days, but they're quite edible, though rather hard, when still freshly baked.

Cream the shortening; gradually cream in the sugar; beat until fluffy. Add the eggs one at a time, beating well after each. Beat in the cinnamon, cardamom, cloves, nutmeg, anise seed, and pepper.

Sift together the flour, salt, and baking soda; beat the dry ingredients into the creamed mixture. Work into the dough the lemon zest, almonds, citron, and candied orange peel.

Wrap the dough and refrigerate it for an hour or two, until it's stiff.

Shaping the cookies: Wet your hands and shape chunks of the dough into ¾-inch balls, a little higher than they are wide. Arrange them on waxed paper as they're shaped. Leave the cookies uncovered at room temperature overnight, or for at least 8 hours—the idea is to let the outsides dry so the cookies will have an attractive cracked surface after they are baked.

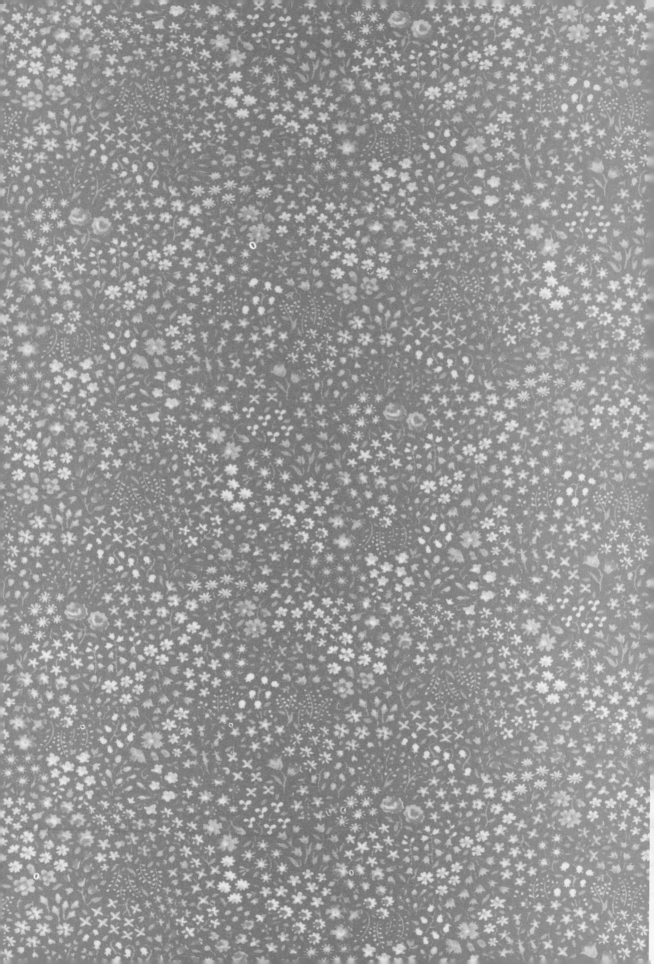

A FEW
BASIC RECIPES
&
NOTES

The most frequent question which I have been asked about this book ... is "Where do you get all your recipes?" The answer, in most cases, is that I have eaten them.

PETER GRAY, *THE MISTRESS COOK*

A NOTE ON ALL SHAPES: Serve either warm or hot; or cool on rack and store, wrapped, at room temperature for a day or so; or bag airtight and freeze for a month or more.

Reheating: Bundle biscuits, rolls, or buns in foil and heat in a preheated 400° oven until hot through, about 10 minutes if the rolls are at room temperature, 15 minutes or more if frozen.

ANGEL OR "RIZ" BISCUITS, ROLLS, OR COOKOUT BUNS

his four-way recipe for angel or "riz" biscuits—which are double-leavened, tender morsels that seem to have come from the South—is all you need to make your choice of biscuits, rolls, or two shapes of buns. Best of all, the dough, in contrast to most yeast breads, requires only one rising, which comes after the dough is shaped and plunked on the pans. (Some angel biscuits call for yeast, baking powder, *and* baking soda, plus the acid of buttermilk, to raise the dough—a little like wearing suspenders and two belts to hold up your trousers.)

For this set of breads I've adapted the angel biscuit method of cooking expert and gastronomic friend Jeanne Voltz, which is one of the simplest and best I've come across (it's in her *Flavor of the South.*) Some angelic biscuit recipes require elaborate kneadings and chillings of the dough; Jeanne's doesn't.

I like to keep a bagful of these rolls in the freezer, ready to be warmed for a variety of meals. The cookout buns aren't for cookouts only: the hamburger size is just right for Perfect Tomato Sandwiches (page 54), or for stuffing, wrapping, and heating in the oven as a sandwich, or, split, for excellent toast. As hot or cold Lobster Rolls (page 43), the frankfurter buns reach their highest and best use.

Elsewhere in the book you'll find Buttery Breadsticks (page 225), long, crisp batons made from this very same dough.

Makes about 5 dozen biscuits or rolls; or 1½ dozen hamburger or oversize frankfurter buns

2 cups buttermilk, or 2½ tablespoons white vinegar plus low-fat milk to make 2 cups
3 tablespoons (envelopes) active dry yeast (see Buying Yeast, page 268)
1 tablespoon salt
2 teaspoons granulated sugar
½ teaspoon baking soda
6 to 7 cups all-purpose flour, plus more for kneading
6 tablespoons (¾ stick) melted butter, cooled but pourable
Optional glaze, for buns:
1 large egg, beaten with 1 teaspoon water

GETTING STARTED WITH YEAST: Baking with yeast is a bugaboo to some very competent cooks, really without reason. I hope any such will make these easy, buttery biscuits, which are lighter in texture but lower in fat than baking-powder biscuits, and not a bit more complicated to make. They're quick, too, as yeast rolls go— they can be ready to serve a little more than an hour after you've started to mix the dough.

If using the vinegar-milk mixture, let it stand 2 to 3 minutes. Warm the buttermilk (or the vinegar mixture) to lukewarm, 100° to 105°. (The liquid will curdle.) Whisk together the yeast, salt, sugar, and baking soda in a mixing bowl. Add the buttermilk and stir until the drys have dissolved. Stir in 2 cups of the flour, then the butter. Stir in just enough of the remaining flour to make a moderately soft dough.

Flour a kneading surface; turn the dough out on it, invert the mixing bowl over it (or cover it with a towel), and let it rest 10 minutes. (This rest, and the rest in the next step, relaxes the dough and makes it easier to knead and to shape.)

Knead the dough 2 to 5 minutes, just until it is smooth and elastic, working in more flour if necessary to prevent sticking. Cover; let rest 5 minutes.

Follow the directions below for shaping the biscuits, rolls, or buns you're making; or see page 225 for directions for shaping Buttery Breadsticks.

ANGEL BISCUITS OR ROLLS: Pat or roll the dough out ½ inch thick. Cut into rounds with a biscuit cutter of whatever size you prefer.

Arrange the cutouts on buttered baking sheets 1 inch apart if you want crusty biscuits, close together for soft sides; or place them ½ inch apart in greased shallow baking pans for kissin' rolls (they will touch when finished). Cover the pans; let the biscuits rise until doubled, about 45 minutes. (When rising is complete, light finger pressure on the side of a roll will leave a dent.)

A few minutes before rising should be complete, preheat the oven to 400°.

Bake risen biscuits or rolls in the center of the oven, exchanging pan positions midway if two panfuls are baked at a time.

Spaced-out biscuits will be done in 10 to 12 minutes; if set close together they need about 5 minutes longer. Biscuits are done when bottoms are crisp and tops are golden-brown. Remove them promptly from the pans so the bottoms don't become steamy and soft.

HAMBURGER BUNS: Roll or pat the dough out ⅔ inch thick. Cut rounds with a 3½-inch cutter, a 4-inch English muffin ring, or a large-size canning-jar ring (about 3½ inches), or a topless and bottomless tuna can, which is about the same diameter.

Place the buns an inch apart on buttered baking sheets; let them rise until doubled, about 45 minutes; optionally, brush the tops with the egg glaze. Bake at 400° about 20 minutes, or until firm and well browned. Remove

BUYING YEAST: Buy your yeast in a four-ounce jar rather than quarter-ounce envelopes, if your market has it. It keeps a long time in the refrigerator and is both handier and less expensive than fiddly little packets. (Yeast can also be purchased in larger quantities from mail-order suppliers.)

promptly from the pans to prevent soggy undersides.

BIG FRANKFURTER BUNS: Pat the dough into an oblong measuring 12 by 15 inches. Cut the dough crosswise into 3 sections (I use a pizza cutter), then cut 6 strips crosswise from each section. Flatten each strip to lengthen it to about 6 inches, brush the strips lightly with water, fold them lengthwise, and place them, seams to one side, almost touching in rows on a buttered jelly-roll pan or baking sheet.

Place on pans and let rise as for Hamburger Buns (they will touch closely when fully risen); brush the tops with glaze if desired; bake about 20 minutes, or until firm and well browned.

Remove from the pan to cool on a rack, if not used at once.

CLARIFIED BUTTER

larified butter is sweet (unsalted) butter that has been simmered to cook out the surplus moisture, then skimmed of foamy impurities and carefully poured off its sediment. These steps eliminate moisture, which is undesirable in both baking and sautéing, as well as the milk solids that can burn easily and spoil a job of sautéing or pan-frying.

After chilling, clarified butter is a hard, golden fat that keeps indefinitely, so it's worthwhile to prepare a jarful at a time. Keeping it on hand is a good resolution for any time of year; its preparation is simple.

Melt a pound (or more, up to half of the capacity of your pan) of unsalted (sweet-cream) butter in a heavy saucepan over very low heat. Once melted, cook it slowly, without letting it brown even faintly, for about 20 minutes, checking often to prevent overheating; it will foam and bubble as moisture evaporates.

When the crust on top looks dry, remove the pan from the heat and let the butter settle briefly; skim off the crusty foam, then pour the clear liquid into a perfectly dry jar or jars, leaving the sediment in the pan. (The last few drops and the flavorful sediment can be saved separately to season vegetables.) Cool, cover, and refrigerate.

A pound of butter will yield about 1½ cups of clarified butter.

CULTURED CREAM (CRÈME FRAÎCHE)

 ultured Cream is close to but not exactly the same as the French crème fraîche because it is not made with the culture used in France. All the same, it's delicately tangy— the chief charm of the Gallic original—it's denser than plain cream, and it also keeps much longer. It can be whipped, and it resists curdling when used in hot sauces. In short, a wonderful thing to have in the fridge.

If you can help it, don't even try to make this with ultrapasteurized cream; it may not work, or may not work as well as it should. If there is no other kind of "fresh" cream to be had (now *that's* a scandal, if you like), it's worth a try.

Makes about 2¼ cups

2 cups heavy (whipping) cream
¼ cup freshly purchased dairy sour cream, at room temperature

Warm the heavy cream over very low heat, stirring, until a drop feels neutral on your inside wrist, or an instant-reading thermometer reads between 90° and 95°.

Whisk the sour cream thoroughly into the warmed cream. Pour the mixture into a scalded and well-drained glass jar, cover it, and let the cream ripen at room temperature for 8 to 12 hours, until it has thickened. (This takes longer in cool weather than in warm.)

Stir the cream and refrigerate it overnight; it will thicken further as it chills.

The cultured cream will keep 2 weeks or longer, refrigerated.

A NUTTY SPREAD OF YOGURT "CHEESE": To a cupful, more or less, of dense (long-drained) yogurt, add ½ cup of chopped toasted hazelnuts (for toasting, see page 275) and 3 tablespoons (or more, if you like) of minced sweet red pepper (bottled pimientos are okay). Season with salt and white pepper; in chive season, add snipped chives to taste; a pinch of minced garlic, with or without the chives, is also good. Let the spread mellow awhile before it's served.

THICK YOGURT

ere's a highly satisfactory lower-calorie stand-in for sour cream, or, if drained longer for increased density, for cream cheese. It's preferable to undrained yogurt for most uses in cooking—it has more body and less acidity.

Drain a pint or more of yogurt for several hours, until it's as thick as you wish, in a sieve lined with fine cheesecloth and set over a bowl. In warm weather, this can be done in the refrigerator. The whey that drains off is an asset for breadmaking.

Thick Yogurt can be any consistency from that of sour cream to that of cream cheese. (The "cheese" may be seasoned with herbs and garlic to make a spread.)

Thick Yogurt keeps for at least a week under refrigeration.

WHIPPED COTTAGE CHEESE

hen calories *do* count, this is a dandy replacement for sour cream; it can be used in cooked sauces if 1 teaspoon cornstarch is blended in (per cup) before the mixture is exposed to heat.

Just whirl regular or low-fat cottage cheese in a blender or food processor until it is completely silky, with no sign of graininess. Be patient; this job takes a few minutes. Scrape down the sides of the container once or twice as you go.

Taste and decide whether you want to add a few grains of salt. This keeps, chilled, as long as "straight" cottage cheese does.

DRIED PEEL FOR A TOUCH OF CITRUS WHEN WANTED

THOUSAND-YEAR TANGERINE PEEL & OTHER IMMORTAL INGREDIENTS: Treasured by Chinese cooks (and by me), dried tangerine peel gets better as it gets older. The most ancient vintage commands the highest price, so don't hesitate to keep a batch in the pantry from one season (or decade) to the next.

Other Oriental ingredients that keep more or less forever, if you're getting into Chinese cooking, are fermented black beans; cellophane noodles; the many soy sauces (except low-sodium soy, which needs refrigeration); dried clams, scallops, squid, jellyfish shark's fin, and oysters; dried red dates; rock sugar; the many kinds of dried mushrooms; salted duck; and lily buds.

Stash in the refrigerator anything in the line of plum or duck sauce, bean pastes and bean sauces, hoisin sauce, oyster sauce, sesame oil and paste, and especially chili paste, which stays hot only if it's kept cold.

or this you need foresight in wintertime (when the whole citrus tribe is at its best) and, for equipment, nothing more than a wire rack.

Dried tangerine peel isn't for Chinese cookery alone—its flavor is helpful to a surprising range of dishes beyond the barbecued pork ribs on page 50. Dried orange peel is a good thing to add to fruit being stewed—wonderful with rhubarb, apples, and pears—and I toss a few chunks into the pan when making otherwise plain cranberry sauce.

Just peel your tangerines, clementines, or oranges, first scoring the peel into quarters if neatness counts. Use the edge of a teaspoon to scrape off a layer of the white pith inside each piece, then spread the bits of peel on a cake rack and leave them to dry in a warm spot until brittle—a matter of hours sometimes, or a day or two other times, depending on the ambient humidity. (To speed up the job, put the rack in the oven and leave the door ajar with the oven light on.)

Store the peel in a closely capped jar. Soak it or not, as you prefer, before use—Chinese cooks usually soak the peel in warm water before making orange beef and a lot of other good things.

A CORDIAL NIP: Tangerine cordial is a snap to concoct. Steep the dried peels of 6 to 8 tangerines in a pint or so of good vodka, keeping the jar covered. Shake the brew daily for two weeks, then strain out the peel and stir in ½ cup (or more, if you like) of sugar syrup—see Lemonade or Limeade Base, page 56. Store, well capped, at room temperature.

MAYONNAISE

ne of the most sensible kitchen utensils I've ever met was a "mayonnaise mortar"—I don't know what it was actually called—my mother had when I was a kid. It was a narrow stoneware crock with a rounded bottom perfectly shaped for the operation of a rotary egg beater, and "Wesson Oil" was emblazoned in blue on the side. In that crock, tutored by my mother, I learned to make mayonnaise without a hitch or a failure. (Failures came later in life, when I tried a highfalutin' method or two.)

I still make mayonnaise with a whole egg, as Mother did; there's very little difference between that sauce and one made with yolks alone, and I suspect it's harder to fail with a whole egg when in a rush—as who isn't, once in a while?

The sauce may be made in a bowl with a whisk, an old-fashioned wooden spoon, or an egg beater, or in a blender or a food processor.

Place the egg (or yolks) in the container with 1 teaspoon of the vinegar, the mustard, the salt, a good pinch of white pepper, and the optional paprika. Beat just to mix well; don't let the mixture become foamy.

Add about a third of the oil very slowly, a drop or two at a time, beating constantly. When the sauce has become quite stiff, beat in the remaining vinegar and the lemon juice. Begin adding the rest of the oil a small dollop at a time, or pour oil in a small steady stream while continuing to beat constantly. Beat a moment longer after all the oil has been incorporated; this makes a lighter sauce.

Taste and add more salt, pepper, mustard, and/or lemon if any or all are needed; beat again. Scrape the sauce into a clean, dry jar, cover, and refrigerate for storage.

MANY MAYOS—VARIATIONS: The sky is the limit if you have made a good basic batch. (If you're going to build on the preceding recipe for other sauces, you may wish to omit or reduce the mustard and add it later if it's wanted.)

Mayonnaise is the base of tartar sauce, herbed may-

Makes about 2 cups

1 large egg, at room temperature (or 2 large egg yolks, at room temperature)

2 teaspoons tarragon vinegar

1½ teaspoons smooth Dijon-style mustard

¼ teaspoon, or to taste, salt

White pepper, to taste

Pinch of mild paprika, optional

1½ cups salad oil (olive, corn, peanut, safflower, etc., or a mixture)

2 tablespoons, or to taste, strained fresh lemon juice, or 1 to 2 tablespoons tarragon vinegar or other mild light-colored vinegar, or a mixture

STORAGE: Mayonnaise will keep for several days with perfect safety if it is kept properly cold. However, because the sauce is so easy to make once the knack is acquired, there's no real reason to make a vast quantity at once.

onnaises (and green sauces) of endless variety, dressings for fruit salad (see the suggestion with the recipe for White Chocolate Marshmallow Sauce), and countless savory dressings seasoned with tomato purée, orange juice (preferably from bitter oranges), curry, anchovies, capers, or, sublimely, a whole *lot* of garlic, in which event it becomes a version of Provençal aïoli sauce and cries out for the Provençal platter of poached fish and vegetables that makes up a *grand aïoli*, which I hope I'll taste one day on its native soil.

WAYS AND MEANS: Cooks who have problems with mayonnaise, even though they know their way around the kitchen very well, might note one clue to getting egg and oil to emulsify readily: the shape of the utensil used for mixing. The deep, narrow shape of the "mayonnaise mortar" discussed above is perfect. The question is what comes closest today.

The general idea is reflected in the deep beaker accompanying a gadget I've recently tried, a wandlike, hand-held, fairly low-speed electric blender. The beaker's shape makes it a snap to make mayonnaise in moments.

CLASSIC VINAIGRETTE SAUCE

isputes have been breaking out lately in the foodie world over the definition of "vinaigrette." The crowd that likes to bend the classics has come out for some (admittedly very tasty) so-called vinaigrettes that are thickened with raw egg, which, to me, moves the sauce over into the mayonnaise department, but we're not here to argue. I'm quite happy with the classic ingredients for vinaigrette, which make a sauce that can be tailored to suit with herbs, shallots, capers, hard-cooked egg yolk, and so on. The recipe below is flexible, which is the general idea of this sauce anyway.

Makes about 1 cup

1 small clove garlic, peeled
¼ teaspoon, or to taste,
  coarse (kosher) salt
½ teaspoon, or to taste,
  smooth Dijon-style
  mustard, optional
3 tablespoons vinegar
  (white wine, red wine,
  Oriental rice, or other)
White pepper, to taste
¾ cup, or more as needed,
  salad oil (olive, corn,
  peanut, walnut,
  safflower, avocado, or
  other)

CLASSIC VINAIGRETTE SAUCE (CONTINUED)

Crush the garlic in a bowl with the salt until it is a smooth paste. Mix in the mustard, then the vinegar; add a pinch of freshly ground white pepper; stir in the oil and beat vigorously until mixed and slightly thickened.

Taste the sauce and adjust its seasoning by adding more salt, pepper, mustard, or acid, or by adding more oil if the flavor seems overemphatic. (In theory, adjustment could go on indefinitely.)

Beat the sauce again just before it's used, as it will separate upon standing.

———

A FEW VINAIGRETTE VARIATIONS: Omit the mustard; use lemon juice in place of vinegar, or use half lemon juice and half orange or other tart fruit juice, and sweeten the sauce lightly with a dab of honey. (For salads containing fruit.)

Include chopped or minced herbs to taste. Ditto chopped capers, sour pickles, or anchovies. (Good for cold meats.)

Increase the garlic, or supplement its flavor with a teaspoonful of minced shallot. (For any green salad or any hot or cold vegetable, if you like the Alliums a lot.)

Add a pinch or two of mild paprika to the salt at the beginning. (Adds a blush of color, not much else.)

POWDERED BAY LEAVES

his used to be a grocer's spice-shelf item, but the product has dropped out of sight. Even if we didn't have our own supply of aromatic fresh bay leaves (and dried bay leaves from the fall pruning of several sizable plants), the powdered form would be worth preparing from a purchased supply of leaves. It adds savor very handily to dishes (such as the wild-rice stuffing for turkey in this book) in which it isn't feasible to use whole or crumbled leaves, and it's good for last-minute flavor adjustments to soups and stews.

What I do is whiz dried bay leaves in the blender (you need quite a lot of leaves to engage the blades sufficiently) or in a small spice mill. Once ground, the powder is pushed through a fine nylon strainer (this removes any intractable bits of stem), then packed into a little jar with a tight cork, and there you are.

As E. S. Dallas wrote of bay leaves in *Kettner's Book of the Table*, "This is indeed poetry in the pot, Daphne at our lips."

TOASTED NUTS = MORE FLAVORFUL NUTS

oasting improves even perfectly fresh and carefully stored nuts, which can sometimes be flabby and/or bland; it's highly recommended for almonds, pecans, and walnuts, and it's essential for hazelnuts, which have a brown coat that can't be removed any other way I've ever heard of. (Toasting also greatly improves such exotic nuts as cashews, Brazil nuts, and unroasted macadamias. Ditto peanuts.)

After toasting a supply of nuts, I subtract enough for the recipe I'm using and refrigerate or freeze the rest in an airtight container; they'll keep for months.

For slicing toasted nuts, using the ultra-thin-slicing disk of a food processor is the easiest method. For chopping, use the food processor's metal knife on a small batch at a time and pulse the machine on and off quickly to avoid making nut butter without meaning to.

THE NUT EXCHANGE: For most culinary uses, certain nuts can replace certain others, often with interesting results.

You can usually interchange *hickories, pecans, English walnuts,* and *butternuts* (or white walnuts; quite rare). *Black walnuts* are a special case because of their strong and distinctive flavor; it's best to use them in recipes written just for them.

Brazil nuts, when lightly toasted, are a good alternative to almonds, as are unsalted *cashews* and *macadamias,* two of the most costly nuts.

Chestnuts, because of their mealy texture after the necessary cooking, aren't a good substitute for other nuts; like black walnuts, they're best when they do their own thing.

Hazelnuts can replace *almonds, pecans,* or *hickory nuts,* besides starring in their own recipes.

Pistachios, pine nuts, and *peanuts* are unique, too, and have their own best uses; this is also true of the flesh of *coconuts,* if you consider coconuts to be nuts at all.

PECANS & WALNUTS

Spread these nuts on a cookie sheet and bake them at 325°, stirring and turning them often—every minute or two—until they smell toasty and extra-nutty and a sample is crisp when cooled a little and broken open. Toasting takes about 10 minutes and requires the cook to watch carefully to prevent scorching.

Walnuts are further improved by being rubbed in a cloth to remove as much loose skin as possible, but this step isn't essential.

Cool the nuts before using them.

HAZELNUTS

Spread whole hazelnuts on a baking sheet and bake them in a 350° oven until their skins are crisp and the nuts smell heavenly and look a little darker in color in the spots where the skin has dropped off, which should take 10 to 15 minutes; shake the pan and stir the nuts often to toast them evenly.

A handful at a time, rub the hot nuts in a rough towel to remove as much brown skin as you can; it won't all come off.

Cool the nuts before using them.

ALMONDS

Preliminary blanching: To blanch natural almonds, drop them into boiling-hot water and leave them for 2 or 3 minutes. Drain them and pop them out of their skins with your fingers. They will be rather moist, so they'll require longer toasting time than almonds in their skins.

Even though they may seem to be crisp enough when they're purchased, either blanched or natural almonds will have more flavor and better texture after they're toasted. Spread them on a baking sheet and bake them in a 325° oven, stirring them every minute or two, until they smell decidedly toasty. Blanched nuts will have turned pale gold; if you're toasting natural nuts, their already golden color will deepen a bit but you'll have to judge mainly by their fragrance. Count on about 15 minutes' baking, perhaps a little longer for freshly blanched nuts.

Cool the nuts before using them.

TOM PINCH AND RUTH (MAINLY RUTH) MAKE A PIE IN THEIR LODGINGS:
"First, she tripped downstairs into the kitchen for the flour, then for the pie-board, then for the eggs, then for the butter, then for a jug of water, then for the rolling-pin . . . making a separate journey for everything, and laughing every time she started off afresh. . . . It was a perfect treat to Tom to see her with her brows knit, and her rosy lips pursed up, kneading away at the crust, rolling it out . . ."
—CHARLES DICKENS, *Martin Chuzzlewit.*

PIE TIME AT AN AMERICAN BOARDING HOUSE: *"It was a solemn and an awful thing to see. . . . Spare men, with lank and rigid cheeks, came out unsatisfied from the destruction of heavy dishes, and glared with watchful eyes upon the pastry. What Mrs. Pawkins felt each day at dinner-time is hidden from all human knowledge. But she had one comfort. It was very soon over."*
—CHARLES DICKENS, *Martin Chuzzlewit.*

PASTRIES FOR PIES & TARTS, & HOW TO SHAPE & BAKE THEM

he Tender Pie Pastry is as close to fool-proof as a dough can get; it owes its amiability, tenderness, and flavor to the inclusion of an extra ingredient or two that have been known to practiced pie-makers for a long time. For beginners, it's a good pastry to start with, as it will forgive rerolling that would make most other pastries into cardboard.

The Flaky Pastry is a classic type that's ideal for many uses, but it's not as easy for beginners to handle as Tender Pie Pastry. Two or three pies' worth of practice should be enough to master it.

A third type of pastry that makes a cookie-type crust will be found as part of the recipe for Hazelnut Cheese Tart (page 151).

Which pastry to use: For a tart, choose either the tender pastry or the cookie crust just mentioned. However, you can use the flaky pastry if you prefer its texture for a tart.

For a pie, use either of the two pastries described in the recipes on the following page.

Quantity of pastry to make: For a two-crust pie, double the ingredients listed in the recipes that follow. You may have a little more pastry than you need, but that's better than trying to stretch a stingy amount, especially if your pastry-making skills are being learned, so to speak, at your own knee, not Granny's. Any surplus dough can be rerolled and cut into cookie shapes; sprinkle them with sugar and cinnamon, and bake them on a cookie sheet. (This is a great project for any child who is yearning to get into the act.)

TENDER PIE PASTRY

Enough for an 8- or 9-inch pie shell or a 10-inch tart shell; or the top of a deep-dish pie

1¼ cups all-purpose flour
2 teaspoons granulated sugar
¼ teaspoon salt
¼ teaspoon baking powder
½ cup chilled vegetable shortening
1 large egg yolk
1 teaspoon vinegar
1 tablespoon water

Sift the flour, sugar, salt, and baking powder into a bowl. Cut in the shortening with a pastry blender (or two knives, wielded crisscross like the blades of scissors) to make a coarse, mealy mixture.

Mix the egg yolk, vinegar, and water and sprinkle the mixture over the dry ingredients. Toss everything lightly together with a table fork until the dough begins to cohere, then press it lightly into a ball, wrap in plastic or waxed paper, and refrigerate 1 hour to as long as overnight.

To shape a crust and prebake a pie or tart shell, see the notes following Flaky Pie Pastry.

FLAKY PIE PASTRY

Enough for an 8- or 9-inch pie shell or a 10-inch tart shell, or the top of a deep-dish pie

1¼ cups all-purpose flour
½ teaspoon salt
½ cup chilled vegetable shortening, or half shortening and half chilled unsalted butter
2 to 4 tablespoons, as needed, ice-cold water

Stir the flour and salt together. Cut in the shortening with a pastry blender or two knives until the particles are the size of rice grains. Sprinkle the ice water gradually over the mixture, tossing everything with a fork as you go, until just enough liquid has been added to make a crumbly dough.

Form the dough lightly into a ball, wrap it in plastic or waxed paper, and chill it for an hour (or more, if possible) before using.

To shape a crust and to prebake a pie or tart shell, see the notes below.

ROLLING OUT PASTRY & SHAPING A CRUST

Beginning: Flatten the ball of chilled dough, dust it with flour, and roll it out on a well-floured work surface with a floured rolling pin. (A canvas pastry cloth and a stockinette rolling-pin cover, both coated with flour that has been well rubbed in, are the most helpful pastry-rolling aids I know.)

Technique: Roll outward from the center of the dough to the edge, fanning out the strokes in all directions. Don't roll back and forth, which would toughen the pastry. Try to make a reasonably uniform circle. If the edges split too much, moisten the edges of the tears and patch them with a bit of dough cut from the area outside the circle you're making.

To test the thickness of the dough, poke a skewer into it vertically and mark with a fingernail the point where it emerges from the pastry; measure the distance from skewer tip to fingernail with a ruler or by eye. For most pies, pastry is rolled ⅛ inch thick. Tender types of pastry are sometimes rolled out much thicker, especially for tarts.

Size of round to roll: For a crust to line a 9-inch piepan, make a 12-inch round.

To fit a piepan or tart pan of another size, make the round 3 inches larger in diameter than the top of the pan, measuring between the outer edges of the rim.

For a top crust, make the round 1½ inches larger than the top of the pan.

Fitting pastry to pan: Lay the rolling pin across the center of the dough, fold one half of the round over the pin, and lift the pin and pastry together, holding the pastry in place with your thumbs. Lower the pastry onto the piepan, centering it more or less. Set aside the pin and coax the pastry downward into place—don't stretch it even slightly. The idea is to fit the pastry well down into the pan while keeping it relaxed. (Stretched pastry will shrink and become tough when it is baked.)

Trimming: For a single-crust pie, trim off excess pastry with shears or a knife, leaving a margin extending about 1 inch beyond the rim of the pan. Turn the margin under all around, making a doubled rim. Using the fingers, press the pastry into upstanding scallops if you want a fluted edge; or crimp the pastry onto the pan rim with a pastry crimper or the tines of a fork.

For a two-crust pie, trim the lower crust to leave a half-inch margin extending beyond the rim. Moisten the margin with water, set the top crust in place over the filling, and trim its edges to match the lower crust. Fold the doubled edge under all around, then flute or crimp it to make an ornamental edge.

Vents: For a double-crust pie, don't overlook the need for slashes or other openings in the top crust to let out steam. These may be cut before the pastry is lifted into place or afterward, and may be simple slashes or elaborate decorative patterns. Or you can set an old-fashioned china pie bird in the filling and let its head emerge through the top crust; the steam is vented through the open beak.

Glazing: Brush the top crust with egg or cream as directed in some recipes; use a pastry brush to make a thin, uniform coating without soaking the dough.

For baking: Follow the directions in each pie or tart recipe. For baking an empty shell, see below.

ADVICE FROM ANGELO:
"Learn a few basic principles and get a firm grip on this solid, heartening fact: the American housewife—man or woman—is potentially the best of all possible cooks ... she has in shameful abundance all the necessary ingredients.... All she needs is the will to take advantage of her opportunities."

—ANGELO PELLEGRINI, *The Unprejudiced Palate.*

BAKING AN EMPTY SHELL

For many tarts and some pies, the shell is partly or fully baked before it's filled. (Makes for a crisper result.)

Here are some how-to's for a fully baked shell. If a recipe calls for a partially baked shell, bake the shell only 2 minutes or so after removing the weights.

For a tart, use a loose-bottomed tart pan, the kind with a low, fluted rim. For a pie, use any piepan. Dust the pan evenly with flour.

Fit the pastry into the pan in the relaxed way described above. Make a fluted or crimped edge for a pie. For a tart, don't trim the pastry as you would for a pie; instead, run the rolling pin across the top to cut off the surplus flush with the pan rim. Then, using a fingertip, go around the sides and press the pastry firmly into the flutings; the pastry will rise above the rim as you do so. Don't trim it again.

Prick the bottom all over with a fork (this helps prevent buckling). Fit a large square of foil or waxed paper loosely into the shell and spread about an inch of a weighty substance over the lining. Rice or beans are traditional pastry weights, or you can use aluminum or ceramic "beads" made especially for the purpose. (Or use well-washed and completely dry gravel or fine pebbles.)

Bake the shell in an oven preheated to 425° for 10 minutes, then lift out the lining and its cargo of weights. If the bottom of the shell has bulged upward, press it flat again. Lower the oven setting to 375° and continue to bake the pastry until it's golden-brown and crisp, which will take another 5 to 10 minutes. Keep an eye on its progress, and cover the edge with foil if it's browning too much. Cool the shell on a rack before filling it.

Before serving, remove the rim of the tart pan by setting the whole business on a sturdy base (such as a can of food) that's smaller than the pan; then ease the rim downward and free of the pastry. Before doing this, check for any spots where the pastry may have stuck to the pan rim; free the crust with the tip of a thin knife before attempting to unmold the tart.

The tart may be left on the pan base for serving (just slide the base onto a serving plate), or it can be shifted onto a serving platter *sans* base. Do this cautiously, first sliding a long thin spatula beneath the tart to be sure it isn't stuck; then coax it from pan base to platter with the spatula. (If in doubt of success, I'd leave it on the base; the transfer of a fragile tart can be tricky.)

THE LAST WORD ON PIE:
"Your apples should have a sort of tingling tartness. No half-hearted sourness or full-confessed sweetness will do. . . . Bake [the pie] until the crust is brown and flaky and the apples are tender, transparent, and gleaming in their rich juices. Serve hot, if possible, with generous slabs (not flimsy wisps) of cheese. Serve a big jug of golden cream for those whose waistlines need no attention. Better serve it anyway. They can diet next week."

—ANN BATCHELDER.

TART PASTRY, FURTHER:
It's almost impossible to overbake a tart shell made from the classic rich pastry doughs you'll find in specialized baking books, so long as you don't let the crust become too brown. (In this book, the nearest thing to those special doughs is the pastry in the recipe for Hazelnut Cheese Tart on page 151.)

If you'd like to make a long-baked and especially crisp crust to fill with custard and/or poached or fresh fruit of your choice, use that dough and follow the baking hints on these pages, but lengthen the suggested baking time of the second stage to 30 minutes. Keep an interested eye on progress and cover the edges with foil if necessary to prevent overbrowning.

Cool the shell completely before filling it. If the filling is a juicy one, you might brush a coat of egg white over the inside about 10 minutes before taking the shell from the oven.

PASTRY TROUBLESHOOTING

Too wet, too dry: If pastry dough is too moist, it sticks to everything. If it's too dry, it crumbles when you try to roll it.

To remedy the first problem, gather the pastry into a rough mass and dust it generously with flour; knead it a stroke or two, no more, then repeat the flouring if necessary to cure the wetness.

If the dough is too dry to hold together, sprinkle a *few* drops of ice water over it, then gather the crumbles together (a pastry scraper is perfect for such maneuvers) and fold it gently into a ball. Wrap and chill it for at least half an hour to allow the moisture to distribute itself.

The rolling surface: Before rerolling problem pie crust, scrape and reflour the board (and the pin, if it isn't wearing a floured stockinette cover). Do this even if the surfaces are not visibly sticky or lumpy. Your pastry scraper, again, does this job best.

Repairs: If the pastry should tear during rolling, brush or dab a very little water around the edges of the tear and lay a patch (cut from the peripheral pastry) over it. Roll the spot gently once or twice to seal the patch in place.

If pastry should tear when it is put into the pan, repair it in the same way, but press the patch in place with the fingers. The filling will cover a multitude of sins, and baking will also improve such blemishes as a slightly raggedy edge or a patched top crust. Sheer perfection needn't be the beginner's goal—there's always a next time.

SWEDISH CUCUMBERS

 n cucumber season a jarful of these sweet and tart refrigerator pickles almost always stands ready to be served with sandwiches, cold meats, seafood, or chicken, or just with a snack of cheese and crackers. (In Sweden, cucumbers prepared along these lines are always among the delicacies on the smorgasbord.)

In the recipe there's wiggle room—use your choice of vinegars and, if you like a low-calorie sweetener in place of sugar. Cucumbers pickled this way, then sauced with sour cream and dill, are especially good with fish or seafood.

Peel the cucumbers, halve them lengthwise, and scoop out the seeds. Slice them ¼ inch thick to make horseshoe shapes.

Mix the vinegar, sugar, salt, and pepper and combine with the cucumbers in a quart jar. The slices should be covered; if not, add more liquid, maintaining the general ratio of ingredients. Cover and refrigerate at least overnight. (They keep for weeks.)

At serving time, fish out as many cucumbers as needed and garnish them with minced parsley (traditional) or fresh dill (my choice).

Makes 1 quart

2 or 3 firm cucumbers
1 cup distilled white vinegar plus ¼ cup water (see Other Vinegars, right)
1 cup sugar or other sweetener (see Alternative Sweetenings right)
A little salt and white pepper
Garnish: Parsley or dill, optional

CUCUMBERS IN SOUR CREAM WITH DILL: Combine Swedish Cucumbers and a little of their liquid with a generous quantity of minced dill leaves (or, out of season, dried dillweed) and enough sour cream to make a sauce. Let the flavors swap around for an hour or two before serving. Leftovers will keep for a day or two.

OTHER VINEGARS: Use 1¼ cups of Oriental rice vinegar or white wine vinegar in place of combined white vinegar and water.

ALTERNATIVE SWEETENINGS: Those concerned about consuming sugar may prefer some such sweetener as Aspartame, marketed as Nutrasweet. (Don't just reduce the sugar in the recipe—that destroys the balance of flavors.)

Aspartame, unlike some earlier sugar substitutes, imparts no bitterness, but for the non-mathematical it's a nuisance to figure how many of the single-serving packets equal a given amount of sugar. The solution is to stir the sweetener into the liquid packet by packet, tasting it often.

KEEPING THE JAR FILLED: As cucumbers are used, more slices may be added to the jar. Taste the liquid after you do so and add vinegar, sugar, salt, and pepper as needed to keep up its pickly character.

SOME EQUIPMENT ABSOLUTELY NOT TO BE WITHOUT

ike most people professionally and/or recreationally entangled with cuisine, Mrs. Witty is interested in kitchen equipment the way a skier is interested in skis.

Professionally, she has evaluated a lot of kitchen stuff, both as an equipment consultant and as senior editor of *The Cooks' Catalogue*, a big, fat, groundbreaking book of the mid-1970s. (Still most useful for its general as well as specific information, if you can find a copy.)

Personally, she's fascinated with the way things work and she's never bored with trying new wrinkles, so her kitchen is often crammed with things to try. Beyond the basics found in every kitchen, here are some items that make it more pleasant to feed family and friends.

BRILLIANT INVENTIONS

Since the introduction of the Cuisinart in the early seventies, the *food processor* has merely changed our cooking lives, that's all. It can do nothing that knives, grinders, graters, blenders, and mandolines can't do, but it does what it does so easily and well...Nevertheless, the *blender* is still worth its counter space because it purées certain foods (and mixes beverages) better than a processor. (And neither one can replace the *electric mixer*. We have a big, sturdy Hobart because it will knead a good-sized batch of the breads we often bake.)

The *microwave*: We're now using a microwave, after ignoring the existence of such for a long time because of tasting some awful early-microwave-era dishes. It's not an essential, but it's obviously a good right hand to anyone who has little time (or inclination) to prepare meals the old-fashioned way. For someone who, like me, cooks a lot in the line of duty, it speeds up preparatory steps—melting, thawing, softening, precooking—and it dries fresh herbs without destroying their flavor.

ANCIENT ARTIFACTS

Without a *wok*, Mrs. W, who was probably born Chinese in a previous incarnation, couldn't be happy; a skeptic will see why after a little wokking of food of any national origin, not just Chinese. Most of the Witty woks are blue-steel jobs of a design as old as China, but one newer one—called a *Peking pan*—is flat-bottomed and exceptionally versatile. Electric woks can't be recommended; they just don't produce enough heat. Wok tools include metal *wok shovels*, shaped to fit the pan; huge bamboo-handled *mesh strainers* for lifting ingredients (or a whole fish); and long, strong *cooking chopsticks*. If they can be found, long bamboo *shovel-shaped spoons* or *spatulas* with slanting ends are a delight, as quiet against the pan as other woods but more durable and easier to keep clean.

Also venerable, and haling from the other side of the world from China, is another item, the hand-cranked Italian *pasta machine*, peerless for noodles wide and noodles narrow, and fresh ravioli dough as well.

STOVETOP STUFF

But before the stuff, the stove itself: We cook with gas (but have electric ovens—regular, convection, and microwave) because stovetop gas is flexible and infinitely controllable; and Mrs. W would advise anyone who has a choice to do likewise. She has another reason for choosing gas—the supply of electricity is a sometime thing here, even when we aren't having a hurricane. Our prize storm to date, Gloria by name if not by nature, left us powerless—lightless, heatless, waterless, ovenless—for a solid nine days; but we could cook, with water hauled from the firehouse.

For the stovetop, the valuable pots, in addition to the usual basics, include a *stock pot* of large capacity (20 quarts or more) that can hold many pounds of bones and vegetables for stock, or a brisket of corned beef, or lobsters or pot au feu for a crowd; it also serves as a waterbath canner for the putting-up of preserves. Good metals are stainless steel (most versatile), aluminum, anodized (dark) aluminum, or costly but wonderful-looking copper lined with nickel or stainless steel rather than tin. Among saucepans, the flared type called a *Windsor saucepan* (or a *fait-tout*) is astonishingly useful, as its slanted sides make stirring

easy—get a big one, 4 or 5 quarts. Also indispensable: a *cast-iron skillet*, large and thick, which can be safely heated white-hot for stovetop steaks...a *cast-iron Dutch oven*, with an absolutely tight cover, for slow braising...*enameled-iron casseroles*, which hold heat as well as thick iron but won't interact with acid ingredients ...an *unlined copper preserving pan*, not really a luxury if you make jam, jelly, and other preserves. A *pressure cooker* remains the cook's friend when time is tight, and it cooks vegetables as well and as fast as a microwave and without the need for arranging the pieces just so.

FAVORED BAKING HELPERS

A *marble rolling pin* is heavy enough to do the work almost on its own, after a push to get it started. For delicate doughs that a heavy pin would squash, the best bet is a long, straight French-type *wooden pastry pin*. A *marble slab* makes a cool, easily cleanable rolling and kneading surface; it's handiest if built into a countertop. Lacking such, a portable substitute is a slab of rigid, pebbled transparent or white plastic, which can double as a counter-protector on a butcher-block surface. Other desirables: Sturdy, professional-style *wire cake racks* large enough to cool a big sheetful of cookies or two cake layers...*air-cushioned baking sheets*, which prevent delicate cookies from overbaking...a set of *thin firebricks* (from a building supply yard), fitted together on an oven shelf to make a "hearth" as large as the shelf for baking pizza, pita, and super-crusty country loaves...*pastry brushes*, a whole jarful in several sizes, for basting as well as glazing baked things... a *dough scraper*—a blunt rectangular blade—to clean up work surfaces fast, be they ever so sticky, and to help when kneading soft doughs...a *pizza cutter*, which is not for pizza only; use it to slash pastry strips for pie tops, dough strips for breadsticks.

SMALL UTENSILS & IMPLEMENTS THAT EARN THEIR KEEP

Professional-quality stainless-steel *cooking spoons*, plain and perforated...a fine-meshed stainless-steel *skimmer* and several fine *strainers* of the same material ...a long, sturdy *pot fork*...a *ladle* (nylon is excellent) with an oval bowl...*rubber spatulas*, several sizes...*long tongs*... sturdy *whisks* from tiny to balloon size... a *food mill*...a porcelain or marble *mortar and pestle*, for crushing jobs nothing else does as well.

KNIVES

It takes time to discover which knife shapes and sizes suit your hand and your style, so most people try (and replace) several blades over time. Once you've decided on what you like for the long haul, do avoid gimmicks and buy good knives. Knives made of no-stain high-carbon steel are now very good; they hold their edges better than the old "stainless" type, they sharpen easily, and they don't need the anti-rust care required by carbon-steel.

A basic trousseau might include an excellent *paring knife* or two, of a shape that pleases you (there are many)...a straight-edged *utility knife* midway in size between a parer and a small chef's knife, and perhaps a *straight, narrow serrated knife*...A good-sized *chef's knife*...A heavy Chinese *cleaver*...A *serrated bread knife*...And a long, sharp *slicer*. Desirable extras are a *boning knife*, for meat and poultry, and a *filleting knife* that makes it easy to deal with fish.

Good *sharpening equipment* will keep your knives delightful (and safe) to use— it's absolutely true that a dull knife is dangerous, because it bounces off food, or slips, instead of cutting where you want it to cut. *Oilstones* and *diamond-surfaced whetstones* do a good job if elbow grease is applied, but the Wittys now rejoice in a four-slot "professional" *electric knife sharpener* that quickly restores even a neglected blade and keeps knives well whetted between sharpenings.

AND NOW FOR THE GADGETS...

Certain widgets make fiddly jobs easier. A *strawberry huller* costs pennies and plucks pesky pinfeathers, too....A *salad spinner* makes short work of washing grubby mushrooms (yes, you can wash mushrooms—just do it fast) as well as greens....A *citrus zester* strips fine slivers of peel from oranges or lemons, thus doubling as a grater....A *tortilla press* shapes tortillas that are fresher and finer than those most of us can buy....An *electric spice mill* (or a small coffee grinder) crumbles dried herbs and grinds spices just before they're used and lets you make your own seasoning mixtures....A *nutmeg grater*, either a small tinned half-cylinder or a grinder resembling a pepper mill, is essential if you want to know the full flavor of nutmeg....*Skewers*, the long and the short, the fat and the thin, are endlessly useful, as is a ball of strong, soft *kitchen twine*....An old-fashioned *glass lemon reamer* puts to flight all metal models....*Pepper mills* are essential, one for white peppercorns, one for black, and so is a *salt mill* for grinding coarse sea salt (which does indeed have flavor, not just saltiness) at the table or for cooking.... An instant-reading *thermometer* can do most temperature-taking jobs around the kitchen except those involved in candymaking and deep-frying, which require special thermometers....A *collapsible steaming basket* fits into pans of several sizes, is valuable for vegetables....Your *bulb baster* should be made of stainless steel, not plastic.

SOURCES OF QUOTATIONS AND A FEW FOOD BOOKS TO READ FOR PLEASURE

Never trust a cookbook that calls itself "complete."
—A COLLECTOR'S MOTTO

For the interested cookbook-worm, here are particulars of the principal books quoted in the text. They are delightful reading, and so are the works on the second, longer list.

Batchelder, Ann. *Ann Batchelder's Cookbook*, rev. ed. New York: Barrows, 1949.

Beeton, Isabella. *The Book of Household Management*, facsimile of 1st (1861) ed. London: Jonathan Cape, 1968.

Dallas, E.S. *Kettner's Book of the Table* [1877]. London: Centaur Press, 1968.

Freeling, Nicolas. *The Kitchen: A Delicious Account of the Author's Years as a Grand Hotel Cook*. New York: Harper & Row, 1970.

Gray, Peter. *The Mistress Cook*. New York: Oxford University Press, 1956.

Pellegrini, Angelo M. *The Unprejudiced Palate*. New York: Macmillan, 1962.

Revel, Jean-Francois. *Culture and Cuisine: A Journey Through the History of Food*, trans. Helen R. Lane. Garden City, New York: Doubleday, 1982.

Shand, P. Morton. *A Book of Food*. New York: Knopf, 1928.

Thorne, John. *Simple Cooking*. New York: Viking, 1987.

ALSO RECOMMENDED...

... To those who enjoy bedtime (or anytime) reading about food. (Many of these are good to cook from, too.) The list represents only a fraction of the titles I treasure most. Many of the books are out of print, but reprints can always be hoped for, and meantime, there is the joy of rummaging through second-hand bookshops.

Adamson, Helen Lyon. *Grandmother in the Kitchen*. New York: Crown, 1965. Like a shoeboxful of old recipes.

Baker, Charles. *The Gentleman's Companion*, 2 vols. New York: Crown, 1946. Exotic eats and, especially, drinks.

Beard, James. *Delights and Prejudices*. New York: Fireside/Simon & Schuster, 1971. Memoir of a palate and its possessor.

Boulestin, X. Marcel. *The Best of Boulestin*, ed. Elvia and Maurice Firuski. New York: Greenberg, 1951.

Brillat-Savarin, Jean Anthelme. *The Physiology of Taste*, trans. and annot. M.F.K. Fisher. New York: Alfred A. Knopf, 1971.

Capon, Robert Farrar. *Capon on Cooking*. Boston: Houghton Mifflin, 1983.

——*The Supper of the Lamb*. Garden

City, New York: Image Books/ Doubleday, 1974. A culinary reflection.

Casas, Penelope. *The Foods and Wines of Spain*. New York: Alfred A. Knopf, 1982.

Courtine, Robert. *The Hundred Glories of French Cooking*, trans. Derek Coltman. New York: Farrar, Strauss & Giroux, 1973.

David, Elizabeth. *An Omelette and a Glass of Wine*. London: Robert Hale, 1984. And, almost needless to say, any other book by this peerless writer/cook.

Davidson, Alan. *Mediterranean Seafood*, rev. ed. London: Allen Lane, 1981.

——*North Atlantic Seafood*. New York: Viking, 1980. Davidson also edits, from London, the esteemed periodical *Petits Propos Culinaires*.

Douglas, Norman. [Pilaff Bey]. *Venus in the Kitchen: Or Love's Cookery Book*. New York: Viking, 1953. Aphrodisiacs, by a skeptic.

Dumas, Alexandre. *Dictionary of Cuisine*, ed. Louis Colman. New York: Simon & Schuster, 1958.

——*Dumas on Food: Selections from Le Grand Dictionnaire de Cuisine*, trans. Alan and Jane Davidson. London: Folio Society, 1978.

Field, Carol. *The Italian Baker*. New York: Harper & Row, 1985. Read it tonight, take it to the kitchen in the morning and *bake*.

Grabhorn, Robert. *A Commonplace Book of Cookery*. San Francisco: North Point Press, 1985. Savory quotes; handsome format.

Grass, Günter. *The Flounder*, trans. Ralph Manheim. New York: Harcourt Brace Jovanovich, 1978. A brilliant novelist considers men, women, history and "the cooks inside me," wielders of spoons and cookpots since the Paleolithic.

Gray, Patience. *Honey from a Weed: Fasting and Feasting in Tuscany, Catalonia, the Cyclades and Apulia*. New York: Harper & Row, 1987.

Grigson, Jane. *The Art of Charcuterie*. New York: Alfred A. Knopf, 1968.

——*Good Things*, New York: Alfred A. Knopf, 1971. And, come to think of it, any Grigson title; only Elizabeth David is her peer among food writers.

Harris, Marvin. *Good to Eat: Riddles of Food and Culture*. New York: Simon & Schuster, 1985.

Hartley, Dorothy. *Food in England* [1954]. London: Macdonald and Jane's, 1975.

——*Lost Country Life*, New York: Pantheon, 1979.

Herman, Judith, and Herman, Marguerite Shalett. *The Cornucopia*. New York: Harper & Row, 1973.

Hess, John, and Hess, Karen. *The Taste of America*. New York: Penguin, 1977. From a set of splendid curmudgeons, all-too-accurate observations.

Hieatt, Constance B., and Butler, Sharon. *Pleyn Delit: Medieval Cookery for Modern Cooks*. Toronto: University of Toronto Press, 1979.

Kamman, Madeline. *The Making of a Cook*. New York: Atheneum, 1982. Memoir with recipes.

Kennedy, Diana. *The Art of Mexican Cooking*. New York: Bantam, 1989.

Lin, Hsiang Ju, and Lin, Tsuifeng. *Chinese Gastronomy*, with preface by Lin Yutang. New York: Harcourt Brace Jovanovich, 1977.

Matson, Ruth. *Cooking by the Garden Calendar*. Garden City, New York: Doubleday, 1955.

——[as Ruth A. Jeremiah Gottfried] *The Questing Cook*. Cambridge, Massachusetts: Washburn & Thomas, 1927.

McGee, Harold. *On Food and Cooking: The Science and Lore of the Kitchen*. New York: Scribner's, 1984.

McNeill, F. Marian. *The Scots Kitchen: Its Lore and Recipes*, 2nd ed. London and Glasgow: Blackie & Son, 1962.

Olney, Richard. *The French Menu Cookbook*, rev. ed. Boston: David R. Godine, 1985.

——*Simple French Food*. New York: Atheneum, 1975. The complexities of splendid simplicity.

Pomiane, Edouard de. *Cooking in Ten Min-*

utes, trans. Peggie Benton. London: Faber & Faber, 1957.

———Cooking with Pomiane, trans. Peggie Benton. New York: Roy Publishers, 1961?.

Roden, Claudia. A Book of Middle Eastern Food. New York: Vintage/Random House, 1974.

Root, Waverley. Eating in America: A History. New York: Ecco Press, 1981.

———Food. New York: Simon & Schuster, 1980.

———The Food of France. New York: Vintage/Random House, 1977.

Stern, Jane, and Stern, Michael. Roadfood and Goodfood. New York: Alfred A. Knopf, 1986.

———Square Meals. New York: Alfred A. Knopf, 1984. Good-natured guides on a tour of estimable to near-awful U.S. food.

Stobart, Tom. Cook's Encyclopedia: Ingredients and Processes. New York: Harper & Row, 1981.

———Herbs, Spices and Flavorings. Woodstock, New York: Overlook Press, 1982. Erudite, graceful; for both reading and reference.

Toklas, Alice B. The Alice B. Toklas Cookbook. New York: Doubleday Anchor Books, 1960.

Tolbert, Frank X. A Bowl of Red: A Natural History of Chili con Carne. Garden City, New York: Doubleday, 1966.

Toulouse-Lautrec, Henri de, and Joyant, Maurice. The Art of Cuisine. trans. Margery Weiner. New York: Holt, 1966.

Tudge, Colin. Future Food. New York: Harmony Books, 1979. For the 21st century.

Wheaton, Barbara Ketcham. Savoring the Past: The French Kitchen and Table from 1300 to 1789. Philadelphia: University of Pennsylvania Press, 1983.

White, Florence. Good Things in England. London: Jonathan Cape, 1932. A classic delve into roots and relics.

Wolcott, Imogene. The Yankee Cookbook, rev. ed. Brattleboro, Vermont: Stephen Greene Press, 1981.

Wolfe, Linda. The Literary Gourmet: Menus from Masterpieces. New York: Harmony Books, 1985.

SEASONAL RECIPE LISTS FOR COMPOSING YOUR OWN HOME-STYLE MENUS

These lists are arranged by type of meal and, within meals, by seasons of the year. Dessert lists—also seasonal—appear after the listings for Breakfasts, Lunches, Cookouts, Dinners, and Suppers. You'll notice that many if not most of the suggestions in each meal category are suitable for any season.

For the whereabouts of individual recipes, check the Index. See the Index, too, for some recipes not included in the lists below—additional breads, sauces, salads, condiments, syrups, and vegetable dishes.

BREAKFASTS

DISHES FOR ANY SEASON
Banana-Nut Pancakes
Butter-Poached Apples
Blueberry Corn Bread or Muffins
Chipped Beef in Cream
Corn Oysters
Angel Biscuits or Rolls
Curdled Eggs
Eggs à la Hotrod
Hot Biscuits or Buttermilk Biscuits
Dad's Brainy Dish
Cinnamon-Capped Apple Muffins, or the
    blueberry version
Uncooked Lime or Lemon Curd (as a
    spread for toast)

FOR SUMMER
Summer Fruit Shortcake
Gingery Melon Mold
Fresh Corn Popovers
Bread & Butter Pudding with Berries
Sautéed Red & Green Tomato Slices

FOR FALL AND WINTER
Amber Apples
Finnan Haddie in Cream
Pennsylvania Dutch Scrapple
Ambrosia
Updated Home-Style Sausage
Summer Fruit Shortcake
Swiss-Style Skillet Potato Cake
Richard's Celtic Soda Bread with Raisins
    & Caraway

LUNCHES

DISHES FOR ANY SEASON
Basic Lobster
Fritto Misto of Brains & Artichokes
Baked Ham
Pretty Good Chili con Carne, and Beans
    for Chili
Pre-Pasta Macaroni Salad, any version
Cucumber Shreds with Sesame & Soy
Tacos
Tomato Aspic with Avocado

Buttered Lobster or Buttered Crabmeat &
    Lobster
Sorrel Egg-Flower Soup
Marinated Jerusalem Artichokes
Hot Seafood in a Roll
Classic Chicken Salad or Fruited Chicken
    Salad
Eggy Potato & Bacon Salad, or Summer
    Potato Salad
Classic Lobster Salad
Yankee-Mex Beans
Savory Chicken & Veal Loaf
Coleslaw (see Index for choices)
Linguine with Clams & Pancetta
Superb Lobster Stew
See also Desserts (below)

FOR SUMMER
Corn on the Cob
Fresh Corn Popovers
Lobster Rolls
Tomato Sandwiches
Corn Oysters
Farmstyle Salad Platter
Steamed & Chilled Clams with Lime,
    Chive & Mustard Mayonnaise
Herb-Broiled Chickens
Sautéed Red & Green Tomato Slices
See also Desserts (below)

COOKOUT DISHES

Eggy Potato & Bacon Salad, or Summer
    Potato Salad
A Grillful of Sausages
Swedish Cucumbers
Citrus-Glazed Pork Ribs
Pre-Pasta Macaroni Salad, any version
Marinated Jerusalem Artichokes
Barbecued Bread
Farmstyle Salad Platter
Tacos, and Guacamole for Tacos
Pretty Good Chili con Carne, and Beans
    for Chili
Carnitas
Cauliflower Slaw
Celery & Sweet Corn Salad
Coleslaw (see Index for choices)

Steamed & Chilled Clams with Lime,
    Chive & Mustard Mayonnaise
Corn on the Cob, or Corn Grilled in the
    Husk
Cucumber Shreds with Sesame & Soy
Crisp Garlic Garbanzos or Garlic Garban-
    zos to Go with Chili
Masa Cheese Sticks
Orange & Lemon Salad with Mint, or Or-
    ange & Onion Salad

DINNERS

DISHES FOR ANY SEASON
Ann Seranne's Great Hunk of Beef
Baked Ham
California Succotash
Pretty Good Chili con Carne, and Beans
    for Chili
Lemon Chicken My Way
Linguine with Clams & Pancetta
Fritto Misto of Brains & Artichokes
Antipasto
Carnitas
Orzo "Risotto"
Panned Cherry Tomatoes
Panned Spinach
Pan-Seared Sirloin
Poached Radishes in Marjoram Cream
Red Cherry Rice Pilaff
Slunk (oven-baked chowder)
Chinese Cabbage Coleslaw, two versions
Marinated Jerusalem Artichokes
Spicy Sweet-Potato Sticks & Sweet-
    Potato Sticks with Orange & Honey
Crisp Garlic Garbanzos
Swiss-Style Skillet Potato Cake
The Real Mashed Potatoes
Tomato Aspic (Three Ways)
Masa Cheese Sticks
A Tapenade of a Different Color
Turkey Sausages in Garlic Cream
Quick Citrus Coleslaw
Creamy Potato Gratin
See also Desserts (below)

DISHES AT THEIR BEST IN SUMMER
Herb-Broiled Chickens

Corn on the Cob
Fresh Corn Popovers
Farmstyle Salad Platter
Old New England Corn Pudding
Sautéed Red & Green Tomato Slices
Steamed & Chilled Clams with Lime,
     Chive & Mustard Mayonnaise
Swedish Cucumbers
Corn Oysters
Cucumber Shreds with Soy & Sesame
See also Desserts (below)

FOR FALL AND WINTER
Baked Beans—Better-Than-Yankee or
     Vermont-Style
Ham Scalloped with Potatoes à la Jac-
     ques, or Creamy Potato Gratin
Nanny's Braised Wineburgers
Cauliflower Slaw
Fricasseed Rabbit with Creamy Gravy
Iron-Pot Duckling
Red Cherry Rice Pilaff
Pristine Pot Roast & Gravy
Red Cabbage Braised with Cranberries
Old New England Corn Pudding
Remolded Broccoli (or Cauliflower)
Slow-Baked Minimalist Pork Ribs
Hearty Cornbread Skillet with Bacon &
     Whole-Kernel Corn
Buttered Crabmeat & Lobster
Beanpot Chicken & Noodles, or Beanpot
     Chicken with Gravy
Onions in Sage Sauce
Salad of Chinese Cabbage with Fruit &
     Nuts
Red-Wine Beans with a Ham Bone
Turkey for Thanksgiving
See also Desserts (below)

SUPPERS

DISHES FOR ANY SEASON
Baked Ham
Amber Apples
Chipped Beef in Cream, with or without
     baked potato
Richard's Celtic Soda Bread
Six-Seafood Chowder

Cinnamon-Capped Apple Muffins, or the
     blueberry variation
Sorrel Egg-Flower Soup
Classic Chicken Salad or Fruited Chicken
     Salad
Tacos
Classic Lobster Salad
Blueberry Corn Bread or Muffins
Curdled Eggs
Chinese-Cabbage Coleslaw
Eggs à la Hotrod
Buttered Lobster, or Buttered Crabmeat
     & Lobster
Corn Oysters
See also Desserts (below)

FOR SUMMER
Summer Fruit Shortcake
Tomato Sandwiches
Savory Chicken & Veal Loaf
Swedish Cucumbers
Fresh Corn Popovers
Farmstyle Salad Platter
Pre-Pasta Macaroni Salad, with added
     meat or fish
See also Desserts (below)

FOR FALL AND WINTER
Christmas Eve Oyster Stew (or mussel
     stew)
Baked Beans—Better-Than-Yankee or
     Vermont-Style
Hearty Cornbread Skillet with Bacon &
     Whole-Kernel Corn
Finnan Haddie in Cream
Red-Wine Beans with a Ham Bone
Ham Scalloped with Potatoes à la Jacques
A Big Soup of Beef & Okra
Corn Oysters
Superb Lobster Stew
Pretty Good Chili con Carne, and Beans
     for Chili, or Garlic Garbanzos for
     Chili
Wild Rice & Porcini Soup
Pennsylvania Dutch Scrapple
Baked Potato Stuffed with Chipped Beef
     in Cream
Slunk (oven-baked chowder)
Beanpot Chicken, with gravy or with
     noodles
Old New England Corn Pudding
Salad of Chinese Cabbage, Fruit, & Nuts
See also Desserts (below)

DESSERTS

(See the Index for additional, informal dessert suggestions)

FOR MEALS IN ANY SEASON
Blueberry & Pound Cake Pudding, and Bread & Butter Pudding with Berries
Bundled Blueberry Pastries
Cream-Filled Boston Stack Cake
Dark Chocolate Mousse with Raspberry Sauce
Frozen Maple Mousse
Hazelnut Cheese Tart, or Crustless Hazelnut "Cheesecake"
Honey Pecan Pie, Maple Walnut Pie
Just Gingerbread
Little Lemon or Lime Tartlets
Old-Fashioned Sugar Cookies
Pineapple Cake for the Fern Dell
Raspberry & Rhubarb Parfait
Raspberry & White Wine Ice
Richard's Recaptured Angel Cake
Twice-Baked Orange & Nut Cookies
Uncooked Lime or Lemon Curd
Upside-Down Fruited Ginger Cake
Very Chocolate Ice Cream

FOR SPRING
Rhubarb Fool
Springtime Fruit Tart
Berry Bavarian

FOR SUMMER
Springtime Fruit Tart
Berry Bavarian
Cherry, Blueberry, or Plum Picnic Cake
Raspberry & Rhubarb Parfait
Gingery Melon Mold
Plum Velvet
Green Tomato Fool, or soft-frozen version
Nectarine & Almond Custard Pie
Rhubarb Fool

FOR FALL
Amber Apples & A Tart of Amber Apples
Berry Bavarian
Plum Velvet
Green Tomato Fool, or soft-frozen version
Pumpkin Brûlée, gingered or honeyglazed
Cherry, Blueberry, or Plum Picnic Cake
Rummy & Raisiny, Topless & Bottomless Sweet-Potato "Pie"
Cranberry, Raisin & Nut Pie
Pecan or Black Walnut Graham Torte

FOR WINTER
Amber Apples & A Tart of Amber Apples
Ambrosia
Cranberry, Raisin & Nut Pie
Pecan or Black Walnut Graham Torte
Peppernuts for Christmas
Pumpkin Brulée, gingered or honeyglazed
Rummy & Raisiny, Topless & Bottomless Sweet-Potato "Pie"

INDEX

Y

Z